Quille Sep 18		

To renew this item, please call the renewals hotline on 0115-9293388 or renew online at http://enfield.llc.dshost.info

ENFIELD
Council

Also by Roger Maynard

*Ambon: The Truth About One of the Most Brutal POW Camps
in World War Two and the Triumph of the Aussie Spirit*

Milat

*Hell's Heroes: The Forgotten Story of the
Worst POW Camp in Japan*

Fatal Flaw

Where's Peter?

*Life at the Top: Triumphs, Travails and Teachings
of Australia's Top Business Leaders*

Milat: Belanglo, the Next Chapter

HERO
OR DESERTER?
Gordon Bennett and the
Tragic Defeat of the 8th Division

Roger Maynard

EBURY
PRESS

An Ebury Press book
Published by Penguin Random House Australia Pty Ltd
Level 3, 100 Pacific Highway, North Sydney NSW 2060
www.penguin.com.au

Penguin
Random House
Australia

First published by Ebury Press in 2017

National Library of Australia
Cataloguing-in-Publication entry

Maynard, Roger, author
Hero or deserter?: Gordon Bennett and the tragic defeat of the 8th division / Roger Maynard

ISBN 978 0 14378 3 923 (paperback)

Bennett, Henry Gordon, 1887-1962
Australia. Army. Division, 8th – History
Capitulations, Military
Governmental investigations – Australia
Escapes – Singapore
Generals – Australia – History
World War, 1939–1945 – Campaigns – Singapore

Cover design by A⟨ ⟩
Maps by Alicia Fre⟨ ⟩
Internal design by ⟨ ⟩
Typeset in 12.5/17 ⟨ ⟩
Printed in Austral⟨ ⟩ 14001:2004
Environmental Ma⟨ ⟩

Penguin Random⟨ ⟩
recyclable product⟨ ⟩ ewable and
and manufacturin⟨ ⟩ The logging
regulations of the ⟨ ⟩ ironmental

CONTENTS

This book is dedicated to Arthur Kennedy, Bart Richardson, Jack Boardman and Noel Harrison, who lived to tell the tale, and to all the men of the 8th Division who have shared their memories.

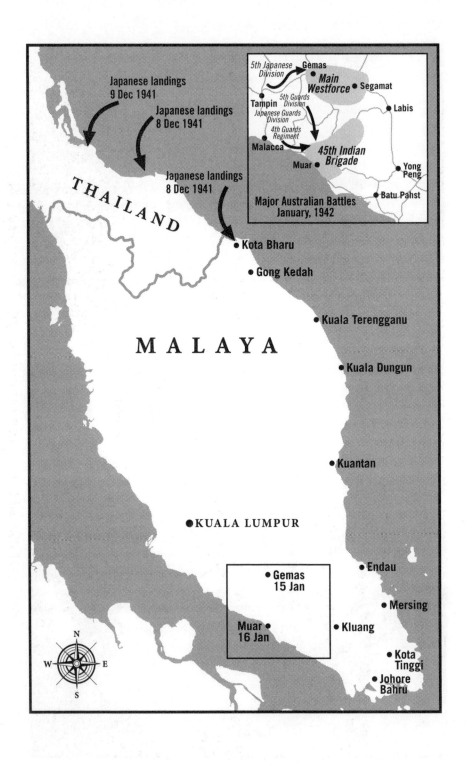

Japanese landings
9 Dec 1941

Japanese landings
8 Dec 1941

Japanese landings
8 Dec 1941

THAILAND

MALAYA

Kota Bharu

Gong Kedah

Kuala Terengganu

Kuala Dungun

Kuantan

KUALA LUMPUR

Endau

Gemas
15 Jan

Mersing

Muar
16 Jan

Kluang

Kota
Tinggi

Johore
Bahru

N
W — E
S

5th Japanese
Division

Gemas

Main
Westforce

Segamat

Tampin

5th Guards
Division

Labis

Japanese Guards
Division

4th Guards
Regiment

Malacca

Muar

45th Indian
Brigade

Yong
Peng

Batu Pahst

Major Australian Battles
January, 1942

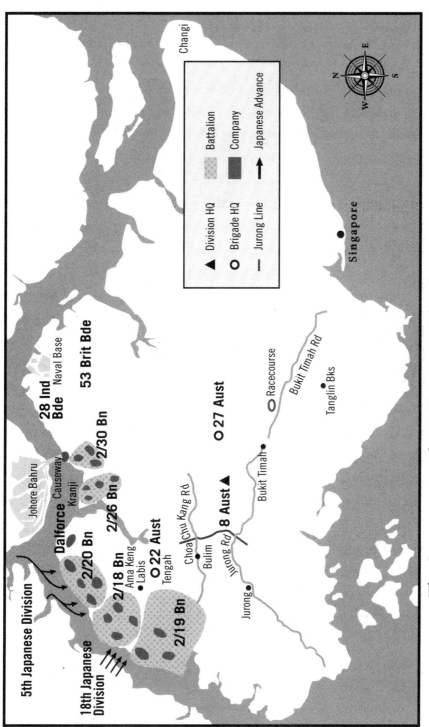

The Japanese attack on Singapore Island, 8 February 1942

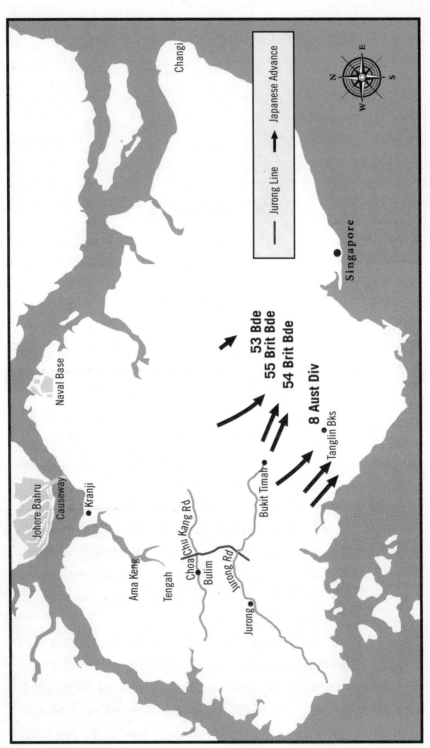

The Japanese attack on Singapore Island, 13 February 1942

INTRODUCTION

The men of the 8th Division woke with aching hearts as dawn broke over Singapore on 15 February 1942. The city was in chaos; both military and civilians had suffered heavy casualties over the previous 24 hours. Fuel, food and ammunition supplies were running low and the army hierarchy was faced with the inevitability of surrender.

These were tense times. The enemy had already been sighted advancing past Pasir Panjang towards Singapore's commercial hub and, despite heavy shelling from the Australian military, enemy troops continued to progress along Bukit Timah Road. The Japanese seemed unstoppable and the Allies knew it.

With no firm plans for their defence, Australian and British commanders chose to call a meeting at Fort Canning to discuss strategy. Senior officers with Malaya Command, including Lieutenant-General Arthur Percival and Major-General H. Gordon Bennett as well as representatives from the civil service, were to assemble at the heavily fortified military bolthole at 11 am.

Bennett, conscious of the risk of aerial bombardment, ditched his staff car and requisitioned a truck to ferry him there. His aide-de-camp, Gordon Walker, took the wheel. The two men drove up to the security gate to be informed that only generals' cars were to be admitted to the compound. The sentries on duty couldn't believe that the commander of the 8th Division would turn up in an old utility and not a gleaming, chauffeur-driven limo, so at first refused to let him through.

Doubtless Bennett's sharp tongue quickly changed their mind and he was let through. Inside the building the atmosphere was as gloomy as the poorly lit interior. Overnight there had been reports of intense bombing, with roads and buildings suffering extensive damage. To add to the growing anarchy, a number of prisoners had been released from jails on the island, and some had attacked the police who were trying to maintain order. Bennett revealed he had even heard that the ex-inmates had bombed detectives, though how they had obtained the explosives was unclear.

By the time the Allied top brass assembled around the table, it was obvious that the days of British rule over Singapore were numbered. How much longer could they hold out?

A.H. Dickinson, Inspector General of the Straits Settlement Police, and Brigadier Ivan Simson, whose local role was as the British Army's Chief Engineer, painted a hopeless picture of a city in disarray. The emergency services were so depleted that they were unable to rescue those trapped and injured in fallen buildings.

The number of casualties was so high that nobody could provide a reliable estimate of the total. At one of the few operating civilian hospitals, medical staff and patients had been without water for the previous 24 hours. Indeed water and food supplies were practically non-existent among the civilian population. Overall the army had only enough to feed themselves for the next three days, although the Australian Imperial Force (AIF) was said to be in a slightly better position, with an estimated 15 days of food supplies and 400 rounds of artillery ammunition per gun.

It was morale that posed the biggest challenge. An unknown number of battle-weary stragglers – both soldiers and civilians – was now roaming those parts of Singapore which had already fallen to the enemy or were about to. Percival, like most of the others in the room, was clearly exhausted. Unable to conceal his despair any longer, he produced a letter signed by the Japanese commander, General Tomoyuki Yamashita, who advised him that he had no choice but to surrender. Yamashita even outlined the way the Allies should relay their response. Hoist a white flag atop Government House and then drive down Bukit Timah Road in a car flying a white flag and the Union Jack.

Accepting that capitulation was inevitable, Percival and those assembled around the table agreed to ask for a ceasefire at 3.30 pm and an unconditional surrender. They also wanted to retain some of their own troops under arms in an effort to keep law and order. The rest of their equipment would be destroyed so that it would be of no use to the enemy.

The military and civilian chiefs shuffled uncomfortably in their seats as Percival brought the meeting to a close. Afterwards Bennett was driven back to his HQ at Tanglin

Barracks, where he summoned his lieutenants to brief them on the latest developments.

The news came as no surprise to most of them, who realised that the sacrifice of so many lives could not continue. The dead and injured were littering the streets and the number of Allied troops still able to wage war had dramatically reduced.

One man, however, refused to accept the inevitable. He was thinking along very different lines. Major-General Gordon Bennett, while realising that his men were about to become prisoners of war, was in no mood to share their fate. Secretly, and with the connivance of a few brother officers, the commander of the 8th Division was privately planning his escape. As he later recalled in his wartime memoir: 'I had determined I would not fall into Japanese hands.'[1] His idea was to pass through enemy lines west of Bukit Timah village following the end of hostilities and get away to the mainland by boat. Once ashore he would make his way north to Malacca or Port Dickson, where he would hire a fishing vessel to take him the 50 miles (80 km) to Sumatra. It was a dangerous strategy but Bennett thrived on risk.

Apart from anything else, he viewed it as his duty to escape to tell the Australian government what had happened on the Malay Peninsula and more specifically how it could have been avoided. Above all, Bennett was in no mood to accept responsibility for the military debacle that had taken place between 8 December 1941 and 15 February 1942. And he was determined to get his own version in first.

In truth he was not the only member of the Allied forces planning to leave Singapore and attempt a last dash for freedom. As thousands of Australian and British servicemen roamed the island, many of those separated from their units made for the harbour in the hope of bagging a berth on a commercial liner or native vessel. Eyewitness accounts of the time talk of men barging and pushing their way on board. Women and children certainly didn't come first. It was not the Allies' finest hour. There was widespread looting, drunkenness and a total breakdown of military discipline.

Although Bennett made it back to Australia, not all of the escape attempts were successful. Many of the fleeing vessels were sunk at sea by the Japanese Navy or Air Force, those on board captured by the enemy in Java and either executed or sent back to Singapore to spend the rest of the conflict as prisoners of war. Come the Allies' surrender, around 15,000 Australians found themselves prisoners of war in Singapore, many of whom were to die in labour camps on the Burma–Thai Railway, in Sandakan and Japan. Those servicemen who were fortunate enough to make it back to Australia were often ostracised by the community or by their comrades-in-arms when they eventually got home.

Bennett himself, who had anticipated a hero's welcome on his return, was to be sorely disappointed. While Australia's Prime Minister, John Curtin, praised the commander's actions, many of Bennett's fellow officers on the army staff were highly critical of his behaviour. Some believed his motivation had more to do with saving his own skin than bringing back important information about the enemy's military strategy to aid the government's war effort.

A few even used the dreaded D word. Whether or not Gordon Bennett could be classified as a deserter depended on how the law was interpreted. If he had been officially a

prisoner of war at the time he slipped away, he was legally
obliged to try to escape. But if he was not, he could only have
left his post legally if his superiors had allowed him to do so.
And so far as Major-General Percival was concerned, no such
permission had been granted.

But was Bennett under the authority of the British
General Officer Commanding (GOC)? Or as commander of
Australia's 8th Division, was he his own boss and did not have
to answer to the British?

Then there was the question of the timing of the surrender.
When the British agreed to a ceasefire to take effect from
8.30 pm on 15 February, did this constitute a surrender under
the terms of international law? If so then Bennett, who left
sometime around 10 pm, may have been within his rights.
But not everyone was convinced that the Allied troops officially became prisoners of war at 8.30 pm. Many have since
argued that the surrender happened much later, after all the
men had downed arms and completed the long march to
Changi, where they were classified as POWs.

Regardless of the legal niceties, Bennett's actions and the
subsequent inquiries into the rights and wrongs of his escape
captivated Australians for decades. There can be no more
damning an indictment of an officer's behaviour than that he
deserted his men. That when the chips were down he turned
his back on the soldiers he was there to lead and protect.

Sadly the case of Major-General H. Gordon Bennett has
also left a stain on the division he commanded. His name has
become synonymous with a military controversy that refuses
to die. The events surrounding his departure and the fall of
Singapore have tended to overshadow a courageous fighting
force who have been much maligned over the years.

Their courage and sacrifice in the face of Japanese might is without question. Yet this has not deterred a few historians and armchair generals from condemning these brave men as an ill-disciplined rabble led by an irascible, unpredictable and pompous man who was not up to the job.

Is this assessment of Bennett fair or is it a gross calumny on an individual who was also smart, innovative, dogged, inspirational and always determined to take the battle to the enemy? His strategy was always attack, attack, attack. Retreat was never part of his lexicon. Here was a soldier who had served with distinction in World War I, becoming a general at 29, a man who had carved out a successful career in civvy street during the 1920s and '30s and whose military ambitions were so driven that he even wrote to then Prime Minister, Robert Menzies, offering his services as the 8th Division's top-ranking officer.[2]

There were, however, two hindrances to Bennett's lofty career objectives. Firstly the poor relations he had with staff officers, who looked down on Bennett for leaving the army after World War I, even though he continued to play a role in the Army Reserve which was more generally known as the militia. And secondly his lifelong beef with arch-rival Sir Thomas Blamey, who in 1939 was given command of the 6th Division of the AIF in the Middle East.

The two men originally fell out over a comparatively trivial incident in which Blamey accused Bennett of pushing him into a horse trough during a training exercise in 1912. Bennett denied his involvement, insisting it was a case of mistaken identity. Then in 1916, when both were serving in France, Blamey infuriated Bennett by reducing the number of days on his leave pass, which he had obtained in order to get married in London. The mean-spirited deed was never forgiven by Bennett, leading to a lifetime of rivalry and animosity between the men.

Through such acts of disharmony are friendships fractured and careers endangered. While the hand of fate might fashion crucial moments in history, much more minor events can sometimes have an equal impact.

Such is the case of Major-General H. Gordon Bennett, whose life was plagued by crises great and small and whose name will go down in history as one of the most unconventional and controversial leaders in Australian military history. Yet for all the criticism he attracted, the men who served under him remained surprisingly loyal. He may have left them to get on with it after the fall of Singapore, but when the POWs of the 8th Division sailed into Sydney Harbour after the war some had signs declaring their loyalty to Bennett, who was at the dockside to greet them.

At Bennett's funeral in 1962, thousands lined the streets to honour him as the cortege left St Andrew's Cathedral in Sydney. Was this the response of a people who viewed Bennett as a deserter? Clearly not. They were paying their respects to a man whose career was prematurely terminated by an officer class who took issue with his behaviour and, rightly or wrongly, made him pay for it for the rest of his life.

As to the conduct of the men of the 8th Division, history speaks for itself. The division had also sent battalions to Ambon, Timor and Rabaul, three smaller theatres of war which also took their toll. Hostilities on the Malay Peninsula, Singapore Island, Ambon, Timor and Rabaul claimed the lives of more than 10,000 men from the 8th Division, a quarter of them killed in action. During the

Malay–Singapore campaign, 73 per cent of those who died in battle were members of the 8th Division, a figure all the more astounding given that they represented only 13 per cent of the Allied forces. Their extraordinary sacrifice is remembered every year on 15 February in Sydney's Martin Place and other sites around the country, when the 8th Division Association holds a service and wreath-laying ceremony to honour those who fell and the courage of those who survived to tell the tale.

The year 2017 saw the last such service. As the number of members has dwindled, the Association decided that the 75th anniversary commemoration of the fall of Singapore would be the last. But the division's rich history will endure, as will the controversy surrounding the man who led them.

Gordon Bennett was a remarkable leader. Cocky, short-tempered, selfish, argumentative, distrustful – he was all of these. His life was an extraordinary adventure which, for good or ill, was to have a dramatic impact on the 8th Division. Their histories are entwined, their legacies forged on events which spanned much of the 20th century and part of the 19th, when Henry Gordon Bennett entered the world.

This is their story.

Chapter 1

THE EARLY DAYS

Henry Gordon Bennett – who always answered to Gordon – was born in the eastern suburbs of Melbourne on Friday 15 April 1887 in Balwyn. In those days it was a semi-rural area, green and lightly wooded. It was a tightly knit community, with its own post office and school. Gordon's father, George, who was born in South Africa, was the village headmaster, which meant the family lived in the schoolhouse.

Australia was a different country in the latter years of the 19th century. If you lived in this part of the world you saw yourself as a resident of the colony of Victoria, whose name-sake was to reign supreme as sovereign for another quarter of a century. People knew their place and respected those above them. In Balwyn's hierarchy the Bennetts were near the top of the ladder.

There were nine kids from two marriages (George's first wife died). Gordon was the eldest child from his father's second marriage and inherited many of his dad's characteristics, including his enormous energy, fierce patriotism and glowing pride in a job well done. Those who knew Gordon well also detected a hint of precociousness in his behaviour, a quality that would make him unpopular in later years.

Born with red hair and a fiery temper to match, Gordon was heavily influenced by his father's Christian work ethic and love of all things military. There was no question that every boy had to enlist in the school cadets, which was no hardship so far as Gordon was concerned. Throughout his formative years he yearned to be a soldier, an ambition that became even more pronounced as a teenager.

There was no shame in nationalism and Gordon took every opportunity to wave his flag at passing military parades as army units marched through Melbourne on their way to the Boer War. On the relief of Mafeking, which was celebrated by a half-day holiday at school, he led his own tin-can band through the streets of Balwyn to mark the occasion.[1]

Intellectually he showed promise, but his nerves often let him down at examination time, a weakness he was determined to conquer. As with many of the challenges Gordon Bennett faced in adult life, he set about overcoming this obstacle with a mixture of military-style precision and sheer willpower. It worked. Eventually he won a scholarship to nearby Hawthorn College, where he excelled in mathematics, a talent which was to help mould his career in civilian life.

After matriculating in 1902, he gained his first job as a clerk with the Australian Mutual Provident Society and began studying as an actuary. However, he continued to be obsessed by thoughts of soldiering, and intended to join the militia, an extension of the army cadets beloved of many schoolboys at the time, as soon as he was old enough. Immediately after his 21st birthday he approached a near neighbour who was commanding officer of a Victorian infantry regiment. Colonel J. McLaren was so impressed by Bennett's demeanour and enthusiasm that he told him to report to the headquarters of the 5th Australian Infantry Regiment on the next drill night.

Bennett was immediately accepted as a recruit officer and ordered to attend training four nights a week, as well as each Saturday afternoon. This was no hardship for the young man. For the next six months he learned all he could about tactics, infantry drill, administration and military law and he was soon on his way to becoming a second-lieutenant. After his commission was confirmed towards the end of 1908, Gordon Bennett became driven by an all-consuming passion for his part-time role as a civilian soldier. By the beginning of World War I he held the rank of major and had been appointed second-in-command of the 6th Battalion AIF. The 6th Battalion was one of the first infantry battalions to be raised during World War I and was later sent to Egypt.[2]

Bennett's meteoric rise through the ranks ran parallel with the progress of another ambitious soldier, Thomas Albert Blamey, who was three years older. Like Bennett, Blamey came from a large family and joined the cadet corps at school, where he was similarly inspired by developments in the Boer War. Blamey spent his childhood at Wagga Wagga in New South Wales and he, too, made no secret of his desire for military status. In 1906 he gained a commission in the Cadet Instructional Staff of the Australian Military Forces and became a staff officer.

Blamey's elevation came 18 months before Bennett was appointed an officer within the militia. Despite their similarities of talent, temperament and approach, unlike Blamey,

Bennett was classified as a civilian soldier. This had ramifications in terms of status and career prospects, and it was a bitter pill for Bennett to swallow. Over the years, the pair would fight to better each other in seniority and power. While Blamey was made a captain four months before Bennett, Bennett was elevated to the rank of major a full two years ahead of Blamey. Bennett was put in charge of his own brigade at Gallipoli, 18 months before Blamey enjoyed the same level of command in France. Competition between the two men and real or perceived offence by one against the other cemented their life-long rivalry. It would haunt their careers and ultimately impact on the very course of Australia's role in World War II.[3]

But this was all in the future. For now Gordon Bennett was more concerned with carving a reputation for himself in World War I. It did not take him long. As second-in-command of 6th Infantry Battalion he hit the ground running, leading his men ashore at Gallipoli on 25 April 1915 with an aura of invincibility that few could match. His bravery under fire even caught the attention of C.E.W. Bean in his official history of the war as he recorded Bennett's fortitude during an advance from Sniper's Ridge: 'When the men, who realised that everything had miscarried, were suggesting a retirement, Bennett told them that he would lead them, but it would be forward and not towards the rear.'[4]

Even two gunshot wounds on the same day failed to deter him from further action, as Bean also noted.

'From their position on Pine Ridge at last they caught sight of a party of the enemy. This was a group in front of the Turkish guns which were in plain view on the Third ridge opposite. Major Bennett at once began to direct the fire of his men upon this group. He stood up for this purpose, and had opened a map, when he was immediately shot in the wrist and shoulder. Handing over command to an officer of another battalion, he went to the rear to have his wound dressed. He was sent to a hospital ship, but next day found an opportunity to desert and rejoined his battalion in the front line.'[5]

If Bennett thought he was bulletproof, this should have been a reminder of his own mortality but, outwardly at least, he showed no sign of fear in combat. The major's undoubted courage clearly impressed his men but those of higher rank were not so sure. Word got about that he often lost his temper and did not take kindly to criticism.

But while some regarded Bennett as foolhardy and a risk-taker, others viewed him as resourceful and more than capable when commanding his troops on the front line. By the age of 29 he was a temporary brigadier and put in command of the 3rd Brigade of the AIF. He also served in France, seeing action at Bullecourt, Passchendaele and on the Hindenburg Line.

It was at Pozières in July 1916 that Bennett had his closest shave. He later described Pozières as nothing short of 'Hell itself', the enemy bombardment as devastating.[6] His memories of that time depict a man neither immune to fear nor controlled by it. 'Bodies of hundreds of Australians were strewn along the road where they had fallen,' he recalled. When stopping for a rest he noticed a runner in his late teens who was 'scared stiff'.

'So was I,' Bennett admitted.

'One shell landed at my feet. The blast tore off the sleeve of my tunic and ripped it up the back. It did not touch me – but it was close. The runner almost panicked but I talked to him and he quickly gained control of himself. On we went with shells falling all around.'

As with his earlier struggle to overcome exam nerves, Bennett's self-mastery in battle was an act of will. Months earlier, at the Battle of Krithia in Gallipoli, he had been forced to face his demons. Until then he had been wont to insist that he was 'not in the least affected by danger'.

Later he would write: 'I could push fear to the back of my mind almost automatically. Now I found that my dreadful experience there had shattered my complacent approach to the problems of facing dangers squarely in battle. I realised that I could not possibly allow this new weakness to rule me. If I could not fight down the dread and the fear I could not go on commanding men in battle,' he added. 'Of course I had decided that no one must know that my nerve had cracked. That had to be concealed at all costs. It was this consideration that helped in restoring my self-control.'[7]

This was a surprising admission given Bennett normally exuded total confidence. Here was a man who was willing to admit to his fears, doubt and fallibility, but only to himself. Perhaps if he had shared his anxiety with others he might not have made mistakes in later life, but this was a world in which men could not show their true feelings and where post-traumatic stress disorder was unrecognised.

On 18 November 1916, at the Scottish National Church, Chelsea, London, he married Bessie Agnes Buchanan, whom he had met in Melbourne. Bess stayed on in England, and the couple's only child, Joan, was born early in 1918.

Come the end of December 1916, Bennett was confirmed in the rank of brigadier-general. It was an extraordinary achievement for someone of his relative youth. Later he would look back on his time as commander of the Australian 3rd Infantry Brigade with something approaching fondness, despite the associated horrors. Indeed for the rest of World War I it seemed he could do no wrong; on one occasion he was personally congratulated by Britain's Commander-in-Chief, Field Marshal Sir Douglas Haig.

Bennett's medals and citations piled up, including the Distinguished Service Order, Companion of the order of St Michael and St George and Companion of the Order of the Bath. To add to his reputation he was also mentioned in despatches no fewer than eight times. By the end of the war, of all the fighting generals produced by the first AIF, Brigadier H. Gordon Bennett, CB, CMG, DS, was the youngest. He was still only 32.[8]

———·——·———

While some were surprised at Bennett's decision to leave the regular army at the end of the war, he planned to continue as a civilian soldier and resume his work as an accountant. Perhaps a little battle weary, he was keen to settle down to family life with Bess and their daughter back home in Melbourne. He remained a citizen-officer and continued to involve himself in military affairs, commanding the 9th Infantry Brigade in 1921 and rising once again to lead the 2nd Australian Division in 1926.

Throughout the 1920s and much of the '30s Bennett threw himself into business, running a clothing manufacturing company and becoming president of the Australasian Institute of Cost Accountants. He was president of the NSW Chamber of Manufacturers and fought continuously for the production of munitions in wartime.

Even in civilian life he never softened his drive, and sometimes he infuriated his opponents. In his draft memoir, held at the Mitchell Library in Sydney, there are references to his 'persistence as a fighter', and when he believed in a cause he 'fought continuously and stubbornly to the end'.[9] But like many former army men, peacetime was vaguely unsatisfying for him. Commercial life could never match the whiff of war and the drama of a combat zone. By the late 1930s he sensed his time might come again. However, to secure a top military appointment, he needed to work the system to his advantage, and this wasn't at all Bennett's style.

Bennett was 52 years old and the second-highest-ranking citizen-officer in Australia when World War II broke out. His exemplary service in World War I had earned him immense kudos. A proven commander, he still had the energy of a man half his age and he expected to be made the commander of an Australian Expeditionary Force. When his old adversary Thomas Blamey won the top job over him, Bennett was incandescent with rage.

The problem was that Bennett had a knack of upsetting his military superiors. Well before the outbreak of World War II, he got the top brass off-side with a series of articles published in Sydney's *Sun*. In one he declared that nothing was being done to train senior officers in the militia for high command. Instead only staff officers were being appointed to lead divisions, to the exclusion of militia officers like himself who, in his view, were much more capable. All potential leaders should be encouraged to make themselves fit enough for high command, and training for the rank and file should also be stepped up, he urged.

Not surprisingly, full-time professional officers were apoplectic. Bennett's impudence sent retired colonels and serving members of the Staff Corps into paroxysms of rage.[10] Finally, a heavily promoted article by Bennett on Australia's defence proved too much. The *Sun* was instructed not to publish his views anymore. Instead an apology appeared in the newspaper alerting its readers to a decision by the Military Board forbidding 'this distinguished officer' from having any further communication with it.

'It may be easily understood that General Gordon Bennett is not the favourite of a self-satisfied military administration,' the *Sun* opined. 'He is bold in his opinions, plain spoken in his assertions and pugnacious in temperament,' it added. 'Military red tape has put its stranglehold on the throat of Major-General H. Gordon Bennett.'[11]

A lesser man might have given up the fight and continued to make his way in commercial life but Bennett was made of sterner stuff. Further, he knew he also had his backers, especially in politics. The *Sun* series had created enough interest for Bennett's views to become the subject of intense debate during a Federal Cabinet meeting, which decided to take no action against him for his critical remarks.

By the beginning of hostilities in 1939, Bennett was first commander of the Volunteer Defence Corps in New South Wales. Within a few months he was also in charge of training depots in the state. But he still had his eye on a much bigger prize. Nothing less than the leadership of a division would suit his purpose, yet his ambitions were to be thwarted.

Thomas Blamey, who had also returned to civilian life and served in the militia but unlike Bennett had kept his nose clean, pipped his rival to the post when in October 1939 he was appointed to command the 6th Division. Bennett was ropeable. Five months later the government decided to form another AIF division, the 7th, and amalgamate the two under Blamey's command. That was not the end of it. Once again Bennett was given the cold shoulder when Lieutenant-General Sir Vernon Sturdee was given the leadership of the 8th Division on 1 August 1940.

As Lionel Wigmore's *The Japanese Thrust* makes clear, Bennett's aggressive temperament and public criticism of his superiors was a recurring theme in his career: 'The references to the Staff Corps in his newspaper articles had caused resentment among professional officers. Bennett thus had become a controversial figure and when leaders were sought who could command general support, strong points of resistance to his being chosen were encountered.'

Bennett was left in no doubt that he did not meet the requirements for top office when he was told by General Sir Cyril Brudenell White, Chief of the General Staff, that he had 'certain qualities and certain disqualities' for an active command. This was extremely galling for a man with such a high opinion of himself.[12]

Then came the hand of fate. In a tragic twist, White was killed in a plane crash at Canberra airport on 13 August 1940 which claimed the lives of ten people, including three members of the Australian Cabinet.

Sturdee, who had only been in charge of the 8th Division for a couple of months, was given General White's job, leaving the government and military with another hole to fill. Never backward in coming forward, Bennett sat down at his home in Sydney's Elizabeth Bay and typed a letter to Prime Minister Robert Menzies: 'I am very anxious to be appointed to the command of the 8th Division AIF which has been vacated by General Sturdee.

'My age [53] and my service in the last war and in the Citizen Forces since then, surely justify my appointment. The only reason for my suppression is the attempt on behalf of the Permanent Staff to have all the high appointments in the A.I.F. reserved for themselves. This is not in the interest of the A.I.F. nor of the Citizen Force officers.

'I would appreciate your support when your Cabinet considers the matter this week.'[13]

Little did Bennett know at the time, but Sturdee was lobbying for him to take over. The newly appointed Chief of the General Staff believed that on the basis of Bennett's experience alone he deserved the job. When the matter came before Menzies and his ministers, the War Cabinet agreed to accept Sturdee's recommendation.

Major-General Gordon Bennett was now the commander of the 8th Division, the third of what was to be a series of four Divisions enlisted for World War II. There was a certain symmetry to his appointment, for General Sir John Monash, who had been Bennett's hero in World War I, had been commander of the 3rd Division of the 1st AIF. As Bennett was to reveal in his personal papers, 'The 8th had the same shaped colour patch as the 3rd – the oval, popularly known as the Eggs A-Cook.'

He was now following in the footsteps of the man he regarded as 'Australia's most famous and most brilliant war General'.

Sadly their reputations and careers would not chart the same course.

Chapter 2

READYING FOR WAR

The 8th Division drew its force from all over Australia. The 22nd Brigade, comprising the 2/18th, 2/19th and 2/20th Battalions, came mainly from New South Wales. The 23rd Brigade's 2/21st and 2/22nd Battalions were made up of men from Victoria, while the 2/40th Battalion's ranks consisted of Tasmanians. The 24th Brigade's battalions came from Queensland, South Australia and Western Australia and formed the 2/26th, the 2/29th and 2/30th.

There were also artillery regiments, including the 2/9th, 2/10th, 2/11th, 2/14th, 2/15th Field Regiments, and the 2/3rd and 2/4th Anti-tank Regiments. Other units were the 2/4th Machine Gun Battalion from Western Australia, the 2/3rd Pioneer Battalion and the 8th–9th Divisional Cavalry.

Finally came the Royal Australian Engineers, who comprised men from the 2/10th Field Company in Victoria, the 2/11th Field Company from Queensland, the 2/12th

Field Company of New South Wales, and Western Australia's 2/4th Field Park Company.

They were an eclectic mix: farmhands from the bush, tradies from the suburbs, and white-collar workers who were more used to pushing pens than pushing their luck on the battlefield.

In the early days of the division, developments within the war in Europe and the Middle East demanded changes to the 8th. In December 1940 the 24th Brigade was sent to Egypt, which meant another brigade was required to complete the infantry of 6th, 7th, 8th and 9th Divisions. As a result, the 27th Brigade was formed from recruits attached to other divisions who were from all over Australia. Over the next few months brigades and individual units continued to be transferred from one division to another in response to emergencies, and this meant that various parts of 8th Division were doing their training in locations scattered across Australia.[1]

On 4 July 1940 the temporary headquarters of the new division had been established at Victoria Barracks in Sydney, but in less than a month it was transferred to Rosebery Racecourse, in the city's south. As the year progressed, thousands of men signed up at enlistment halls in towns and villages across Australia, most of them raw recruits who had never handled a gun in their life. The rookie soldiers were sent to hastily prepared training camps. In New South Wales these were set up at Ingleburn and Walgrove in Sydney's west. Among the new recruits were Joe Byrne and George Daldry, both Sydney boys with a reputation for fighting.

In the Sydney of the 1930s life could be tough and it always helped to get in the first punch in the event of trouble. Originally from Kogarah in Sydney's south, Joe Byrne had been working on commercial shipping in Darling Harbour and was desperate for a new challenge. The army seemed an appropriate career choice at the time for a young man handy with his fists. 'I had a short fuse and I'd rather fight than eat,' he would later say.[2]

Like Joe, George Daldry knew how to protect himself. 'I was in the local boys' club and I soon learned how to throw a straight left and not to leave my head open.' He was also in the militia so he knew what he was getting into when he turned up at the enlistment office in Paddington. Still only seventeen, he was under-age but the recruiting officer turned a blind eye. 'I shouldn't have been accepted because of my age but there were others younger than me,' he told me.[3]

Cas Cook had grown up on the land, at Springwood on the lower slopes of the Blue Mountains. After volunteering he ended up in C Company of the 2/20th. Don Alchin, from the state's rural southwest, was barely sixteen and the army was an attractive option, even though he was also under-age. After finding somewhere to live in Redfern he turned up at the Sydney Showground, where the military didn't care how old you were. Not to be outdone, his elder brother Merv signed up on the same day. Soon they were in uniform and sent to Walgrove, where they were bashed into shape.

The officers in charge were hard men who brooked no quarter. They included Brigadier Harold Taylor, commander of the 22nd Brigade, who had served with distinction in France during World War I as an infantry officer. Below him as brigade major was Major Clarence Dawkins, from Korong Vale in Victoria, who was in his late thirties. Perhaps understandably he favoured officers who had also served in the last war or were in the militia. He chose men such as Brigadier

Arthur Varley, who was put in charge of the 2/18th Battalion, Brigadier Duncan Maxwell from Hobart, who became CO of the 2/19th, and Lieutenant-Colonel Bill Jeater, of Newcastle, who was made commanding officer of the 2/20th. Jeater was an especially hard taskmaster who delighted in putting his men through rigorous procedures, including trench digging and longer and longer marches.[4]

Walgrove was tough, particularly for those boys who were used to Mum's home cooking. Army rations were often inedible and, with eight men to a tent, sleeping conditions were cramped. The windswept plains of the western suburbs were uncomfortable in winter and hot and dusty in summer.

At least new facilities were being built at Ingleburn near Liverpool, where the emphasis was on infantry training. The accommodation was better and the camp was much cleaner. There was a noticeable improvement in morale once men had been transferred there.

By November they were off again, this time to Bathurst on the other side of the Blue Mountains, where the training would be even more intense in readiness for their deployment overseas. The 8th Division replaced the camp's earlier occupants, members of the 7th Division, who were on their way to the Middle East. The 2/18th, 2/19th and 2/20th Battalions had assumed they would be bound for the same part of the world, a view reinforced when their kit arrived and included desert fatigues. Even their training replicated the dry conditions of the Middle East and North Africa, not the clammy tropics where they would eventually end up.

Basking in the early summer sun of the Central Tablelands, the men reckoned Bathurst was a plum posting, albeit of a temporary nature. They were becoming stronger and fitter by the day. Friendships were formed and camp camaraderie bode well for the future.

With Christmas leave approaching, their new divisional commander, Major-General Gordon Bennett, who had by now been in charge for a little over three months, sent them a seasonal greeting reminding them of the challenges ahead: 'Though we are impatient to set out on the task for which we enlisted, we are fortunate that we are able to spend the festive season among relatives and friends in sunny Australia, rather than among the discomforts of an alien land,' he wrote. 'May the year 1941 see the 8 Aus. Div. participating in decisive victories against our enemies so that we may soon return to our homes to enjoy a real peace on earth with goodwill to all men.'[5]

Precisely who the enemy would be at this stage was a matter of speculation. Japan's military intentions were unclear, although Australia had good reason to be concerned, given the ten-year pact signed on 27 September 1940 between Germany, Italy and Japan. This committed the signatories to 'assist one another with all political, economic and military means if one of the high contracting parties should be attacked by a power not at present involved in the European war or in the Sino-Japanese conflict.'[6]

Throughout the latter half of 1940 thousands of Australians continued to heed the call to arms, and by now the army was having difficulty accommodating them. In Victoria, Shepparton Showground was running out of space so training camps were springing up in other parts of the state to train what was a mostly motley crew – unfit, undisciplined and untested in warfare. It would take many months to instil the necessary physical and mental resolve to transform them into soldiers.

Initially the 2/21st Battalion set up shop at Trawool near
Seymour, close to rail communications but wet and bitterly
cold in winter. Later, the decision to move the men to
Bonegilla, near Albury on the Victoria–New South Wales
border, provided some relief from the weather but the training
was hampered by a lack of suitable weaponry. A lot of the
guns were World War I vintage and there was no rifle range.

But for all its faults the camp slowly turned the members of
the 2/21st Battalion, now officially part of the 23rd Brigade
of the 8th Division of the AIF, into men of war. Among them
was Eddie Gilbert, who grew up in St Kilda and went on to
get a job with the State Electricity Commission, where his
father, Ulric, worked. Enlisting for the army liberated him
from life behind a desk and Eddie revelled in it. At Bonegilla
he spent every waking hour improving his physical fitness by
running, jumping and wading through water. 'The training
was pretty intensive but . . . it was a great camp and I was
happy there,' he said.[7]

One of the few who had experience with a rifle was Walter
Hicks, who had spent part of his early life in the country
and regarded himself as a crack shot. By the late 1930s he
was working at the State Savings Bank in Melbourne. The
day Australians heard on the radio that Neville Chamberlain
had declared war against Germany, a chance meeting with a
World War I veteran in a Melbourne street on the way home
from work left an indelible impression. The old soldier pulled
up his trouser leg to reveal a wartime injury. 'Are you going
to war?' he asked.

Walter didn't need any more convincing. Within a year he
was on his way with the 2/21st.[8]

Unlike members of the 2/20th and other battalions

within the 8th Division, he would not be bound for Malaya. The military had other plans, which would sideline him and thousands of other Australians to smaller theatres of war in Timor, Ambon and New Guinea. Though each was to be no less exacting in terms of death, injury and sheer brutality.

As 1941 began and the perceived threat from Australia's north appeared more serious by the week, the 8th Division prepared to set sail for foreign waters, although few knew where.

The 2/20th first got wind of an imminent departure when their CO, Lieutenant-Colonel Jeater, was despatched to Sydney on 1 February 1941 to become officer in charge of training on the *Queen Mary*, which was being converted into a troopship. The following day the battalion left by train for Darling Harbour, where on 3 February the men boarded ferries for the luxury liner, now anchored off Bradleys Head in Sydney Harbour. The 2/20th was the last of three battalions to climb aboard the vessel. Other units included the 8th Division Signals, 2/10th Field Regiment, 2/4th Machine Gun Battalion, 2/9th Field Ambulance and 2/5th Field Hygiene Section.

By the time the transfer was complete there were nearly 6000 men crammed into the twelve-deck, 1020-feet long liner, which, as a merchant ship, was only built to hold 1957 passengers. With three times that many on board it looked like the men would be sleeping cheek by jowl.

On the morning of 4 February the governor-general, Lord Gowrie, inspected the troops and after mess parade they were allowed on deck. A small armada of pleasure craft carrying relatives and friends of those on board was jostling for position as the *Queen Mary* prepared to weigh anchor. It was a period of intense emotion as flags and signs were waved and last-minute shouts from well-wishers wafted across the morning breeze. At precisely 1.30 pm the ship slowly headed towards open waters.[9]

'It was a glorious day, with hundreds of small craft bobbing about to farewell her,' remembered Jack Mudie. He was in his early thirties and had been a teacher in Queanbeyan before signing up.[10]

As Don Wall wrote in *Singapore and Beyond*, the 2/20th's official history, 'There is something symbolic about the Heads of Sydney Harbour – having passed through them there was a feeling of achievement, at last we were on the way to active service. The canteen opened and beer flowed, drinkers borrowed spare dixies from non-drinkers to get their quota while it was available.'[11]

The party had begun and the voyage was underway. If only they knew where they were going. Given the Cunard liner's reputation for five-star luxury the men half-hoped they'd enjoy accommodation to match. Mudie, who had been in the militia and had NCO status, was lucky enough to be given a private berth, but other ranks got a hammock and told to make do.

Private Jack Boardman, who was born at Bogan Gate, in the central west of New South Wales, belonged to Brigade Headquarters and thought he'd get a state room. 'Instead they put us right down in the bowels of the ship. But it didn't matter, we were so pleased to be there,' he recalled.[12]

Once out of the harbour the *Queen Mary* was joined by two other converted troopships, the *New Amsterdam*, which was carrying men from New Zealand, and the *Aquitania*. The voyage would take them to Melbourne, Adelaide and across the Great Australian Bight to Fremantle in Western Australia, where locally raised units would join the flotilla.

Other troopships would follow in the coming months, including the *Johan Van Oldenbarnevelt*, which set sail in July with the 8th Division's 27th Brigade and reinforcements for the 22nd. The 2/30th Battalion, under the command of the legendary Senior Lieutenant-Colonel Frederick 'Black Jack' Galleghan, was also on board. An officer with a fearsome reputation for discipline who demanded strict compliance from his men, Galleghan assumed full command of the *Johan Van Oldenbarnevelt* and ruled the ship with an iron fist.

As before, the first few days at sea saw something of a party atmosphere, with the lower ranks drinking and gambling away their money with reckless abandon.

Lance-Corporal Henry Dietz, who had been working on a sheep farm at Quandialla near Young when he enlisted, encountered Galleghan's formidable presence when he was ordered to keep his men under control.

'My, did he give us a lecture,' said Henry. 'This is wrong, that's wrong, things are getting out of hand – you've got to do something about it.'

On leaving Black Jack's cabin Henry did just that. Disillusioned with the responsibility of power, he ripped the lance-corporal's insignia from his shoulder and headed back downstairs to C deck to join a game of two-up. He lost. It was a salutary beginning to a four-year journey that would take him to Malaya and Japan before he was able to return home.[13]

The voyage along Australia's southern coast was often hampered by rough seas, especially in the Great Australian

Bight, where it was almost impossible to stand straight. Even so daily deck drill continued regardless of the weather. The standards achieved in the training camps at Walgrove, Ingleburn and Bathurst had to be maintained. They might be passengers on a luxury liner, but this was no holiday cruise.

And to remind them of the ever-present threat, RAAF Hudson bombers flew low overhead to guard them. While Australia was not officially at war with Japan, there was good reason to fear that it was only a matter of time. Japan's unopposed invasion of Indochina the previous year had increased tensions in the region and Australian shipping was deemed at risk, if not from the air, then from a Japanese torpedo.

On troopships packed to the gunwales, the ratio of passengers to lifeboat seats did not instil confidence that a seaborne rescue was achievable if the worst happened.

Don Alchin admitted, 'We were really frightened about submarines and really worried about what might happen if we were torpedoed.'[14]

Rumour was one of the greatest threats to morale but sometimes it could work the other way. Jack Boardman overheard a conversation on the *Queen Mary* as he made his way through the mess room one day. 'We had to go through a middle section where the British, who ran the ship, would congregate and as I came along they had the BBC on the radio. There was a rumour on it that the *Queen Mary* had been sunk by the Japs. As quick as a flash one of the old sea dogs observed, "Thank God it's only a rumour."'[15]

What everyone wanted was certainty about their destination. Was it to be the Middle East or Asia? It was Jack Mudie who got the first solid clue about their intended route when a box of papers fell open as they were being loaded during a stopover in Fremantle. The box was marked Elbow Force, and in it was a booklet about Malaya.

'They contained a little bit about the people and some language tips, so we knew immediately where we were going,' said Jack.[16]

The convoy, now joined by the *Mauretania*, which was carrying reinforcements to the Middle East, set sail from Fremantle on 12 February. Given all the grapevine talk of their destination being Malaya, army chiefs decided to clear the air with an announcement that the *Queen Mary* was bound for Singapore.

A few days later, at some point south of Sumatra, the British destroyer *Durban* joined the fleet. By now it included the Australian cruiser *Canberra*, which had taken over the job of escort duty from the *Hobart*. What followed was enough to stir the spirit of the entire convoy, which now consisted of roughly 12,000 men. Slowly the *Queen Mary* swung to port, encircled the other ships and, when they were in formation, accelerated past them full steam ahead at 26 knots. It was a majestic scene: bands played and the massed throng of soldiers and sailors aboard their ships whooped with joy, cheering each other as the 81,000-ton pride of the Cunard Line set course for the tropics. The *Queen Mary* sounded her horn and the rest of the convoy replied in unison.

The initial contingent of the 8th Division arrived in Singapore on 18 February. It was to be the first time any Australian troops had set foot on Malayan soil.[17] As they assembled on the deck of the *Queen Mary*, the Australians noticed a welcoming party on the quayside, including their commander, Major-General Gordon Bennett, who had flown there by plane earlier in the month. Also dockside to greet them were the Singapore governor, Sir Shenton Thomas, and a group of naval and army officers.

Intrinsically disrespectful of authority, the men of the 8th seized the opportunity to make light of the reception down below by throwing coins on the military and government leaders. Despite being foreign to the ways of his colonial cousins, Thomas took it in good part and went on to say how impressed he was with the athletic build of the young Australians.

———·—·———

When the *Johan Van Oldenbarnevelt* eventually berthed at Singapore on 15 August, the first two people to climb the gangplank were Bennett and Brigadier Duncan Maxwell, who had recently been appointed brigadier of the 27th Brigade. Maxwell had previously been a medical officer with the rank of captain in the Riverina Regiment and there was bad blood between him and 'Black Jack' Galleghan. As the senior lieutenant-colonel in New South Wales when war broke out Galleghan felt, perhaps with good reason, that he should have received the brigadier's job.

This also soured Galleghan's relations with Bennett, who'd made the appointment. How could the commander favour a man who was not a soldier but a medical officer, did not have Galleghan's experience in infantry tactics and had had only brief army service? Galleghan was so furious he'd threatened not to serve under Maxwell and to return to Australia to seek another appointment. Once the news got out the brigade was sent into turmoil, with officers wondering how they would cope without a strong leader such as Galleghan.

Several heated discussions ensued and finally Galleghan,

who was nicknamed 'Black Jack' because of his West Indian ancestry and swarthy good looks, was persuaded to change his mind. Despite the obvious blow to his pride, he was man enough to offer his full support to Maxwell and Bennett and did not waver from that assurance throughout the war. Maxwell would in fact make a habit of seeking Galleghan's advice on tactics before issuing orders for the day.[18]

Galleghan would go on to become a key player in the Malaya campaign and its aftermath in the Changi POW camp. The iron discipline he imposed would instil new pride into 8th Division's achievements and end up saving many lives.

Of course all this was in the future. As the *Johan Van Oldenbarnevelt* unloaded its human cargo onto the Singapore dock, the invasion of Malaya was still nearly four months away.

Also there that day were a handful of Japanese civilians, assiduously trying to blend into the crowd while attempting to estimate the number of troops disembarking. It had long been suspected that many Japanese who had supposedly legitimate jobs in Singapore were actually spies who were reporting direct to Tokyo.[19] Japanese intelligence chiefs were amassing an encyclopaedic knowledge of the region and, more especially, the island that sat at the bottom of the peninsula.

Not that this worried most Singaporeans, who regarded the so-called Lion Island as an impregnable fortress. The British colony was thought invincible to outside aggression. Hadn't the government back in Blighty promised to send its military might to the east in the event of threatened invasion? Such guarantees were more than enough to allow the ex-pats to rest easily as they sipped their *stengahs* and ate and danced the night away at Raffles or Government House.

Gordon Bennett himself was quick to take advantage of the social scene, attending dinner with the governor while his men were being transported north over the causeway that linked Singapore with the mainland. Then it was on by train up the west coast towards Kuala Lumpur. The 2/18th and the 2/20th would be based at Port Dickson for the time being while 2/19th set up temporary home at Seremban, just inland.

The boys could not have been happier. They had money in their pockets and plenty of booze and entertainment on which to spend it. With beer at ten cents a bottle and 3 cents for a packet of cigarettes, even lower ranks could afford to splash out from their army pay of 30 shillings a week.

From time to time some of the officers even made it down to Singapore, where the party life was in full swing. A few were lucky enough to get invited to the palatial residence where Sir Shenton and Lady Thomas held court over evening cocktails. Others were welcomed as weekend guests at the grand homes of the Singaporean business elite or the country estates of plantation owners.

For those with excess energy there was plenty of sport, including cricket, soccer, rugby, hockey and athletics, while in the evening those with a theatrical or musical leaning presented battalion concert parties. For the more literary minded, locally produced newsletters with names like *Thumbs Up* and *Second Two Nought* always provided plenty of laughs for the men on the ground and their families back home.

Within a few months a little slice of Australia had been transplanted to the equator. But how long would it last?

War? What war? While the discipline and training were constant reminders of why the 8th Division was there, it was easy to forget that much of Europe was in flames and that Asia might be about to follow suit.

Not that Gordon Bennett was oblivious to the threat. War or the perceived threat of it required only one response, he believed.

Attack, attack, attack!

But would the Allies be up to it? Would they share his ethos? Or would they be part of Malaya's downfall?

Chapter 3

'GIVE US MORE MEN'

By the middle of 1941 some 6000 Australian soldiers had been deployed in Malaya, a tiny proportion of the nation's total population of 5.5 million. Although further Allied troops were on their way, it was not a large force to protect a country that spanned 400 miles (645 km) from north to south. To add to the challenge the tropical Malayan climate could be exhausting and much of the jungle-covered terrain was inaccessible. The temperature rarely fell below 81 degrees Fahrenheit (27°C) in the shade throughout the year and the sheer humidity came as a shock, especially to the boys from Victoria, with its cold, blowy winters.

Training in such inhospitable conditions was uncomfortable and debilitating, especially those energy-sapping exercises which saw men hacking their way through heavily forested terrain for days on end.

Bennett thought long and hard about how his men could accustom themselves to jungle life. Conventional training was clearly not enough. Instead he told his men to take a lead from those who knew the conditions best of all: indigenous tribespeople. The Sakai people had lived in the dense forest since the third century, surviving as nomadic hunter-gatherers and wearing little more than loincloths made out of tree bark. Their greatest skill was the ability to move quickly and silently through the wilderness with the agility of a wild animal. And because they were surrounded by bamboo, most of their furnishings and receptacles were made from cane. They used it to make beds to lie on, rafts to sail on and even cups to drink from.

Inspired by the ingenuity of the tribespeople, Bennett organised for some of his men to meet and learn the ways of the jungle from the Sakais. They stayed with them in make-shift camps and ate the traditional salt meals, which invoked friendship.[1]

This unique experience would later enable members of 8th Division to make the jungle their home and undoubtedly to strengthen their warrior-like skills against the Japanese. What they didn't know at the time was that the top brass back in Australia had other plans, and these plans had little to do with the law of the jungle. In fact Army HQ had earmarked the Malayan force for duty elsewhere.

Bennett had already been told that his division was only there as a temporary boost to the country's defences and would ultimately join the Australian Corps in the Middle East. Certain that the Japanese threat would not eventuate, Thomas Blamey, who was in command of the 6th and 7th Divisions, was urging the General Staff to hasten the deployment of Bennett's division to the Middle East, insistent that his need was much greater than Malaya's.

No doubt Blamey would have been glad to know the men of the 8th were equipped for desert warfare, much as it was the bane of their existence in the wet and steamy conditions of the jungle. They would have preferred light footwear and headwear, not boots that left tell-tale prints in the mud and steel helmets that clattered against the vegetation, advertising their location. To make matters worse their rifles were too bulky to handle in confined spaces and their brown-coloured uniforms, which were fine for the desert, were hardly suited to the jungle.

In anticipation of a sudden move to the Middle East, the division's transport had also been designed for rapid mechanised movement along well-built highways and open country, not densely vegetated terrain where roads were few and enemy soldiers might be hiding in the trees and bushes.

Then there were the rivers, which could often only be negotiated by swimming. The fact that a third of the men couldn't swim was an obvious disadvantage which the officer class had somehow overlooked in their training. Nobody had thought of making swimming lessons compulsory.

Yet for all the initial hardships the Australians proved to be remarkably adaptable to the Malayan conditions. Perhaps it was the outdoor lifestyle they'd enjoyed back home or the 'can do' Aussie spirit, but they would often put their British counterparts to shame in training and in battle. Bennett observed that the British units and their junior leaders were not given enough training in how to plan and wage small battles. In close country, he asserted, all depended on an instant reaction to the enemy, whatever the situation.

'Instead too much attention seems to be paid to barrack-square discipline, immaculate guards and sentries, spotless turnout and all the other outward and visible signs – highly necessary if kept in due proportion – of an efficient unit,' he wrote. 'As a result too little attention seems to be paid to tactics which alone enable soldiers to fulfil their reason for existence, that is to fight and beat the enemy.'

This was to be a recurring theme in Bennett's musings in his diary and later in his memoir. 'In war, a good soldier must be physically aggressive and a good commander must be mentally aggressive,' he declared.[2]

Only the 2/Argyll and Sutherland Highlanders, who were part of the 12th Indian Brigade, seemed to be up to the challenge, both as a fighting force and their response to conditions. Like the Aussies the Scots recognised the problems posed by a tropical environment and trained accordingly.

The 12th Indian had arrived in Malaya in 1939 so had a head start against the new arrivals but it did not take long for the Australians to acquire the same level of skill. Urged on by AIF HQ to become 'jungle minded', the men of the 8th Division were told that thick country did not favour static defence and that only offensive action would work against the enemy. An army booklet issued in 1940 stressed the necessity of training all ranks in moving through the jungle since 'the difference between trained and untrained troops is immense'.[3]

It was a message with which Gordon Bennett would have doubtless concurred, but other army thinking contained conflicting views on the military prowess of the enemy.

In 1940 Army HQ warned that the Japanese likely possessed a high standard of armament and technical training, great physical endurance and few bodily requirements compared with British troops.

They were also ruthless, had a talent for misleading their opponent and ample experience of landing operations.

Such guidance proved to be remarkably prescient, yet a year later AIF Headquarters in Malaya described the enemy as poorly trained and weak. Previous experience had shown that the Japanese soldier was 'peculiarly helpless against unforeseen action by his enemy'.[4]

In reality it turned out to be almost the reverse with Allied forces being largely unprepared for the quick and ruthless tactics of the invader.

It is difficult to understand how such mixed messages could be conveyed when Bennett himself was in charge, but it was, perhaps, symptomatic of a large and unwieldy military machine which was often at odds with the officers who drove it.

There was also the question of the 8th Division's future in Malaya and if it would be replaced or augmented by other battalions which remained on standby in Australia.

Firmly of the opinion that he needed more men in Malaya to counter the Japanese threat, Bennett lobbied hard for his proposals to be taken seriously. He would not have been encouraged by the Deputy Chief of the Australian General Staff, Major-General John Northcott, who was of the view that much of the division should either stay at home or be sent to the Dutch East Indies.

A commitment to send troops to the islands of Ambon and Timor only added to the intransigence. Back in late February 1941 the Dutch had agreed to provide air support in defence of Malaya in return for a similar pledge by Australia to protect Ambon and Timor in the event of Japan entering the war.[5] Under the deal 24 aircraft would be sent by the Dutch to Singapore while Australia would commit three squadrons for the protection of the two islands. But it didn't end there. As part of the agreement Australia promised to send land forces to protect the RAAF, a demand made by Sir Charles Burnett, who was the country's Air Chief Marshal.

The so-called Singapore agreement, which would also commit Australia to providing air support out of the Northern Territory, had significant implications for Bennett who now faced the very real possibility of having to rely on a vastly diminished 8th Division, since it seemed a third of his men would have to stay in central Australia, a third in Darwin or the Dutch East Indies and the rest in Malaya.

Though not Bennett's responsibility, he was becoming increasingly aware of the lack of air cover for Allied forces in the region. The British had a decidedly uninspiring body of aircraft at their disposal including two squadrons of Vickers Vildebeest biplanes, disparagingly known by those who used them as 'flying coffins'.

Lance-Sergeant Kevin Timbs, who grew up near Glen Innes in rural New South Wales, had arrived with the 2/20th in Malaya in February and had learned a lot about the country's military capabilities.

'We were all pretty knowledgeable about what was going on and how prepared the British and Australian forces were to defend themselves, but we were also worried,' he confided.

Earlier in the year he and his mates had seized the opportunity to go straight to the top with their reservations when the Australian Prime Minister Robert Menzies had dropped by on his way to London. 'Seeing Menzies a few of us decided to put him on the spot and voice our concerns,' he explained.

'One of our group asked bluntly, "When are we going to get air support?"

'"Haven't you got it already?" Menzies queried.

'"No," Kevin said bluntly.

'"The only bloody things we've got are three Rooster Buffalos and an old biplane."'

If Menzies was taken aback by the intense questioning from lower ranks, he didn't show it. 'Oh, that'll be all fixed by the time you see action – there'll be thousands of planes,' the prime minister told Kevin.[6]

If Menzies' pledge was verging on the over-optimistic, it was an accurate reflection of so much of government and military thinking at the time. Was it mere PR to boost confidence in the troops or did they seriously believe their own rhetoric?

Even Bennett reinforced the view that the Allies were the superior force when he came to inspect a prisoner of war camp at Mersing on 30 September. It was built, he emphasised, to hold all the captured Japanese who would try to infiltrate Australian positions.

Significantly, the construction of the east coast camp, some 120 kilometres north of Singapore, also gave credence to the rumour that the Japanese might carry out their assault from the north. Even Sir Robert Brooke-Popham, Commander-in-Chief, British Far East Command, was among the VIPs who visited the lads in Mersing to congratulate them on their high standard of workmanship and in particular the design of the barbed-wire fencing.

More troops arrived during October and November. Brimming with energy and enthusiasm, they soon dug themselves in along the peninsula's east coast from Mersing in the south to Endau in the north. To all intents and purposes they were ready for action. What could go wrong? It was a question that few expressed publicly but many considered privately.

As Australia's grand strategy further evolved that year, three new fighting units were created – known as Sparrow Force, Lark Force and Gull Force – all of them made up of men from the 8th Division battalions.

Lark, comprising some 700 men from the 22nd Battalion, would head to Rabaul in New Britain, to the east of New Guinea, where it would protect an Australian Air Force base and flying boat anchorage. Sparrow, which was made up of about 1400 soldiers mainly drawn from the 2/40th Battalion, would reinforce West Timor, a Dutch territory in the East Indies which nestled alongside a Portuguese colony on the same island. And Gull Force would be sent to Ambon, one of the most strategically important islands in the area because of its large, deep-water harbour, which could accommodate a small navy.

Some 1150 members of the 2/21st Battalion, most of them from Victoria, would be earmarked for service on Ambon, where they would join 2600 indigenous troops.

Back in Malaya Bennett realised his position was on the line, with all the loss of power and responsibilities that entailed. He could either stay where he was with a vastly reduced 8th Division, or return to Australia and command the rest of his men. At least that was Northcott's ultimatum.

Bennett, sensing that circumstances would soon change, wisely chose the former, writing in his diary: 'I asked that a complete Div HQ be formed here or alternatively my Div HQ be sent from Australia and that I be authorised to form a complete Base HQ.'

It is a measure of Bennett's determined character that he never took no for an answer, firing off letters to General Sturdee and other senior members of the military calling for his division to be kept intact. There was a slight weakening of army resolve when Sturdee agreed to increase Bennett's staff numbers but not his overall force. They included the appointment as his deputy assistant quartermaster-General Major Wilfred Kent Hughes, who had served with distinction in World War I and had been a citizen soldier.

'Kent Hughes arrived like a breath of Heaven – he will be really good. He knows his job,' Bennett noted in his diary.

To add to the good news Army HQ told Bennett that his entire divisional headquarters could join him, as well as a reserve motor transport company, a stores depot and a field park company. Slowly Bennett was getting his own way but it still fell far short of his wish list, which required the presence of his entire division, minus those troops already committed to the Dutch East Indies in the event of war.

The commander of the 8th Division was not only making his presence felt within the military hierarchy, he was also exhibiting a less harmonious side to his character in the way he handled his fellow officers. Bennett's reputation for making enemies was amply demonstrated when relations soured between him and Brigadier Harold Taylor, who commanded the 22nd Infantry Brigade. The two men, both citizen soldiers, fell out during a defence exercise which involved troops moving from Malaya's west coast to the east. Taylor was slightly younger but equal to his boss in terms of aggressive nature and opinionated manner. Both men had their own way of doing things and did not countenance interference, so when Bennett decided to monitor the exercise in person, Taylor was ready for trouble.

Tempers exploded when Taylor decided to interrupt the exercise in order to give his men a couple of hours' break for breakfast. The sight of an entire brigade downing eggs and toast and piping hot mugs of tea sent Bennett into a rage. Finally, frustrated by the time it was all taking, he ordered his brigadier to get his men moving at the double. Taylor, who was already upset over his commander's eagle-eyed presence, turned around and, in so many words, told his superior where to go.

Bristling with indignation, Bennett threatened to send Taylor back to Australia. Taylor sensed he had gone too far and sought the intervention of Bennett's chief signals officer, Colonel James Thyer, who had witnessed the altercation. Thyer engineered a meeting with the two men to patch things up, but just as Taylor left the room he foolishly quipped, 'I still think I am in the right.'[7]

The two officers were never going to agree and from that moment on tried to avoid any professional or social contact. Once again Bennett's giant ego had got in the way of common sense. He sorely needed friends and confidants and Taylor, while verging on the insubordinate, was to prove himself a courageous soldier in the coming months.

Other officers were to fall foul of Bennett's volatile temperament and not-so-thinly veiled criticism, especially members of the Staff Corps, whose military philosophy would always be at odds with his own. There was also a perception that Bennett did not get along with his British counterparts – a suggestion that is hard to believe given his respect for the Empire and Australia's colonial ties with the mother country.

In fact he was to become a staunch supporter and admirer of the man who would become Britain's General Officer

Commanding, Malaya, General Arthur Percival. A World War I veteran who had commanded a battalion and won three decorations, Lieutenant-General Percival was appointed GOC on 16 May 1941. His military pedigree was certainly impressive: he had graduated not only from the Army Staff College but the Naval Staff College. He also had an intimate knowledge of Malaya, after serving there in 1937 as a staff officer and preparing a dummy plan of attack on Singapore from a Japanese perspective.

In many ways Percival was the exact antithesis of Bennett. He was quiet, tactful and patient, with a firm but positive resolve. In Bennett's judgement this meant Percival was probably the best candidate for the job but in the final analysis was unable to beat the system hoisted upon him by the British government.

Percival also shared the view that stronger forces were urgently needed in Malaya, the two men thus acknowledging the dire repercussions of a Japanese invasion and what it would mean for Singapore.

The sense of foreboding added to the stress of training and containing a fighting force several thousand miles away from home. As Lionel Wigmore, the official historian, was to acknowledge in *The Japanese Thrust*: 'The 8th Division from its commander downwards was now undergoing a test to which Australian troops had not hitherto been put . . . [they] had been dispersed far and wide on garrison duty of a kind not contemplated by the officers and men when their units were formed. In tropical conditions, which themselves imposed nervous strain, this resulted in a sense of frustration and the sort of grumbling by which men relieve their feelings.'

One example of this could be found in the Northern Territory, where the 2/21st Battalion was still kicking up its heels. The men had arrived there in April 1941 and faced several months of boredom and frustration before they were finally sent to Ambon. Dumped in scrubland several miles outside Darwin, they drank like fish and played cards to while away the time.

Max 'Eddie' Gilbert, who was part of B Company, said it was like living in a wild-west town. 'Fellas either boozed or gambled or did both,' he recalled, though fortunately he was able to occupy himself as a member of the mortar team.[8]

Lieutenant-Colonel William Scott, who would later command Gull Force, claimed the battalion was out of control. He cited indiscipline, drunkenness and fighting among the men as the main complaints, although it would later emerge that the officer had a vested interest in badmouthing the troops, after falling out with their CO, Lieutenant-Colonel Len Roach.[9]

Family ties were also being stretched to the limit after newspaper articles published in Australia unwittingly gave the impression that those troops stationed in Malaya were enjoying the high life. Wives and girlfriends writing letters from home said they'd seen how their menfolk were 'leading exotic lives in the tropics'. Sometimes a wife or girl would add that she too knew how to have a 'gay time'. Such remarks, made in ignorance of the toil, sweat and tedium of the men's lot, bit into the feelings of many.

While the joke was on them, they accepted the mocking tone, referring to themselves satirically as 'Menzies' Glamour Boys' and naming a row of huts 'Pansy Alley'.[10]

While there is no doubt that training and conditions in Malaya were hard for the 8th Division, they also enjoyed a good social life.

Conscious of his men's needs, Bennett helped to establish a leave club in Kuala Lumpur, with British ex-pat women cooking the meals and even waiting on the officers. Soon an Anzac Club was opened in Singapore, financed by a local resident as a 'mark of an Englishman's appreciation of the Dominion troops'.

The Aussies, who were always up for a party, were regarded as a bit of a novelty and while the peace continued there were abundant opportunities to down a few ales and make small talk with the locals.

Gordon Bennett was also beginning to enjoy himself, some reports of the time suggesting a tendency to 'going native'. Certainly his dress sense was frequently out of character when compared with the full uniform he wore as 8th Division commander.

Alfred Duff Cooper, a prominent British politician whom Churchill would send to Singapore as Resident Minister of Far Eastern Affairs, clearly found it difficult to know what to make of Bennett when he paid a visit to his headquarters and his 'pansy hat – wide brimmed straw with a multi-coloured scarf around it' incited sniggers.[11]

Bennett also donned a sarong on occasions, though he was not alone in this. In the tropical conditions it was a practical garment and became increasingly popular among males relaxing under the heat of the midday sun.

As his social circle grew, Bennett took full advantage of the hospitality on offer, particularly that provided by the Sultan of Johore, who was said to be among the world's wealthiest monarchs. The head of one of Malaya's richest states, Sultan Ibrahim enjoyed high living and the company of beautiful women. He was an anglophile, having been sent to public school in Britain, where his father had been a friend of Queen Victoria. As commander-in-chief of his own battalion, he also enjoyed the trappings of military life, so when the 8th Division's Headquarters was established in Johore Bahru, he was quick to extend a royal welcome to its commander.

Gordon Bennett and the Sultan got on famously, and the friendship extended to the Australian troops, who were to enjoy full use of his polo field to play football. The largesse included whisky and cigars for Bennett, who also got on well with the Sultan's wife. Gossips suggested that the relationship with her was more than platonic, though this may have been a scurrilous rumour invented by Bennett's enemies.

Major John Wyett, who was a member of Bennett's staff, was later to recall how he found a compromising photograph of the Sultan's fourth and much younger wife, Marcella, the daughter of a Romanian migrant, in the commander's personal belongings after the fall of Singapore.

'She was very pleasant, youngish and easy to talk to,' he told author Peter Thompson. 'I think it was a bit more than that with him. They were flirting with each other – the Sultan didn't seem to mind,' Wyett added.[12]

Whatever the truth, the strong ties between the 8th Division and the Sultan clearly had mutual benefits. Not only did Bennett's troops share in the Sultan's generosity, but the ruler himself felt safer in the knowledge that the 8th Division was there to protect his state.

Interestingly those close relations did not stop the Sultan from charging the Australians a royalty of five Malayan dollars for every tree they felled for defence or training purposes. The thinking was that as the Sultan owned everything in the state, he had to be recompensed for everything taken. By December 1942 the AIF had handed over 100,000 Straits dollars to the Sultan's coffers. Not a bad little earner for a country that was relying on the Allies to protect them.[13]

———·—·———

Bennett decided to place part of the 22nd Brigade at Mersing, in order to block the road to Singapore in the event of a Japanese attack down the east coast. In the meantime he still continued to do battle with his masters back in Australia. With the arrival of the 27th Brigade in August, the AIF's total force in Malaya was now 15,000. They included 2/26th Battalion, 2/29th Battalion, 2/30th Battalion, 2/15th Field Regiment, 2/12th Field Company, 2/6th Field Company and 2/10th Field Ambulance. But while Australia was providing more men on the ground, air and sea support were sadly lacking.

There were a mere 143 aircraft based in Malaya, comprising 22 Vildebeests, six Catalina flying boats, 60 Buffalo fighters, 12 Hudson and 43 Blenheim bombers.

Naval support was little better. After pressure on London, the Admiralty recognised the need for a battle fleet to be sent to the Far East. Initially it recommended that four 'R' class battleships be sent to the Indian Ocean followed by reinforcements early in 1942, including two more battle-ships, a battle cruiser and, in the event of an emergency, an aircraft carrier.

Churchill rejected this proposal but in early October the decision was made to send the recently completed *Prince of Wales* and an older but faster battle cruiser, the *Repulse*, which would head almost immediately to the area. The aircraft carrier *Indomitable* would join them in Singapore, but on the way she struck a reef in Jamaica, an accident that would have tragic consequences. The *Indomitable* was carrying 45 aircraft with which to defend the small naval task force despatched to Singapore. Without the carrier, the *Prince of Wales* and the rest of the flotilla were exposed and hopelessly vulnerable to attack by enemy planes.[14]

While the increased naval presence was a welcome step, Bennett continued to press for more troops and he had not given up on his request to transfer the 23rd Brigade, who continued to languish in the Northern Territory. To reinforce his demand, he offered to fly to Darwin for a formal inspection of the brigade which remained under his command. Much to his indignation, Bennett was told that such a visit would be unnecessary as the 23rd were about to be wrested from his control and separated into individual forces for duty in the Dutch East Indies, New Britain and the Northern Territory. This amounted to the official formation of Gull Force, Lark Force and Sparrow Force, which had been under consideration for some months.

However, perhaps he might consider a journey to the Middle East instead, the Military Board suggested. The decision, agreed by the War Cabinet, dismayed and perplexed Bennett who might have guessed that other forces were afoot to unseat him from his present position.

A couple of days later his suspicions were confirmed when his old adversary General Thomas Blamey arrived in Singapore on the way back to Australia from the Middle East and told Bennett in no uncertain terms that he was about to urge the Cabinet to dispatch the 8th Division to the Middle

East. Bennett was shocked and rightly saw it as a thinly disguised move by Blamey to bring the entire AIF under his control in the Middle East. In one fell swoop he would achieve his ultimate ambition and thereby scuttle Bennett's attempts to secure the top job himself.

By now it was early November, just over a month before Japan would enter World War II by blitzing Pearl Harbor and invading Malaya. The clock was ticking but Blamey remained convinced that the Japanese still posed no particular threat.

Meanwhile, Bennett, whose resolve showed no sign of faltering, took advantage of Blamey's absence from the Middle East and headed for Egypt, in accordance with the War Cabinet's earlier instructions. What he found there did not impress him. He described the Western Desert offensive as lacking drive, punch and coordination, with an 'elephantine' headquarters which had grown at the expense of the number of men available to fight.

'Too many officers were so far removed from the battles that were being fought that they lost touch with reality. Departments became watertight and out of touch with other departments. Perfect cooperation was extremely difficult,' he declared.[15]

If this was Bennett's way of getting his own back on Blamey, he need not have worried. The War Cabinet had already rejected Blamey's request to send the 8th Division to the Middle East so the way was now open for Bennett to concentrate on Malaya. It was not a pretty picture. The number of fighting units positioned in Malaya by early December 1941 comprised 86,000 men, of whom many were poorly trained and badly equipped. Most were Indians and locally enlisted troops, who together totalled almost 54,000.

In addition there were now 19,600 British and 15,200 Australians. As well as 31 infantry battalions there were seven field units, one mountain regiment, two anti-tank regiments and two anti-tank batteries.

Although it looked impressive on paper, the figures did not fill Bennett with confidence.

Anxious to get back to his men and aware of intelligence reports that the Japanese had been sending military and political personnel to Thailand for several months, the commander decided to return as soon as possible. He booked a passage on a Qantas flying boat due to leave on the morning of 3 December and wrote in his diary: 'Indo-China has been well prepared as a springboard from which to make the dive into Thailand, Malaya and the Netherlands East Indies. I fear that the move may start before my return so I have decided to push off at once.'

When Blamey got wind of Bennett's early departure he dismissed the idea that Japan was on the brink of invading.

'Blamey pooh-poohed the idea,' Bennett noted in his diary, 'and was very definite in his opinion nothing would happen in Malaya, and that the Japanese would not extend the war there. I quoted what had been happening in Thailand. He was still not convinced.'[16]

The flight to Malaya took several days. Arriving at Government House in Calcutta to meet up with General Archibald Wavell, Supreme Commander, South West Pacific, Bennett also found his boyhood foe Thomas Blamey there. Once again the two men clashed, with each attempting to press home their personal arguments. Bennett was adamant, telling Blamey that the 8th Division would soon be fighting the war against the Japanese in Malaya, but Blamey would not listen.

It was fortuitous that Bennett left Cairo when he did. As the 8th Division's commander resumed his flight, unbeknown to him the Japanese invasion fleet was already heading towards the Malay Peninsula and the east coast of southern Thailand.

Three Australian Hudson reconnaissance aircraft spotted the fleet after taking off from Kota Bharu on Malaya's north-eastern coast on the Saturday morning of 6 December. It was Flight Lieutenant Jack Ramshaw who saw the first three Japanese vessels nearly 300 kilometres out to sea. A short time later he identified a much larger flotilla, consisting of seven destroyers, five cruisers, a heavy cruiser and 25 merchant ships.[17] Because of the monsoonal conditions the aircraft were unable to maintain visual contact but radioed the sighting back to base.

Later, Flying Officer Patrick Bedell of the British RAF spotted the armada from his Catalina flying boat. He was a sitting duck in the circumstances. The Japanese saw him and opened fire to prevent him alerting his HQ back in Singapore. Bedell is believed to have been the first official casualty of the war in the Far East.

In the early hours of 8 December, weather reports from Japanese radio in Tokyo forecast a fair, westerly wind. The Allies did not know it at the time but it was a code for Japanese missions across the globe to prepare for the outbreak of war.

At 3.30 am local time in Singapore, a formation of unidentified planes was reported heading towards the island from the northwest, sending local army, navy and air force units into a frenzy. An hour later bombs started falling on Singapore's airfields.

It was too late to alert the local population as the civil defence officer who had the key to the air-raid siren had gone to the cinema earlier in the evening and could not be contacted. Thus the litany of blunders began to unfold. Singapore's lack of preparedness in the face of a mighty and ruthless enemy would haunt the Allied forces for years to come.

Around the same time, during a refuelling stop in Rangoon, Bennett was given the dreadful news. The Japanese had also bombed the Americans at Pearl Harbor, as well as Manila. Around the same time the Japanese 5th Division were landing at Singora and Patani in Thailand and parts of the 18th were coming ashore just over the border at Kota Bharu in north-east Malaya.

Henry Gordon Bennett's instincts had been proved correct. The war in the Far East was underway. Who knew where it would end?

Chapter 4

ATTACK, ATTACK, ATTACK

In the half-light of dawn on 8 December, the reality of the Japanese attacks was only just beginning to sink in. Although dozens of civilians were reported killed or injured in Singapore, miraculously the pride of the British fleet, HMS *Prince of Wales* and her sister ship, *Repulse*, which were now at anchor at the naval base, had escaped unscathed.

With Australia's 8th Division ensconced further north along the peninsula's east coast, around Mersing and Endau, all eyes switched to the Thai border, where the Japanese were coming ashore in force. Operation Matador, a British plan to invade Thailand and thereby cut off the enemy before they crossed the border into Malaya, had been carefully devised months before the anticipated invasion. But even as enemy forces landed at Singora and Patani in southern Thailand, Matador had still to be put into effect. Incredibly, the 11th Indian Division, which had been in position south of the Thai border for weeks, was still awaiting its orders because of indecision by Air Vice-Marshal Sir Robert Brooke Popham, who was close to nervous collapse. Then Commander-in-Chief of British Far East Command, he was soon to be replaced by Lieutenant-General Sir Henry Pownall.

The Indian troops, led by Major-General David Murray-Lyon, had been champing at the bit all night in the pouring rain and by morning were thoroughly drenched. It was not until early afternoon that they received the message that Matador had been called off.

Eventually 11th Division was given permission to press ahead with its advance across the border, only to be confronted by a group of Thai police who held them up with rifles and light machine guns. The Thais, who had also blocked the road with felled trees, soon realised they were outnumbered and allowed the Indians through to a ridge known as the Ledge. Not long afterwards, the 2/16th Punjabs found themselves in contact with an advance party of Japanese who were backed up by tanks. It was clearly an unequal match. Despite valiant efforts by the Indians to fight their way up the road, enemy soldiers forced them back with mortars and machine guns, inflicting heavy casualties in the process.

'It was said at the time that the failure was due to the unexpected change from attack to defence for which our troops were not properly disposed,' Bennett recorded later in his official report. 'With trained troops this should have made no difference. Leadership was also weak. An encounter battle should have ensued in which our troops, if superior in quality to the enemy and if better led, should have overcome the Japanese.'[1]

Further withdrawals by the Indians followed, notably at Jitra in Malaya's far northwest, where about 3000 soldiers were taken prisoner. It was a humiliating defeat for the men of the 11th Indian Division, who were beaten by a reconnaissance detachment of only 500 Japanese soldiers.

Bennett was so impressed by the way so few men had defeated so many that he sent a staff officer there to investigate the methods adopted by the Japanese to achieve such a decisive and remarkable result.

'The feat demonstrated that battles are not always won by big battalions,' he wrote. 'That a small force of battle trained men possessing the initiative and making use of that valuable weapon, surprise, can quickly overwhelm a numerically stronger force which lacks battle experience.'[2]

But how had they done it?

The answer was to be found in Japanese tactics.

First, they detected a weak spot in the defensive line then, under the cover of darkness, launched their attack. After penetrating the Indian line, they started firing at them from behind. As a result the Allies panicked and the front crumbled.

In this case the Japanese troops involved in the Jitra attack were all veterans of the war in China, where so many civilians were killed. They were already experienced in combat and were not deterred by the clatter of machine guns or the whine of rifle bullets against a background of thunder from mortar bombs and artillery.

Because of the enemy's intense training in night operations they had become experts in nocturnal aggression. These men were familiar with the roar of war and were not frightened by it. The same could not be said for the men of 11th Division, for whom this was their first taste of battle.

But noise itself did not cause casualties, as Bennett knew well from his own experience. 'It is natural for troops being attacked for the first time in their lives to be susceptible to shock and panic,' he would later concede. 'Battle experienced soldiers have learned this lesson and, using their knowledge, are able to develop a battle cunning that quickly tricks the inexperienced and shocks defenders into surrender.'[3]

This was certainly the case with the Japanese but the same lesson had not been learned by the British, whose tactics had more in common with withdrawal than attack, according to the 8th Division's commander.

Bennett was obviously not impressed with the way the war had started. His views on poor leadership and training were a running theme in the subsequent weeks. However, he did not direct his criticism at his own men, although he continued to have rows with fellow officers.

Brigadier Cecil Callaghan, who was acting commander of the division while Bennett had been in the Middle East, felt the full force of his superior's tongue on Bennett's return to Malaya.

During Bennett's absence Callaghan, who had served in World War I and participated in the Gallipoli landing, had taken it upon himself to change the disposition of Australian troops around Endau, fearing an imminent Japanese attack in the area. Bennett was furious that his own plans had been over-ridden by his deputy and immediately ordered a return to the original positions. It did not bode well for the relationship between the two men as they prepared for one of the most intense periods of military activity either had experienced.

Meanwhile, two divisions of Japanese troops, the 5th and the 18th, were now free to make their way into northern Malaya. Others were already coming ashore at Kota Bharu at the northeastern end of the peninsula. The RAAF's No. 1

Squadron based there was a sitting target and soon all British and Indian forces in the area succumbed to the enemy's attack from the sea and in the air. Lieutenant-General Tomoyuki Yamashita, Commander of the 25th Japanese Army, which included the fearsome Imperial Guards Division, was on the warpath and heading south.

The AIF's 8th Division was still nearly 300 miles (500 km) away from the onslaught, which Churchill had described as 'unprovoked aggression' and a 'flagrant violation of international law'. Addressing the House of Commons that same day he told MPs, 'We can only feel that Hitler's madness has infected the Japanese mind.'[4]

The bad news from Malaya did not get any better. Back in Singapore the British fleet, which was supposed to protect the 'impregnable fortress' in the event of war, had already steamed out of the naval base overlooking the Johore Strait and was on its way north.

The *Prince of Wales* and *Repulse* were intending to attack Japanese troopships carrying more men to Kota Bharu, but without proper aerial support they were hopelessly vulnerable.

It did not take long for Japanese spotter planes to relay the exact position of the vessels back to base. Senior officers led by Admiral Tom Phillips, who was in overall command of the British fleet, realised they were an easy target and decided to return to Singapore.

Pint-sized Phillips, who was nicknamed Tom Thumb by his crew, was friends with Churchill, who called him the Cocksparrow, a cockney term for small men with a cocky demeanour. The admiral was 53 and had a high opinion of himself. At first he dismissed the advice of others who believed aircraft always posed a major threat to a well-equipped battleship.[5] Tragically, he was to learn the hard way. Admiral Phillips went down with his ship.

Gunnery rating John Gaynor, who was a member of the *Prince of Wales'* crew, said the power went first, after the ship was hit by two torpedoes, one in the bows and the other in the stern. Being a modern, all-electric vessel nothing worked once the power failed, not even the guns. Soon the battleship was listing to port, which exposed part of the starboard side's underbelly.

'So the Japanese pilots went around again and now they came in on the exposed portion of the ship and in came the torpedoes, because she could no longer fire back at them,' he recalled. 'One minute she was going to port then she rocked back to starboard. I looked over and saw the torpedoes, the wreckage and people hanging all over the place, lots of bodies floating around. It was carnage. This was the time for the survivors of which I was going to be one.'[6]

Although Gaynor lived to tell the tale, 840 crew members from *Repulse* and *Prince of Wales* perished. Incredibly hundreds survived, many of them forced to cling to wreckage in the oily water. A British pilot who flew over the area where the two ships sank was astonished at the spirit of those men trying to stay afloat.

'As I flew around every man waved and put up his thumb as I flew over him. After an hour lack of petrol forced me to leave but during that hour I had seen many men in dire danger waving, cheering and joking, as if they were holiday-makers at Brighton waving at a low-flying aircraft,' he told the *London Gazette*.

News of the calamitous sinking of the British vessels

sent shock waves around the world. In London Churchill pondered the loss in his pyjamas.

'As I turned over and twisted in bed the full horror of the news sank in upon me,' he admitted. 'There were no British or American ships in the Indian Ocean or the Pacific except the American survivors of Pearl Harbor . . . Over all this vast expanse of water Japan was supreme and we everywhere were weak and naked.'[7]

While Bennett and the men of the 8th Division must have been equally as shocked by the naval loss, they could not dwell on it. Their brief was to protect the rest of the Malay Peninsula from the Japanese advance by land. And they were not ruling out a seaborne landing along their own strip of coast from Mersing to Endau.

General Bennett, who by now had established his head-quarters at Johore Bahru overlooking Singapore Island, had deployed his 22nd Brigade along the coast from Mersing to Endau, which he believed was the most likely area for a seaborne assault by the Japanese. The 27th Brigade, which had spent most of the time in Singapore since its arrival, was to be sent to the northwestern Johore region, where it could be made available to support the 22nd Brigade if necessary.

General Percival agreed to the move on the basis that the Australians deserved more responsibility. Bennett was happy because he did not want his force split up. Far better, he reasoned, that they remain together as one formation rather than risk individual units being sent off willy-nilly to relieve the Indians.

As the enemy continued to advance it looked increasingly likely that their progress would depend on securing control of Jemaluang, a road junction just south of Mersing on the east coast, which would allow them access across country to Kluang in the west and Kota Tinggi to the south. With this in mind Bennett proposed to hold the beaches at Mersing and Endau to the north by placing the 2/18th and 2/20th Battalions along this stretch of the eastern coastline. The 2/19th would be positioned at Jemaluang and part of the 2/30th a few miles to its west. The 2/29th would defend Kahang and Kluang along a road which linked the east coast to the western side of the peninsula. As well as being an important transport corridor, the route had two airfields which had to be defended. Further south part of the 2/26th Battalion would guard the road from Sedili Besar northwards.

The 22nd Brigade had already spent many weeks strengthening defences in the area, while the 2/30th used the time to cut tracks through the dense jungle in case the main road became impassable.

Brigadier Harold Taylor, who was in command of the 22nd Brigade, saw its mission as the destruction of any enemy landing on the beaches between Jemaluang and Mersing and to harass them as much as possible. He was under no illusion about the threat they posed. 'We can expect them to be bold,' he wrote at the time. 'They greatly admire German methods and will develop maximum strength in the minimum time. Japanese infantry can maintain themselves for several days without transport in difficult terrain.'[8]

Taylor, who came from Sydney, was one of Bennett's key officers but it was no secret that the two men did not get along. They openly disagreed at a professional and personal level from the time they arrived in Malaya. Like Bennett's rift with Blamey, the gulf between them would outlast the war and have significant repercussions for Taylor's military career.

By mid–December the situation facing the Allies gave little cause for comfort. The news from the north became gloomier by the day, as British and Indian forces were attacked, forcing them into a series of humiliating retreats. General Bennett's men, keen to prove their mettle on the battlefield, had their fingers on the trigger ready for any emergency. 'They are afraid of nothing and nobody,' Bennett wrote in his diary. 'The men earnestly hope that the enemy will attack as they have confidence in themselves and in their position.'[9]

But one question continued to disturb him. How could they resist the Japanese war machine when they were apparently so outnumbered? This worried Bennett more than anything. So much so that he sent a letter to Army Headquarters pleading for reinforcements.

'This is imperative. I also need as much assistance as I can get from Australia at a very early date in the form of additional units,' he added.[10]

He followed that up with a letter to the Minister for the Army, Frank Forde, who was assured that the 8th Division were as 'happy as sandboys at the thought of being able to get our new enemy, the yellow Huns of the East. In my whole experience, including that of my last war, I have never met men with a higher morale.'

But there was a major problem that had to be addressed, he continued. He wanted more troops and he needed them now.

'Our line is thin. The 3rd Brigade of my division would have been a godsend to us now. As you know, it has been repeatedly asked for, and my requests have been repeatedly refused.'[11]

And then there was the air force, or rather the lack of it.

'The air position, of course, gives me great concern,' he stated, 'there being insufficient to do the job adequately.'[12]

The Allies' inadequacy in the air had already been demonstrated over Singapore, as well as off the east coast, where the British fleet was resting at the bottom of the South China Sea. Without the planes Bennett and his men were dreadfully exposed.

A message from Malaya Command on the afternoon of 13 December did not improve the outlook. A convoy of more than 100 Japanese vessels had been reported off the southern point of French Indochina moving in a south-southwesterly direction towards the Malayan Peninsula. Though it was still uncertain where precisely the reinforcements would come ashore it seemed only a matter of time before the full might of the Japanese offensive would be unleashed.

On the west coast of the peninsula the enemy advance had reached Penang, which had given in without a struggle. As enemy planes blitzed the island, Allied forces withdrew in haste, leaving behind their food and supplies. To Bennett the swift withdrawal symbolised all that was wrong with the Allies' strategy – retreat, retreat, retreat.

If only he could be sent 'quality' reinforcements, he wrote to Army HQ in Melbourne. Then at least they would have a chance of stopping the Japanese in their tracks.

'I have seen a total absence of the offensive spirit, which after all is the one great remedy for the methods adopted by the Japanese. Counterattacks would put a stop to this penetration.'[13]

Bennett wanted one division from the AIF in the Middle East to be sent to Malaya. And he urged that HQ consider it as a matter of 'paramount importance'.

While the commander's demands might have irritated the top brass at home, his men were on his side. And he used every opportunity to share his thoughts about what should be their tactical response to the enemy. In an open letter to all ranks he emphasised it was imperative that the offensive spirit be maintained.

'If it is possible for the enemy to create havoc and panic amongst troops by outflanking them, then it is just as possible for us to do that to him.

'Should the enemy endeavour to infiltrate through jungle, it will be our policy to move forward to meet him and attack him at every opportunity.' And in a final rallying call he alluded to the strategy employed by one of his World War I heroes, Field Marshal William Birdwood, who demanded that each of his men should kill ten Germans. 'We might well take a leaf out of his book and urge every individual Australian in the forward zone to accept the risk of killing at least ten Japanese.'[14]

It was stirring stuff and a necessary call to arms given that the Japanese were getting closer. On 18 December, Bennett received word that the garrison at Kuantan further up the east coast road was hard pressed to contain the enemy, which was threatening the Allies' rear position by adopting the now familiar tactic of infiltration.

Over the next few days the situation in Malaya's north-west deteriorated further, with General Percival allowing his commanding officer of Indian 111 Brigade, Lieutenant-General Sir Lewis 'Piggy' Heath, to withdraw further south to the Perak River, the country's second-longest river. How long before Kuala Lumpur, Port Dickson and Malacca would be similarly swallowed?

If the British, Indian and Australian troops were beginning to recognise the perilous nature of their position, the same could not be said for the civilian community in Singapore, where the upper classes continued to turn a blind eye to the chaos unfolding to their north.

Although an Allied conference was held in Singapore on 18 December by the newly appointed British ministerial supremo Duff Cooper to assess the current situation, the champagne continued to bubble on the cocktail circuit. Cooper's actress wife, the glamorous Diana, who had appeared in a couple of prewar movies, was staying in Government House, which she described as 'cool as a fishnet'.

Outside the town was 'enchanting' and the lawns were 'mown by the fingers and thumbs of natives advancing on all fours in a serried row and plucking the growing grass blades'.

Later the couple moved in to some sumptuous digs further out of town, where the servants and their concubines seemed to be employed for the sole purpose of 'our comfort', she enthused.[15]

If Lady Diana was in the grip of Singapore's unreal world, her husband was not. Realising the seriousness of the crisis that was about to befall the island, he fired off a letter to Churchill warning him of the likelihood of Malaya's imminent defeat. In it Duff Cooper was highly critical of the civilian authorities in Singapore, especially those who were responsible for civil defence.

Perhaps surprisingly he did not share his misgivings with the American, British, Dutch, Australian and New Zealanders who had gathered at the Allied conference earlier in the day. For whatever reason he had decided to keep his thoughts to himself and Churchill. Was it all part of the Singapore delusion, in which the obvious went largely unspoken? Why trouble yourself with the unthinkable when life was such a ball?

In truth, life for many of those expats was beginning to unravel. While some put on a brave face, others were already seeking refuge in Raffles Hotel, where families from the rubber plantations up north were beginning to assemble. Separated from their husbands, hundreds of wives and children who were hoping to secure a passage overseas were clogging up the luxury hotel with their luggage and personal belongings. The hotel, which was synonymous with luxury and privilege and where civil servants and the officer class would gather in the Long Bar for a peg of Scotch, was beginning to resemble a refugee camp.

Back on the mainland Bennett and Brigadier Callaghan, who was now acting as his artillery commander, decided to have a look at conditions for themselves and headed for Gemas and Muar, in the southwest of the peninsula, which were the most likely locations for the 8th Division's first real clash with the enemy.

Holding the Gemus–Muar front with one Australian brigade would become Bennett's toughest challenge. Once again he decided to write to Army HQ to alert them to the impending crisis. 'We are living from hand to mouth in the matter of troops and our task will be extremely difficult,' he warned.

With some luck they might be able to hold the enemy, he reasoned, but with insufficient troops to launch counter-blows, the enemy would accumulate and might overwhelm them by dint of numbers. To make their position secure he required at least one more AIF division.

General Percival backed him up and urged Bennett to increase the pressure on Australia to send further reinforcements. Air Vice-Marshal Brooke-Popham, who was about to hand over his position of Commander-in-Chief, British Far East, to Lieutenant-General Henry Pownall, was also inveigled into using his influence on the Australians.

By now British and Indian forces who had been battling the Japanese for nearly a fortnight were exhausted. Christmas was only a few days away and in a welcome nod to the season of goodwill, 23 December coincided with a lull in the fighting.

In the relatively quiet days leading up to Christmas Bennett took the opportunity to see Brigadier Ivan Simson, who was worried about Singapore's defences. Simson wanted permission to install anti-tank obstacles to hinder the enemy's advance.

The divisional commander agreed to let the chief engineer do the necessary, but Simson got the impression that Bennett was not that interested, a view reinforced in *Why Singapore Fell*, in which Bennett revealed his preference for anti-tank weapons rather than physical obstacles.[16]

Throughout the lead-up to the Japanese invasion, Singapore had never taken its defences seriously. Even General Percival was reluctant to install fixed defences because of the negative effect it might have on civilian morale.

Churchill was seething when he learned about the lack of preparedness on the island and ordered his Commander-in-Chief, Field Marshal Archibald Wavell, to urge the entire male population to get involved in defending the island. 'The most rigorous compulsion is to be used, up to the limit where picks and shovels are available,' he stipulated. 'Not only must the defence of Singapore Island be maintained by every means, but . . . the city of Singapore must be converted into a citadel and defended to the death.'[17]

Amazingly it was not until mid-January 1942 that the order was given to prepare field defences. After years of indecision the authorities were at last goaded into action.

It wasn't enough, though. As Brigadier Simson confided in a memo at the time, although as much as possible had been done to construct air-raid shelters and the like, only a small percentage of the real requirements for such a large population were met 'owing to all this work not having begun or even seriously considered until half-way through the campaign'.[18]

The fact was that the British military had given little consideration to the idea that the Japanese might attack from land. The heavy artillery defences, which were placed in an arc from the southwest round to the east, assumed that any invasion would come from the sea. It is why the large-calibre coastal guns were left pointing defiantly to the south. Although they could in theory be turned the other way, they were mostly equipped to fire armour-piercing shells, which were fine for penetrating the steel hulls of warships but useless for attacking infantry targets.

Among all the gloom and doom there were occasional glimmers of hope. Back in Australia, and after much pressure, Lieutenant-General Vernon Sturdee, Chief of the General Staff, agreed to send the machine gun battalion and 1800 reinforcements to Malaya. It was a step in the right direction but fell far short of Bennett's demand for a full division.[19]

If nothing else, the Christmas Eve news provided some cause for celebration. Bennett spent the early evening hosting a party for 80 officers and staff, as well as a group of nurses from his 2/13th Australian General Hospital unit.

The next day he went to church at St Christopher's in Johore Bahru. 'Within the church was the spirit of peace and goodwill – but outside it was war, bitter war,' he wrote in his diary entry for 25 December.[20]

Of immediate concern was how the enemy had become more active in the air, thanks partly to their occupation of Allied airports at Alor Setar, Kota Bharu and Kuantan, halfway down the east coast.

Japanese troops had also managed to cross the strategically important Perak River. Once over the other side they got up to their old tricks of sending soldiers around the flank to the rear of British and Indian forces in the area.

Bennett realised the end game was approaching. 'It cannot be long before the Australians are put to the test. It seems certain that they will soon be moving forward to their battle stations in the north of Johore,' he noted later that Christmas Day.

As for the men themselves, he wondered whether they appreciated they would soon be fighting for dear life. While walking among them as they ate their Christmas lunch of turkey, ham and plum pudding, he found them full of cheer. There was much banter as the officers waited on the lower ranks who addressed their superiors as 'boy' and jokingly demanded better service.

Bennett had a heavy social calendar that day. Soon he was off to lunch with the Sultan's eldest son, Tungku Mahkota, followed by dinner with the Sultan of Johore himself and his attractive European wife, Marcella. It was a convivial evening, with the Sultan promising to stand or fall by the Australians in the war against the Japanese.

Christmas Day had provided a brief but welcome interlude in the depressing saga which was unfolding to Bennett's north. How much longer could the Allies contain the Japanese? And when the hour came would his men be up to the job?

Bennett need have no doubt there. The next few weeks would produce the 8th Division's finest hour.

———·———

By now the division's commander had been forced to accept that most of the men he had left behind in Australia would not be joining him in Malaya. The 22nd Battalion had already been sent to Rabaul in New Britain under the name of Lark Force, which also included an RAAF bomber squadron, a coastal artillery battery and members of the New Guinea Volunteer Rifles. New Britain was then part of Australian territory and close to the Caroline Islands to the north, which would fall under the control of the Japanese. Rabaul's location in the Pacific was of immense strategic importance, providing an airfield for the RAAF and a flying boat anchorage, which allowed the Australians to keep an eye on Japanese movements in the region. As an Allied outpost it was also extremely isolated, so when 20,000 Japanese marines landed on the island on 23 January 1942, Lark Force was quickly overwhelmed.

Around the same time Sparrow Force, which had been sent to Timor a month earlier, came under attack from the Japanese Air Force. Initially 1400 men drawn mainly from the 2/40th Battalion were assigned to Sparrow Force, which also included commandoes of the 2/2nd Independent Company. Even accompanied by about 650 Dutch East Indies troops, the force was no match for the Japanese, who rapidly over-powered Sparrow Force and took control of the island.

Gull Force, which had left Darwin for Ambon in the middle of December, had the hardest job of all. Nearly 1200 soldiers, mostly Victorians from the 2/21st Battalion, were given the task of defending one of the most strategically important islands in the Dutch East Indies, but with insufficient manpower and inadequate hardware. Even their CO, Len Roach, was able to predict the inevitable disaster long before the men arrived there. Not mincing his words, he warned his superiors that if Gull Force was defeated it would not be a case of 'gallant sacrifice but of murder due to sheer slackness and maladministration'.[21]

As the 2/21st Battalion steamed across the turquoise waters of the Arafura Sea on their 520 nautical mile (950 km) voyage north, they were as lambs to the slaughter. Most of them had never heard of Ambon, but the Japanese certainly knew its value. Whoever governed Ambon, with its large deep-water port and airfield, also controlled much of the region.

It was 17 December when Eddie Gilbert and his mates sailed into the island's well-protected harbour aboard the *Patras*, the *Bhot* and the *Valentine*, three inter-island ferries which were being temporarily used as troopships. 'We were on our way to war,' he reflected. 'That's why we enlisted, not to spend eight demoralising months at Darwin digging slit trenches and learning how to be defensive.'[22]

But soon Eddie and his friends would rue the day they ever set foot on Ambon. Like their counterparts in 8th Division to the north, west and east, they were to end up either prisoners of war or dead.

Chapter 5

'IT WAS A BLOODY SHOW, I CAN TELL YOU'

It is a warm spring morning as I set off for Helensburgh, a semi-rural community bordering the Royal National Park, nearly 43 miles (70 km) south of Sydney. I have arranged to meet Arthur 'Bluey' Kennedy, who lives alone in a ground-floor flat and refuses to move into a nursing home. He is as independent now as he was as a boy growing up in Sydney's western suburbs.

Bluey was born at the Royal Hospital for Women in Paddington on 11 September 1917, which makes him 99 on the day of my visit, though you wouldn't believe it if you saw him. He is short but erect with twinkling eyes and a devilish grin. Despite his age he doesn't need reading glasses and has a healthy appetite. (One meat pie a day and perhaps a slice of pizza in the evening are his favourite dishes.)

Perhaps it's because he never smoked or drank alcohol that he has lived so long. Whatever the reason for his longevity he agrees he's had a charmed life. Born during World War

I, growing up in the Depression, captured by the Japanese, imprisoned on the Burma-Thai Railway and bedevilled by all manner of tropical diseases along the way, it is a miracle that he has lived to tell the tale.

He is also one of the last survivors of the battle of Gemas, which is etched in 8th Division's history as a defining moment in Australia's valiant attempt to halt the Japanese advance. Bluey was a member of the 2/15th Field Regiment, which was raised at Rosebery racecourse in Sydney on 12 November 1940. His memory of the war is as sharp today as it ever was, which makes his eyewitness account of what happened during the Malaya campaign so extraordinarily vivid. To hear about the fighting in the Gemas–Segamat sector some three-quarters of a century ago from a man who was actually there is to experience a unique link with history.

By now the 8th Division had been divided into Eastforce and Westforce, with the latter including the 27th Brigade, which was to act as a shock absorber when the Japanese attacked. Their mission: to kill and injure as many of them as possible.

An elaborate plan was hatched to ambush the enemy as they approached the bridge over the Sungei Gemencheh River close to the main road and rail links that connected southern Malaya and Singapore with the north.

It was the perfect spot for an ambush. Dense jungle grew on both sides of the road for about 600 yards (half a kilometre) and included a cutting some 12 feet (3.6 m) high and about 24 miles (40 m) long. The cutting ended about 60 yards (55 m) from the bridge, rendering the enemy totally exposed.[1]

Gordon Bennett called a conference with Brigadier Duncan Maxwell, CO of the 27th Brigade, and Lieutenant-Colonel

'Black Jack' Galleghan, CO of the 2/30th Battalion. They knew that much depended on the success of this operation. As Galleghan told his commanders and staff on the eve of battle: 'The reputation not only of the AIF in Malaya, but of Australia, is in the hands of this unit.'[2]

Galleghan's troops were desperate for action. They'd been so highly trained for so long that they were like a tightly coiled spring. The fact that they would be the first Australians to fight the Japanese only added to their sense of purpose. They were Galleghan's chosen ones and they wore the accolade with pride.

The surprise element was the key to the mission's success. Silence was paramount. Even a snapping twig or muttered Aussie oath from behind a bush could give away their presence.

Captain Des Kearney, who was second-in-command of the ambush, remembered the long wait, 'not moving and hardly daring to speak'.

'One slip on the part of any man and the whole carefully prepared scheme could fall through.'

Hours went by and they were beginning to expect another night in the jungle when they heard a peculiar 'swishing sound such as a swarm of bees might make'.

Kearney looked up and caught his first sight of the enemy.

'As they approached us we realised that the noise we could hear was caused by the cycle tyres "singing" on the tarred road.'

They were overwhelmed by intense excitement as they knew this was the moment for which they had trained so long. 'According to plan, we made not a move as the column rode only 10 feet beneath us, all laughing and chattering and often looking up into the jungle which hid us so well.'[3]

The idea was to wait for the advance party of Japanese to cross the bridge, blow it up and then commence the ambush. As Colonel Charles Kappe described it in his narrative of the operation on 14 January 1942:

> The object was to destroy with one blow not only the forward elements, but also a large proportion of the main force moving against us from Tampin. At about 10.00 hours a small advance Japanese patrol of four or five mounted on bicycles was seen approaching the bridge. This information was quickly passed on to Battalion HQ . . . Behind the patrol at a distance of about 150 yards came a column of about 150 strong (4 or 5 abreast) riding bicycles. Immediately following them was a further group of about 100 or more.
>
> When it was estimated that 250 cyclists had passed beyond the eastern limit of the ambush position and 500 more were in the ambush area itself and a further 400–500 (5–6 abreast) could be seen riding down the road tightly packed in a compact group, Capt. Duffy, the Coy Commander, at 10.20 hours then gave orders to engineers to blow the bridge.[4]

It was an almighty blast. The charge threw timber, bicycles and bodies high in the air. Three platoons of Captain Duffy's B Company hurled grenades at the enemy and swept them with Bren gun fire, Tommy guns and rifles. The noise was so great that when Duffy ordered artillery fire, the artillery forward observation officer thought his own battery's guns were firing.[5]

The Australians who had hidden themselves in and around the cutting overlooking the bridge had opened up with all guns ablazing.

'They were firing machine guns and rolling hand grenades down the slope and the Japanese didn't know what hit them,' Bluey Kennedy recalled.

'It was a bloody show, I can tell you.'[6]

The gunfight lasted for about 20 minutes, with about 800 Japanese killed or injured, for the loss of one Australian. Lance-Sergeant Athol Nagle, aged 32, from Bellingen in New South Wales, would gain the unenviable title of becoming the first Aussie to die in action against the Japanese – on 15 January 1942.

'The Bren gun fire unfolding along the road combined with the explosion at the bridge had accounted for a very large number of the enemy,' Colonel Kappe reported.

'All opposition across the bridge was wiped out with the exception of a few enemy who made for the jungle.'

The ambush had caught the Japanese totally by surprise. They didn't even have time to unstrap their rifles or automatic guns from the bikes.

As Captain Duffy was to relate afterwards: 'The sight from my observation post was a grim one. The entire 300 yards of road was thickly covered with dead bodies and dying men.'[7]

But the Australians also had a problem. At Company HQ the order went out to the forward observation officer to bring down the artillery fire. However, signal orderlies reported that the line was dead.

The advance party of Japanese had found the cable that linked Battalion and Company Headquarters and had severed the line. As a result those enemy soldiers who had managed to cross the bridge unscathed also escaped the follow-up artillery barrage from the Australians.

'The failure to provide an alternative means of communication in the event of lines being cut had allowed the enemy beyond the bridge to remain untouched,' Kappe explained.

It was a valuable lesson and one which would have serious consequences for the success of the Battle of Gemas.

Within hours the Japanese had managed to rebuild the bridge, thanks to material available from a nearby timber mill which had been left intact. Soon the bridge was strong enough to carry light tanks and motor vehicles, allowing the Japanese to continue their advance towards the 2/30th Battalion.

At the same time those of the enemy who had been allowed to pass through the ambush had doubled back and were now engaging the forward posts of the company.

Eyewitness reports from the time spoke of 'dreadful hand to hand fighting and fierce bayonet work until returning Japanese had also been decimated'.[8]

With at least eight Australians wounded no time could be wasted in getting B Company clear. Slowly they moved off in single file to the south. The 8th Division's retreat, which was never part of General Bennett's strategy, had begun.

Enemy gunfire made movement extremely difficult, forcing the Australians to change their direction. To avoid being detected they had to lower their voices, with the result that the company was split into two parties.

It was difficult to know which way to turn. Then came another surprise encounter in the form of friendly fire from the battalion's own mortars. Death by enemy action was one thing, but to be killed by your own side was not the way to go.

As the Japanese advance and aerial bombardment continued, the Australian gunners remained in constant action. Not only did they have to cope with the full might of the Japanese Air Force but also a squadron of light tanks supported by massed infantry. Part two of the battle of Gemas was underway.

A stick of bombs fell on a signals truck, destroying all communications. Incommunicado with his men, 'Black Jack' emerged from his command post quivering with rage, but no-one could hear his voice because of the surrounding noise level.

As Stuart Peach recalls in Stan Arneil's biography of Galleghan: 'He was heading in my direction and I stood petrified. I had never seen such a look on his face and I wondered if he thought we had let him down.

'My first impression was that we had been overrun by the Japanese,' he added.

Black Jack need not have worried. By the following morning Sergeant Hall had scavenged a few items from another wrecked signals truck down the road and purloined several telephones from local homes. It was enough to restore full communications within a few hours.

For Bombardier 'Bluey' Kennedy the fighting was far from over. While returning from the command post, where he'd been asked to deliver a message, he stumbled across four 25-pounder guns that had been left unattended during the withdrawal. There were three shells lying beside one of them, which proved too much of a temptation for the boy from the militia who had trained as a gunnery sergeant. Normally you need the support of a fellow gunner to operate the mechanism, but on this occasion he decided to fire it by himself.

'I put the shell home, loaded a charge and then thought how the hell am I going to fire it by myself? I can't keep on jumping around.'

Somehow Bluey stretched his arm over the barrel and pressed the trigger. 'Well the whole box of dice, the bloody works went up. There was a burst of flame but it didn't harm me.'

Bluey Kennedy had a lucky escape, one of many he was to enjoy as the war progressed.

By now the gun crew had returned but the tractor on which it was placed was out of action, making the weapon impossible to move. Exposed to enemy fire, some of the gunners were hit by slivers of bronze.

Bluey was also struck in the forehead by a piece of shrapnel but as it didn't bleed he thought nothing of it, believing the wound had been caused by a tree branch. Subsequently a medic removed the splinter but the scar remains to this day.

Fortunately no one was seriously hurt and all of the gunners remained on duty, except for the sergeant, who was injured severely enough to be evacuated to Singapore.[9]

The same day, Bluey Kennedy also witnessed an attack by Japanese infantry units who were supported by tanks and dive bombers. It was mayhem.

'The Japanese were firing with rifles, machine guns, mortars and shellfire from an unknown number of tanks. Branches and leaves were falling from the trees and the whistle and thud of projectiles hitting trees could be heard. Ricocheting pieces of shell whirred past with their chilling sound . . . then an attempt was made to force the road block with tanks.'[10]

The attack was quickly thwarted with the combined fire of the anti-tank and two field guns. The Japs got the message and beat a hasty retreat into the rubber plantations.

Excited by the scene, an Aussie infantryman who was directing his mortar crew's fire from a position up a rubber tree roared with delight as one of his mortar bombs dropped precisely down the open hatch of one of the enemy's tanks.

'Give that man a cigar,' he yelled to his cobber on the ground.

While a little larrikin humour did not go amiss, the Australians' dilemma was no joke. Much valour was displayed that day as they tried their utmost to resist the advancing horde. There seemed no limit to the Aussies' fighting spirit, even to the point of a near suicidal bayonet attack, which had more in common with World War I than II.

How this was allowed to happen is a question that angers Arthur Kennedy to this day. It is a scene that continues to dog him and concerns the orders of Lieutenant-Colonel Galleghan, whose reputation for iron discipline and courage in conflict went before him. But was what happened bravery or madness?

To fully understand the circumstances that led to the bayonet attack it is necessary to return to the few remaining authoritative documents that provide a detailed account of events – the Report of Operations as compiled by Colonels Thyer and Kappe.

Couched in the military terms of the day, 15 January 1942 started with two medium-sized Japanese tanks making their way down the road.

The 16 Anti-tank Battalion opened fire on them and the tanks withdrew. Another two quickly replaced them only to be destroyed.

While this was going on the enemy had been using the nearby rubber plantation to dig in, right on A and D

Companies' front. Suddenly the whole of the battalion came under fire from enemy mortars and other weapons.

'Increased enemy movement indicated that the enemy was preparing an attack on the front of those companies,' the report revealed.

It was at this moment, as the enemy was forming up, that Lieutenant-Colonel Galleghan decided to strike. Only one company could be spared for the task, which he fully appreciated required a battalion, but manpower was short.

On receiving his orders, the company commander said he would be ready to attack at 11.45 hours. As 'zero' hour approached, a number of Japanese light and medium tanks appeared, intended to assist the enemy's infantry attack. It meant the postponement of Galleghan's planned counter-attack until the Japanese hardware could be dealt with by artillery and mortar fire.

Confusion followed as HQ and D Troop of 30 Forward Battalion started to withdraw and on arrival at their new position were unable to support the forward infantry. Who gave the order to fall back is not revealed but in the chaos of war, messages and instructions are often lost and this was no exception.

Thyer and Kappe's report suggests the troop withdrew because of fear of being left behind without infantry protection. While the truth will never be known 'yeoman service' was eventually rendered by C Troop.

'Soon a steady and accurate fire from battalion mortars was being poured into the enemy tank assembly area,' it was reported.

Unfortunately this was not enough to deter the enemy. Because of the absence of D Troop and increasing enemy resistance, the artillery tasks were becoming too numerous for C Troop to handle. In addition, the Australians had to contend with a constant battering from enemy mortars, light automatics and small-arms fire, as well as wave after wave of dive bombers from the air. The sound and the fury of armed conflict between two violently opposing forces was almost unbearable, but slowly the men of the 8th Division gained the upper hand.

The enemy had difficulty forming up and their preparations for the next stage of the offensive were becoming disorganised. The Japs were in disarray and Galleghan saw his chance.

The time was opportune to launch D Company on their objective – a hill about 1000 metres forward of the 2/30th Battalion position.

At precisely 12.45 the men of D Company lined up to launch their bayonet attack across open countryside in full view of the Japanese. What was Galleghan thinking? Had he learned nothing from World War I, when men sent over the top were mown down by enemy gunfire in their thousands? Or was he simply willing to sacrifice his troops in pursuit of a minor military advantage?

Stan Arneil, who was in the 2/30th Battalion and wrote extensively about his commanding officer after the war, believed Galleghan 'expected a mass attack from the Japanese at any time so he took the initiative and ordered his troops to advance with the bayonet'.

Bluey Kennedy said the scene left an indelible impression. 'It is something I will never forget and perhaps one of the last of this type of attack ever mounted. It is difficult to believe that men could be sent against the enemy in such a way,' he later wrote.[11]

'The officer was mad. He just lined them up like a parade ground and they were ordered forward.'[12]

Others, including Stan Arneil, saw it differently.

A 'great cry' went up as D Company advanced in open formation across the clearing. 'It was magnificent to see them, each man in place with his rifle held high across his body walking forward as if on a training exercise. We had prepared for this for two years, and as we and others watched, we yelled and roared with excitement to see D Company doing its job so well.'[13]

As the infantry marched on with their bayonets fixed it looked like a most unequal struggle. There was hand-to-hand fighting as the two sides met. Screaming could be heard coming from the trees. For a time it seemed the Australians were facing mass slaughter, but despite the fire-storm, they carried on relentlessly. Evidently exhilarated by their mission, the Australians put up such a fight that the Japanese were badly shaken by the onslaught. Until now the Japs had been used to victory, taking the Indian and British forces they'd encountered along the way with little or no effort. But this was different. The Australians were over-running enemy machine-gun nests and killing the gun crews. This was a band of men who enjoyed the fight and forced the Japanese infantry to withdraw, at least for the time being.

By now other companies behind were also coming under fire. C Company on the right felt the full blast of 12 enemy aircraft and sundry mortars. It got so bad that the company's forward elements had no alternative but to fall back under pressure from a force that was three times bigger than them.

Undeterred D Company's infantry continued on their dogged and seemingly foolhardy advance up the hill until Galleghan and his officers realised that the battalion was in real danger of being annihilated or cut off. Enemy tanks were sighted manoeuvring into position further up the road in an apparent attempt to cut off forward elements. At the same time those companies astride the main road were being heavily shelled. The Australians were in mortal peril of being overwhelmed.

The commanding officer estimated he faced at least three Japanese battalions with artillery and tank support, making the Allies' position west of the Sungei Gemenecheh River untenable. There was no alternative but to withdraw.

By 15.15 hours, a little over five hours after the start of that day's fighting, the Australians commenced their retreat. A, B and D Companies withdrew along the railway line and C Company staggered back through the rubber plantation.

As Bluey Kennedy was to observe, the fact that so few men were killed 'when perhaps some 200 men attacked several battalions of Japanese infantry supported by tanks and aircraft, is almost unbelievable. It was a relic of World War I mounted by an officer of that period.'[14]

In fact the overall Australian casualty rate from two days of fighting around Gemas was surprisingly low. One officer and 16 other ranks were killed, four officers and 51 others were wounded and nine men were reported missing. Equally so it was reassuring that the battalion had taken a heavy toll of the enemy.

During the first few days of the fighting in the Gemas–Segamat sector almost 8000 rounds of ammunition were fired by the 29th and 30th Batteries. The 65th Battery fired almost as many rounds in support of Indian troops who were caught up in the action and later in support of the 2/19th and 2/29th Battalions, who were forced to withdraw from Muar to Parit Sulong. The gunners were in action throughout, suffering heavy casualties in the process, but their bravery under fire almost certainly saved the lives of many more.

After the war the Japanese even went so far as to compliment the 2/30th on their courage. In Japan's official history of the war, special mention was made of 'the Australian troops encountered at Gemencheh–Gemas [who] fought with bravery the Imperial Japanese Army had not previously encountered'.[15]

It was a rare tribute and the only one paid to an Allied unit in a particular battle. At least Galleghan's strategy had impressed the enemy.

The Battle of Gemas was a huge morale booster for the Allies, with talk in Singapore of it being a turning point in the war against the Japanese invaders. General Bennett was even moved to tell the *Singapore Times* that his force would not only stop the advancing horde, but put them on the defensive.

Unfortunately, it was wishful thinking. Although the men of the 8th Division, and in particular the 2/30th, had done themselves proud, they would be no match for the Japanese in the intense few days of fighting that would follow. The Battle of Muar was about to begin.

Chapter 6

KILL OR BE KILLED

It did not take long for the Japanese to set their sights on the coastal town of Muar, barely 60 miles (100 km) to the south of Gemas. They had already attacked it from the air and by 15 January Japanese troops were spotted at the northern approach to the ferry.

Sensing that the mainly Indian units in the area would not be able to put up much resistance, Bennett chose to send in his reserve battalion, the 2/29th, under the command of Lieutenant-Colonel James Robertson from Geelong, who had earned a Military Cross for his efforts during World War I. A troop of the 2/4th Australian Anti-tank Regiment was also allotted to the task.

General Percival was also worried, especially when he heard that Japanese Guards were being deployed in the Muar area. Over the next few days there were countless skirmishes and bloody confrontations as the two sides prepared for the inevitable full-scale fight.

Across on the eastern side of the peninsula at the Jemaluang crossroads, the 2/19th Battalion was waiting for orders. As the battalion's official history puts it: 'The whole atmosphere of Jemaluang was eerie with the very dark night under the rubber trees and the movements and mustering of the various Companies in the old camp area ready for embussing on January 18.'[1]

Maps and papers were distributed to the men revealing that the Japanese had arrived in force in the Muar area and that the 2/19th was being sent there to reinforce the 2/29th. It was the news they'd been waiting for.

If any man was nervous he didn't show it, especially after Colonel Charles Anderson, their commanding officer, had a chance to chat with them.

'There's been a lot of talk about the fanatical fighting of the Japanese – so fanatical as to render them almost immune from fear and to make them unbeatable,' he said. 'But don't worry,' he assured them. 'In view of the battalion's high standards of training, they'd handle them easily and roughly.'[2]

Then they all sat down to a hearty breakfast. For many of the boys sitting around the tables that morning, it would be their last.

'It would have been hard to believe that so many of the men with whom we were talking and joking during that early morning meal would be killed in action during the next few days,' the 2/19th's official history noted.[3]

For good or ill they were on their way. The 2/19th would be deployed at Bakri, where they would join other units in an aggressive defence of the area.

Private Chick Warden was the youngest soldier in the battalion. He shouldn't have been there at all, given he was only 14 years and ten months when he enlisted. Now he found himself part of B Company's 12 Platoon in 11 Section and about to enter the most dangerous phase of the war. Chick grabbed himself a Vienna loaf, tore out the centre and poured in a helping of steak and kidney stew.

'I really enjoyed that meal for it was the last one I was to have for several days,' he recalled.

As he climbed onto a waiting truck he remembered being 'chased around' by Captain 'Horsey' Harris and singing little ditties as they rolled on towards Kluang and finally to Bakri.[4]

It was a dangerous journey, made all the more hazardous by the level of Japanese aerial activity. There was really nowhere to hide along the wide open roads. This was rubber country, with a landscape of gently sloping small hills and plantations as far as the eye could see. At another time it would have seemed idyllic but today the distant rattle of gunfire did not bode well for the boys of the 2/19th Battalion. Suddenly they became alert and apprehensive. This was the real thing.

At midday they were ordered out of the trucks and took up the first of several positions. The sound of battle was getting closer. The 2/19th's commanding officer, Lieutenant-Colonel Anderson, who would effectively be in charge of most of the new Aussie reinforcements, moved along the line to boost morale.

'Don't worry chaps, it's just tin cans and a bit of scrap the Japs are throwing about over there – it won't hurt you,' he lied through his teeth.

Chick and his mates were not stupid.

'We copped quite a bit but no casualties that I know of, for we just dug deeply.'

By now the fighting was intensifying. The next morning 12 Platoon was told to move through an area of bracken fern and to catch some Japs who were known to be in the area.

'We caught them by surprise,' Chick admitted proudly.

By the end of the shoot-out 65 Japanese were dead and several wounded. The platoon had got off lightly in comparison with only two dead, Eddie Goss and Laurie Morris.

It was a sobering experience for youngster Chick Warden, but he learned quickly. He and his mates had a number of narrow escapes that day when wounded Japs suddenly came to life.

'From that first engagement we learnt not to trust their wounded and shortly afterwards we received orders not to take any prisoners and to leave no wounded,' he recalled.

The message was clear: kill or be killed.

The shelling came thick and fast. The enemy was so close Chick could see them rushing from tree to tree, sounding their bugles as they ran. First they were moving along the top of the ridge then quietly making their way back along a creek that ran across 12 Platoon's front. They were alarmingly close and ready to pounce.

Chick's heart was pounding as the first Jap officer, who was dressed in a smart white shirt, led his men in a seemingly suicidal charge across the creek. Everyone in 11 Section saw him at the same time and opened up. The Japanese officer went down in a hail of Bren, Tommy gun and rifle fire, his shirt disintegrating into a thousand pieces.

Night was drawing in but there would be no sleep for 12 Platoon.

'The nips kept trying to move in and the shells and mortars

kept coming over. We were learning the different sounds by now and about where things were likely to land.'[5]

The next morning they were back on the main road, with 12 Platoon leading the way. Lieutenant Howard appeared with a wounded chap from another carrier, which had been caught in a road block further up the highway – so they knew there was trouble ahead. It didn't take long for contact to be made. About two miles (3.2 km) south of Brigade HQ two of the front scouts were shot dead and others were mown down and badly injured.

The Aussies searched the terrain for the source of the shooting and identified a machine-gun nest. Chick Warden was about to hop over a rotting tree trunk when he spied the Jap who'd just killed Tom Howard. He was brandishing a machine gun but somehow, in his haste to bring his gun to bear on the young Aussie, the weapon fell over on its legs and the Jap went with it. All Chick could see was a pair of legs, but seizing the moment he opened fire and shot the soldier in the backside.

'Just as I had fired several rounds I was hit and felt a terrific burning pain in my left shoulder. I looked round and saw Charlie Dutton throwing a grenade into the Jap machine-gun nest. At the same time he was hit badly and his face hit the ground in front of him and he lay still.'[6]

It was a fierce exchange, and bodies from both sides were soon littering the area. Next to go down was Lieutenant Jimmy Quinlan, who had been throwing grenades at the machine-gun nest from about three metres behind Chick and was lying badly injured. They were pinned down and desperately needed support. Then as if by a miracle Colonel Anderson appeared, along with B Company's two other platoons and Captain Frank Beverley's A Company on the left-hand side of the road. The CO aimed his revolver at one of the few Japanese still standing and 'bowled him over'.[7]

Meanwhile, the Jap whom Chick had just shot in the backside was starting to move again, raising his machine gun to his shoulder. For a few terrifying seconds the men of 12 Platoon, or those who were still capable of fighting, went on an orgy of blood-letting.

'I'll never forget the look on Cliff Farlow's face when his bayonet bent on the way into the Nip gunner's body, and to finish things off 'Deadeye' Dick Robinson came charging in firing his Bren from the hip . . .'[8]

As if that wasn't enough Robinson turned his gun on the two other machine-gun nests and cleaned them out too.

12 Platoon suffered heavy casualties that day but it would have been far worse had it not been for A Company's covering fire.

Dr Lloyd Cahill did his best to patch up the injured as stretcher bearers placed them onto trucks. To their sorrow it was too late to do anything for Lieutenant Quinlan and Charlie Dutton, who died shortly afterwards. It was a truly miserable scene, made worse by Chick's close bond with Dutton, who'd been a good mate.

'I was a bit cut up about Charlie, as he was a close friend,' was all he'd say. But at least Chick was alive and he could still wield his one good arm.

Those who were able to do so walked through the night until dawn, when they stopped on the outskirts of Parit Sulong village. There was no time for sleep.

All that day Japanese aircraft, artillery, mortars and tanks continued to pound the 2/19th and other 8th Division units, but it was not entirely one way. A large number of Japanese troops were also killed or injured as the Aussies went on the attack, targeting houses where the enemy was known to be hiding.

Yet amid the mayhem it was still possible to laugh, especially at someone else's expense. Sergeant 'Sonny' Lay got a ribbing when several of his teeth were knocked out – by what is unclear. When he was told it was his own fault for being such a 'loud-mouthed sergeant', he didn't take it kindly. It was hard to have a sense of humour in such circumstances but it got a smile from the ranks.[9]

Events were drawing to a climax now. But how would they escape? A message came through for every man to make his way to the flank and move out in a wide swing around the Japanese. This was their best chance of getting out.

They slept in the jungle that night. It was wet and cold so Chick and Geoff O'Connor curled up and tried to keep each other warm. The next day, with some help from a group of Chinese, they crossed over the Yong Peng bridge and were taken by trucks to the 2/29th Battalion area. For the first time in days they were given a hot meal and a bath. It was a welcome respite for the 2/19th. But not far away the scene was set for one of the bloodiest encounters of the Malaya campaign.

It became known as the Parit Sulong massacre and involved the 8th Division as well as the 45th Indian Infantry Brigade. Making the most of the cover of darkness, the 2/29th's Lieutenant-Colonel Charles Anderson was leading a column through open countryside when he sent one of his men to reconnoitre the bridge at Parit Sulong. It did not go well. The scout was attacked and fled back to his patrol, whereupon

Anderson investigated further. Soon his men were being charged by some 120 Japanese, whom they managed to contain by means of a flank attack. There was rapid gunfire from the enemy, who brought their heavy tanks up to the rear of the column. Strafed from the air and bombed at close quarters, the Australians were in serious trouble. To add to their problems they lost wireless contact with base, but eventually managed to get a message through pleading for assistance. Assured that a relief force was on its way, the column fought on, but the casualty toll was rising and Anderson gave up any hope of his attack succeeding.[10]

The outlook was so grim that defeat seemed inevitable. During a lull in the fighting the distant rumble of approaching tanks was heard, prompting two men to throw themselves into a ditch and hurl grenades at the leading tank. Subsequent shots from an anti-tank gun finished it off, with the target bursting into flames.

For South African-born Anderson and his men the situation became bleaker by the hour. Ammunition, energy and food supplies were all running low. They'd had little sleep and were quite clearly at the point of total exhaustion.

It was time to negotiate with the enemy. Two of the officers, Captain Cahill and Captain Brand, suggested it might be worth asking the Japs if they'd be prepared to allow through the worst of the Allied injured. A volunteer driver got behind the wheel of an army ambulance and approached the Japanese line.

If the enemy had an ounce of compassion surely this was the moment to show it but the Japanese were in no mood to negotiate. Surrender and only then will we take care of the wounded, was their response.

It was a difficult decision for Anderson to make. The badly injured were already at death's door and had little hope of surviving, even if they received treatment. In the end the commanding officer declined the offer, hoping that the earlier promise of air support by morning would save the day.

The more immediate challenge was to last the night. The Australians were falling like ninepins. Captain Maher was hit by shrapnel but survived, only to be killed by a shell that blew up the car in which he had been placed.

Lieutenant Austin, who had been gravely wounded in the neck, still managed to drive back one of the ambulances that had been left on the bridge.

There was no let-up in the barrage as enemy tanks, artillery and machine guns continued their relentless attack. By first light an uneasy calm suddenly replaced the constant clatter of enemy gunfire and the battering by Japanese aircraft. In the eerie and unexpected silence a distant drone could be heard. And it wasn't the enemy.

'Two cumbersome planes came over, dropped the food and morphia for which Anderson had asked and went off after releasing bombs upon the Japanese at the far end of the bridge.'[11]

While Bennett had kept his promise of air support it was too little too late. The bombing made hardly any impact on the enemy, who were still active and were about to make a flank attack. The number of Australian dead and injured was now so high that Anderson's column faced complete decimation. He knew the fight was almost over but like a gambler who always believes the next card will produce an ace, he was determined to give it one more go.

'Test the bridge,' he ordered one of his companies.

Slowly the troop moved forward to gauge the Japanese response. This was a dangerous game to play, with huge stakes, but Anderson was keen to establish whether it was worth giving the bridge a final assault.

The enemy's response was an emphatic no. As artillery, mortars and gunfire rained down on them, Anderson's column was in danger of being obliterated. It was no time to hang around.

It was precisely 9 o'clock on the morning of 22 January that those 8th Division soldiers who had fought so valiantly for so long received the order to destroy all weapons and withdraw through the surrounding swamps and jungles. If Anderson had any doubts about the move, he would have been heartened by Gordon Bennett's message, which arrived soon afterwards.

'Sorry unable to help after your heroic effort – Good luck.'

Slowly the survivors and walking wounded of the Battle of Muar began to make their way eastward through the mud and dense undergrowth which, though difficult to nego-tiate, at least provided useful cover. Some of the officers, including Anderson, Major Vincent, Captain Hughes and Padre Greenwood of the 2/19th, stayed in position to help the others get away but it wasn't long before the exchange of gunfire slowed.

Ben Hackney, a lieutenant in the 2/29th Infantry Battalion who was among the wounded, recalled the gradual withdrawal.

'Our fellows, although so far fewer than the enemy in numbers, had seemed for ages to be sending back nearly as much fire as came into our area, but now there was a noticeable, a definite slackening off of the fire from our position.

'An odd burst from a machine gun and some rifle fire kept going out from our troops, but as time went on there were less and less of our men about,' the 26-year-old Sydneysider wrote. 'In small parties and sometimes singly, we could see our fellows going up the northern bank of the river east of the bridge.'[12]

The 65th Battery had fired more than 6500 rounds during the action from Muar to Parit Sulong. But while it would be seen as a gallant and heroic effort it had come at a heavy price. The loss was the equivalent of a brigade and two Australian battalions, but in terms of sheer Japanese bastardry worse was to follow.

About 150 Australians and a number of Indians were so badly wounded that there was no alternative but to leave them behind. Anderson had privately hoped that the Japanese would make good on their earlier promise of medical care for the injured in the event of a surrender. In the early days of the conflict the full savagery of the Japanese advance and the way they treated their prisoners was yet to emerge. It is only thanks to Lieutenant Ben Hackney's good fortune that what followed the 2/29th's withdrawal became known.

Unable to retreat, Hackney found himself a truck to hide under and blazed away with a Bren gun to help others make good their getaway. Lieutenant Arthur Tibbitts, who had gone in search of more ammunition, kept his fellow officer company on his return and while they awaited the arrival of the Japanese, the two men talked warmly of the little luxuries of life back home. Caked in mud and blood, they fantasised about the joy of washing and the simple pleasure of rest. Of being out of their dirty, torn and bloodstained uniforms and sleeping in a comfortable bed. How they missed things they 'had not known before were so good'.[13]

Tibbitts, born in Melbourne only a couple of months after Hackney, had been a clerk back home in East Kew.

The enemy arrived and took their time inspecting their captives, then suddenly the scene turned to one of frenzy, with Japanese swarming in from all directions, 'chattering creatures . . . often screaming something to somebody not faraway'.[14]

Sprawled on the ground, the wounded Aussies and Indians now found themselves being kicked and cursed, hit by rifle butts and jabbed by bayonets. They were ordered to stand no matter what their physical state; those who were unable to walk were supported by those who could. Tibbitts helped Hackney to hobble across the bridge, and both were subjected to vicious blows along the way.

Of the huddled mass of men who had survived the battle, there seemed to be about 110 Australians and 40 Indians. Now they were made to strip and sit in a circle, while the victors took delight in further acts of cruelty, beating the prisoners and kicking open wounds.

'So great was their satisfaction at any visible sign of pain, that often the dose was repeated.'[15]

During this scene of horror the Australians noticed an English-speaking man of Caucasian appearance and wearing the uniform of a British soldier. He searched the discarded clothes before returning them in a heap. Just who he was has never been revealed, but rumours of fifth columnists and spies in the area had been rife for weeks. Was this the infamous traitor who allegedly fed information to the enemy?

Or a Japanese who might pass as a Brit? It was a mystery that would have no resolution.

Eventually most of the men were herded into a shed that was so overcrowded that many were forced to lie on top of each other, only adding to their pain. They were thirsty but appeals for water and medical aid were rejected. For some the suffering became intolerable. They simply expired, their death a blessed release.

Passing Japanese soldiers viewed the morbid spectacle with glee. The sight of an Australian body propped up against a truck seemed to add to the entertainment. An Indian lying in front of the building, close to death, provided the chance for further amusement when he began to regain consciousness. The Japanese in charge gave him a series of kicks and bashed him several times with his rifle butt. Not satisfied with the result, his comrade repeatedly thrust his bayonet into the man before pushing the corpse into the river.

This turned out to be a warm-up to the final act of savagery. To torment their captives further, helmets and mugs full of water materialised. Packets of cigarettes were also offered. But if the men thought the cruelty was at an end, they were mistaken. The drinks and tobacco were left just out of reach of the thirst-crazed prisoners.

As the sun began to set on that fateful day, death edged nearer for these men of the 2/29th. Whether the Japanese saw it as an act of mercy or military justice, the decision was taken to help the captives on their way. One by one the prisoners were either roped or wired together and led off until only a few were left behind. Ben Hackney, feigning death, was among them. He heard the clank of fuel cans and petrol being poured from the battalion's stranded vehicles. Then came the ratter-tat-tat of machine-gun fire. Struggling to maintain his death-like pose, he briefly opened his eyes to see the distant flicker of flame. Was he about to meet a similar fate?

Night had fallen and in the darkness Hackney, whose legs were broken, endeavoured to slide away. Inch by inch he pulled himself across the open ground to a nearby hut, where he proceeded to sever the rope which bound his wrists. For hours he rubbed against the corner of a foundation block until he freed himself.

Crawling further away, he found water and, much to his amazement, two more Australian survivors who had also feigned death. One of them, Sergeant Ron Croft, helped Hackney and the other man to a spot in the jungle near the river, where the second man tragically died. But thanks to Croft's efforts he and Hackney got away. This was no mean feat given that the Sydney soldier weighed 14 stone (89 kg) and Richmond-born Croft was much weaker and smaller. Somehow he hoisted Hackney over his shoulder and staggered across the river.

'Sheer strength alone did not enable him to carry his burden. It was something more than that – his wish and willingness to help: courage, guts and manliness.'[16]

Croft was to die some three months later, but Hackney's story of survival lives on. Briefly housed by sympathetic Malays, he continued his journey on his hands and knees until he was found by Chinese who gave him shelter.

But five weeks after he escaped from Parit Sulong his luck ran out. He was caught by a party of Malays who handed him over to the Japanese. Ben Hackney was sent back to Parit Sulong, where he was brutally punished for his escape before being imprisoned in Kuala Lumpur, then Changi, and finally was sent to work on the Burma-Thai Railway.

It is largely thanks to his extraordinary survival that the full extent of the Parit Sulong massacre can be told today. Hackney's evidence before Allied war crimes investigators helped to bring to justice those responsible for this act of infamy. It also reinforced the reputation of the 2/29th, whose duty and commitment in the heat of battle became part of 8th Division folklore.

As General Percival was to comment after the war: 'The Battle of Muar was one of the epics of the Malayan campaign. Our little force, dogged by resistance, had held up a division of the Japanese Imperial Guards attacking with all the advantages of air and tank support for nearly a week, and in doing so had saved the Segamat force from encirclement and probable annihilation. The award of the Victoria Cross to Lieut-Colonel Anderson of the AIF was a fitting tribute both to his own courage and to the valour of his men.'[17]

The ultimate military honour awarded Anderson, who was still only 44, was not only in recognition of his bravery but in many respects bore testimony to the men who supported him during such harrowing times. It is also a measure of the man that he acknowledged what he called the 8th Division's 'complete moral ascendancy of the enemy'.

'They outmatched the Japs in bushcraft and fire control, where the enemy's faults of bunching together and noisy shouting disclosed their dispositions and enabled the Australians to inflict heavy casualties at small cost to themselves. When the enemy was trapped they fought most gamely. In hand–hand fighting [the Japanese] made a very poor showing against the superior training and spirit of the AIF.'

The 8th Division's first real taste of battle in the Malayan campaign may not have ended in triumph but it certainly set them apart as a fighting force. Under Gordon Bennett, many of those battalions and smaller units who were among the first Australians to meet the enemy demonstrated a level of skill, strength and sheer guts that surprised and very nearly stymied the Japanese Army.

But would it continue that way? Did these warriors have the resolve to fight to the finish or would they be let down by forces beyond their control?

The next few weeks would provide the answer, and the truth would be unsettling.

Chapter 7

'IF ANYONE TELLS YOU THEY WEREN'T FRIGHTENED THEY'RE A BLOODY LIAR'

'Stay for lunch – would you like a beer?' asked Noel Harrison, who at the age of 98 still had a healthy appetite. We tucked into chicken curry at his aged care home at Hornsby in Sydney's northern suburbs. Television sets in nearby rooms were tuned to the 'great debate,' a live broadcast of Donald Trump and Hillary Clinton battling it out in the first of the presidential head-to-head contests.

In room 108 the battle under discussion happened three-quarters of a century earlier but the events remained as clear to Noel when we met as when they took place. He needed a wheelchair to get around but despite the odd memory lapse could talk for hours about his part in the Malaya campaign and what followed. I feel so privileged to have met Noel for, within a few weeks of our chat, he passed away. It was the last time he would be able to provide his unique insight into the war and the 8th Division's role in it.

Bega-born Noel Harrison was a corporal in the 2/20th's

signallers when he arrived in Singapore aboard the *Queen Mary* in February 1941. He'd been working in Tamworth for the Rural Bank of New South Wales before the war but the exotic Orient beckoned. For a young man on his first overseas jaunt it was like going on holiday. Malaya was at peace and if the locals were concerned about the Japanese threat they didn't show it.

Noel was sent up north by truck to Seremban, where he got his first real sense of the tropics. The heat of the jungle and the chatter of the native population provided an intoxicating mix. Later he was moved by road to Port Dickson on the coast, where the swimming was 'delightful' and the sunsets were 'magnificent'.

'But the highlight of living in Malaya was going on leave to Malacca, Kuala Lumpur and the best of the lot was off to Singapore.'[1]

If the first few pages of Noel's memoir read more like a travel brochure than a war diary it is because it was so difficult to come to terms with the grim reality of what would follow.

There was the training, of course – jungle exercises and route marches to keep fit – as well as the discipline and daily rituals associated with military life. Come Anzac Day 1941 the 2/20th had the honour of parading in the streets of Kuala Lumpur, which required 'a great deal of preparation,' he recalled.[2]

As the months went by Noel and his mates were thoroughly enjoying army life but those with an eye on current affairs reckoned that the good times were about to end. On the other side of the world the war in Europe was moving fast. The Germans had invaded Yugoslavia and Greece, before moving on Russia. In the United States President Franklin D. Roosevelt froze all Japanese government assets and demanded that trade with Japan stop immediately.

On 24 July large numbers of Japanese forces entered Indochina. Reports of military manoeuvres and amphibious training sessions – in readiness, it was suggested, for a seaborne assault on the Malay Peninsula – only exacerbated regional concerns.

As Noel put it: 'Round about September we gathered that the Japs were getting cheeky, overrunning China and moving southwards. So the day came when we were again put into trucks and sent across to the east coast to a place called Mersing.'[3]

The Mersing area was strategically significant because it offered an enemy with superior naval and air power a short cut to Singapore.

By now there was compelling intelligence that the Japanese had been training in Indochina for an amphibious operation. Mersing would seem the obvious location to put that training into practice. There was also an early warning radar installation on a hill near the mouth of the Mersing River, believed to be the only one of its kind in the Far East and therefore of crucial importance to the Allies.[4]

The 2/20th Battalion's job was to fortify the beach and protect the town, which was on the main road from Kota Bharu in the north to Singapore in the south. They went to work with almost manic intensity.

'As it turned out by the time we had finished we had more barbed wire in Mersing than they had on the coast of Singapore facing the Johore Straits.'[5]

Further reinforcements arrived in October and November,

by which time the 2/19th had moved on from Kluang to Jemaluang, about 18 miles (30 km) west of Mersing. By December 1941 the 22nd Brigade Group was well established in the Mersing and Endau areas, in anticipation of a seaborne assault. On the diplomatic grapevine the word was that pressure was being exerted on Thailand to permit Japanese forces to use its facilities. The news only served to reinforce the view that in the event of war, the Japanese would invade Malaya from the north.

When these fears were confirmed on 8 December, Noel Harrison and the men of what would become Eastforce went into action.

As the Japanese made their way south to Kuantan, Gordon Bennett and his team were forced to accept the likelihood that Mersing and Endau would be used as a back-door approach to Fortress Singapore. With this in mind Noel was sent north as part of a signals post for headquarters at Endau and given an extra stripe for his efforts.

School teacher Jack Mudie, from Queanbeyan, adopted a more basic approach to communications. Also posted to Endau, he thought it wise to appoint a few locals to light a bonfire just under two miles (3 km) up the road when they saw the Japanese coming.

'We acted as a forward observation post,' he explained. 'The idea was to let the rest of the battalion know when we saw the enemy and observe what sort of equipment they'd got. Once we'd sized them up, we'd inflict whatever punishment we could and then retire.'[6]

Henry Dietz, the country boy from Quandialla and member of the 2/20th, found himself on a nearby river with C Company. Much of the waterway had been mined.

'When the Japs came down the coast we were supposed to explode the mines and blow the enemy to smithereens,' he recalled.[7] At least that was the plan.

The Endau River, with its many tributaries, was also important because it offered means for the enemy to approach in shallow-draught vessels to the road running right across the peninsula from Mersing through Jemaluang, Kluang and Ayer Hitam to Batu Pahat.[8]

Endau Force, which now comprised men from the 2/20th and 2/19th Battalions as well as the anti-aircraft platoon of the 2/18th, was ready and waiting. The man who would command them in the front line was Major Andrew Robertson, an accountant who had emigrated to Australia with his family from Britain as a child. He would go on to win a reputation as a courageous soldier and a fine leader of men, but tragically would not live to see his wife and two children again back home in Sydney.

By the morning of 14 January, nearly five weeks after the start of the Japanese invasion, there were reports of enemy infiltration north of Endau. A reconnaissance patrol spotted a party of about 30 Japanese crossing the Sungei Pontian, oddly disguised in black coats and khaki shorts.

The following day Endau itself was bombed and machine-gunned. A group of enemy soldiers on bikes was engaged by a platoon led by John Varley, son of the 2/18th's CO, which had been sent forward for the purpose.[9]

Back down south at Mersing the Australians, who had been complaining about their lack of firepower, were reassured to see the arrival of 2-inch mortars and anti-tank grenades. But it was too late to make a difference. As Lieutenant Frank

Gavan, A Company's second-in-command, observed after the war in Don Wall's book *Singapore and Beyond*: 'There were insufficient weapons, insufficient ammunition, insufficient written instructions and insufficient time to train a sufficient number of personnel.'

It was not the sort of judgement to inspire confidence but this was not a time for doubt. The 2/20th was there to defend the east coast and stop the Japanese in their tracks regardless of local conditions.

Lieutenant Bart Richardson, the battalion ordinance officer, had been given four Vickers machine guns as he was the only man who had trained on them. He'd grown up with the Vickers since joining the militia in 1936 so he was well versed in how to set up and operate the weapon. Bart was given a squad of men to train for the job but was shocked by the reaction of his superiors when he started having a go at low-flying enemy aircraft:

A Japanese aeroplane would fly over our area and drop a few bombs so he received a shock when our guns fired on him and hit him too. This became a daily routine for a few days until I received word that we were not to fire on the Japanese as we were drawing the crabs, an army way of saying we were drawing attention to us. I really couldn't believe it as the Japs knew exactly where our defences were . . . the army works in mysterious ways.

The Japanese at that time were coming over daily, one plane at a time. They'd swoop down very low, drop a few bombs and off they'd go. Well one day the boys opened up on them and gave them an awful fright.[10]

Dismayed and frustrated, Bart told his men to down arms. If this reflected Allied policy it did not bode well for the future of the campaign.

Endau and Mersing would continue to be attacked from the air in a bid to soften up Allied troops on the ground. The Japanese were about to move further south. Only Eastforce stood in its way, but for how long?

Henry Dietz had seen a few Jap reconnaissance planes flying over Endau looking for trouble but took little notice until a British Tiger Moth appeared on the scene.

'We tried to wave at him to go back,' Henry recalled. 'He was like a sparrow with two big hawks looking down on him. They got him first go and he crash-landed into a clump of trees on the other side of the house we'd been staying in.'[11]

Rushing outside to help, Henry and his mates were too late to save the pilot and very nearly came close to sacrificing themselves. The two Jap aircraft that had downed the Tiger Moth were on their way back; fortunately they failed to spot the Australians, who by now had taken cover.

———•———

It wasn't until 14 January that Eastforce first came into contact with enemy soldiers, about 12 miles (20 km) north of Endau. New arrivals from the 2/19th ambushed them, resulting in numerous dead and injured. The Japanese did not take long to lick their wounds. Later that same day they retaliated with a vengeance, forcing the Australians, who were well outnumbered, to retreat and seek shelter in a mangrove swamp.

The men of the 2/19th knew they had to move fast to avoid being over-run. Varley, still not 22 and possessing the same steely nature as his father, took it upon himself to swim the fast-flowing Endau River in search of a boat to rescue his platoon. Heavy rain had turned the waterway into a torrent, forcing Varley to struggle against the current. Finally he found a small craft and towed it to shore, enabling his boys to escape unscathed. It was a commendable act of courage which, quite rightly, earned him the Military Cross.

Meanwhile on the other side of the river Jack Mudie was waiting for a puff of smoke that would signal an imminent enemy approach. One of the other members of his platoon was the first to spot it billowing away on the horizon, but Jack would have to wait a couple of days before putting his plan into action.

Further north Merv Alchin from Temora and two others were on a reconnaissance mission aimed at establishing the enemy's progress and keeping a close watch on any natives who might be helping them. Evidence was mounting that Malays were working for the other side, leaving messages and signs for the invading force along the way. Merv had volunteered to join Private Keith 'Donny' Donaldson, also from C Company, and a mysterious Englishman known as Captain Cope, on the mission, which they knew was fraught with risk.

The plan was to head 36 miles (60 km) up the road as far as Kuantan, which by now was deep inside enemy territory. They got away without being seen for two days but their luck then ran out. While grabbing some food at a Chinese eatery one night, they were tipped off that an enemy soldier was in the area; they had to go. The three raced down to the river where Cope had previously requisitioned a small boat, just in case they needed to make a quick dash to open waters. But the craft had disappeared. Their heavy weaponry prevented them from swimming and when shots were fired in their direction they realised the game was over.

Within minutes they were arrested by a party of Japs and their hands were tethered behind their backs. Merv, Donny and Cope – the British officer who was almost certainly an Allied spy – were not going anywhere. Indeed they viewed their future with even more foreboding when their captors locked Cope's handcuffs and threw away the key. The message was unambiguous. The Japs had no intention of freeing them. Fortuitously, the two Aussies had their hands bound with rope because their wrists proved too thick to fit in the metal handcuffs. Merv, remembering an old schoolboy trick, deliberately kept his hands apart as the rope was tied, in the hope he might be able to free himself at a later stage.

For a while their captors probed them about troop numbers and defences. They knew that the longer they refused to talk, the greater the likelihood of them staying alive. The group insisted they didn't know the answers because they had only just been sent to Endau and had no information about what was happening further south at Mersing. Even when one of the Japanese officers made a threatening motion with his sword, sliding it across his neck, the Australians and the Brit refused to be intimidated. But they also knew that their strategy was risky. How much interrogation could a man take before he cracked under the pressure or the Japanese gave up on their prisoners and summarily executed them?

It was a grim outlook, not made any better by their agonising physical state. All three were now suffering from aching and swollen wrists. However, for Merv at least, remembering to place one hand on top of the other and a few centimetres apart was about to pay dividends. In the afternoon as he and the others were enjoying a brief respite, Merv discovered that one of his hands had slipped out of the knotted rope behind his back. He looked around, noting that there was only one guard nearby and he was asleep.

This was his moment. If he did not escape now he never would. Seizing the opportunity Merv brought his hands from behind his back and reached for a steel scrub hook, used by the natives, which was sitting in the corner. It took only a split second for him to raise the guard's mosquito net and thrust the metal weapon into his right temple.

'He was on his side and I drove it in fairly well, but I never finished him off because he pushed me to get out of the way.'[12]

The guard bellowed in pain and threw himself out of bed, screaming for help.

'He jumped up with blood over his face, pushed me arse over head and raced down the steps screaming out of the hut. I would have done him but for the handle breaking.' Quick as a flash Merv 'picked up his rifle and went after him to try and stop him and fell down a well – scrambled out and headed for the scrub'.[13]

Merv had only seconds to act. If he didn't move now the rest of the camp would be after him. Realising there was no time to untie his mates, Merv ran for his life through the long jungle grass, dodging the bullets being fired by his pursuers and eventually falling into the wallowing mud of a mangrove swamp. There he lay in a daze for several minutes, savouring his newfound freedom and pondering his next step.

'It must have been an area where our troops had set up and I went off the track out in the mangroves up to my neck in this wallow and that's probably what saved me.'[14]

But how long before the Japanese sent a search party, he wondered. Pulling himself up, Merv had no option but to slide into the dark, warm waters of the Endau River and doggy-paddle to the opposite bank. By now there was no sign of his battalion or any other Allied troops. His only option was to walk to safety.

———

With the air attacks frequent and merciless on Endau, it was increasingly evident that withdrawal was the only way out, but not before Jack Mudie's C Company platoon had a final crack at the enemy.

Come 17 January, Japan's 56 Regiment was rapidly approaching Allied lines and Mudie had one last trick up his sleeve. The idea was to hide on the southern side of the river bank and fire mortars at the enemy as they gathered on the northern side. Just look at the geography, Jack reasoned. Jungle to the west, and swamp and ocean to the east. The Japs would have nowhere to run. And so it was that Mudie's platoon enjoyed their greatest triumph.

'When the time came there were about 700 Japs across the river,' Jack recalled. 'We could see them shouting and gesticulating. I couldn't understand their language but the meaning was pretty clear: those at the front of the bank were telling those at the rear that there was a problem and they couldn't get across. Anyhow, they all ended up packed into this area not much bigger than a football pitch and when I thought the time was right, I gave the order: "Fire."

'I instructed one of my blokes to fire a mortar at the front of the group and the other at the back, so they couldn't get away. Every time we fired you heard the bumph, bumph sound of the mortar hitting its target on the other side. We must have been firing forty mortars a minute. The destruction was indescribable. I don't think any of the six or seven hundred escaped either death or injury. I had the pleasure of wiping out the whole of that first advance of Japanese.'[15]

The enemy had definitely met their match in Jack Mudie but elsewhere even the best laid military plans were not going as they should.

A few miles down river Henry Dietz was preparing to blow the mines that had been carefully installed a few months earlier, but when the order came to set them off there was a deafening silence.

'It appeared they'd been there so long that the water had seeped into the firing mechanism and it had gone rusty.'[16]

C Company's positions were dotted around Endau and, despite Mudie's successful attempts to stall the enemy, the Japanese were getting closer.

Arthur 'Snowy' Collins, who had grown up at Muswellbrook in the Hunter Valley, was policing the main road into Endau when he first spotted them. They were slim shadowy figures in the distance but Snowy and his four mates soon learned they meant business. All of a sudden the Japs opened fire. With bullets whistling overhead, Snowy decided not to hang around. He and his mates were vastly outnumbered and to remain in position would have meant almost certain death.

'We just ran like hell,' he admitted.[17]

In the bloody confusion of battle it was every man for himself. As Snowy and his mates took off he saw the company cook hit by a bomb.

'All we found afterwards was his arms and legs,' he recalled.[18]

Brigadier Harold Taylor, who commanded the 22nd Infantry Brigade, realised the Japanese were gathering in strength around Endau and ordered the withdrawal of his men. They had fulfilled their role and they did not want to find themselves outflanked by one of the enemy's now familiar pincer movements.

With the front line at Endau now abandoned, Eastforce continued to feel the pressure as it moved south. The Japanese were spreading out and the fear was that some Australian units would become encircled.

The focus switched to Mersing and the surrounding area. On 18 January General Sir Lewis 'Piggy' Heath, Commander of III Indian Corp, visited Brigadier Taylor at his headquarters to consider the implications of Japan's rapid advance. With Mersing likely to fall within days, the decision was taken to protect Jemaluang and the road leading south through Kota Tinggi towards Singapore Island. More men would be required to strengthen this strategically important road link. Some would come from the garrison at Bukit Langkap to the west of Mersing, a jungle outpost that was unlikely to survive for much longer anyway.

Under Taylor's command Eastforce would now comprise the entire 22nd Brigade and all troops and craft in the Mersing–Kahang–Kota Tinggi areas.

The 8th Division's contribution would be the 2/18th and 2/20th Battalions, the 2/10th Field Regiment, the 2/10th Field Company and the 2/9th Field Ambulance. Two companies of the Johore Military Force and the Johore Volunteer Engineers would also boost numbers.[19]

Over the next two days Australian patrols reported a gradual enemy approach to Mersing, with the 2/20th's

Battalion area under regular attack from the air. There was frequent enemy contact on the ground, as well.

On 21 January, Bondi boy Lieutenant Frank Ramsbotham, who was leading a patrol near the north bank of the Sungei Mersing, ambushed a group of Japanese and killed several of them. Those who managed to avoid the Australians' gunfire tried the customary flanking move only to discover they were in the middle of a minefield. Fortunately for them the mines, which had been long immersed in water, failed to explode. Not that it mattered. Ramsbotham and his men mowed them down with machine-gun and artillery fire instead. Later that day another party of Japanese was detected in the same area. This time it was the guns of the 2/10th Field Regiment which neutralised them.

The enemy's more immediate objective was to capture the Mersing bridge, which would allow them to surge south in ever-increasing numbers. The Australians were not prepared to give in without a fight and had wired the bridge accordingly.

For a while the Japanese, wilting under a barrage of mortar and machine-gun fire, were stopped in their tracks. At the same time a section from the 2/20th Battalion crossed the river, attacking enemy gun posts and houses in which it was known the Japanese were hiding.

After suffering heavy casualties in a series of ambushes, the Japanese counterattacked. The two sides were locked in a devastating struggle, which took a massive human toll, but still the Japs kept coming. Was there no end to it?

Merv Alchin's brother, Don, nearly came to grief when a bullet went through his army boot but luckily didn't injure him. The close shave sent a shudder down his spine. A few inches higher and the same bullet could have done him serious damage. There was no time to dwell on the near miss, but he was badly shaken.

'If anyone tells you they weren't frightened they're a bloody liar and I wasn't looking forward to being knocked off,' he told me. 'We knew they were coming, because the intelligence blokes had told us – and by Christ, we soon found out they had plenty of gear.'[20]

Despite the growing number of dead and injured, the 2/20th kept up the fight.

'We were shit scared but we were determined to get out alive, simply because we all wanted to get home one day. That's what kept us going. So I thought, bugger this – I'm going to have a go.'[21]

Francis 'Joe' Wilson, from Orange, came to a similar conclusion after he took over 11 Platoon and managed to clear the enemy from a section post. His courage under fire was to earn him the Distinguished Conduct Medal.

Such acts of bravery, though not always recognised, became commonplace in the 8th Division during the days and weeks ahead. Life became a lottery as the Australians tried to stall the Japanese advance, and you needed luck to survive.

Noel Harrison, who had spent many months enjoying the delights of Port Dickson before the war, was now in the thick of it. Mersing was his patch and communications were his job. He had been sent off on patrol into the jungle looking for enemy infiltration but had lost contact with HQ. For a signals man that could have been embarrassing, but Dame Fortune looked kindly on the boy from Bega, who risked being left behind.

'I'd been sent out with a companion to see if there were any Japs getting through but we never saw anyone. Eventually

I lost contact with my battalion because they were with-drawing from Mersing.'[22]

Stuck in the middle of nowhere Noel climbed a hill in a bid to restore radio contact and managed to pick up a weak signal.

'We were able to make contact and were told to get back to the main road pretty damn quick as the 2/20th were in the process of leaving. Luckily for us we made it or we would have been left behind.'[23]

Such is the lottery of life in war. And as George Daldry was to discover, sometimes you have to make your own luck. George's chance encounter with a Japanese patrol during a bombing raid found him captured by the enemy and impris-oned in their camp. Perhaps because of his slight physique and youthful countenance, the Japs looked kindly on the boy soldier. When the camp was unexpectedly raided one day George found himself unguarded and decided to slip away.

'I just walked out and didn't know where I was going, but eventually ran into a group of our blokes who seemed to know where they were heading. So I teamed up with them,' he explained.[24]

It was as simple as that. George Daldry who had acciden-tally fallen into enemy hands had, with consummate ease, managed to extricate himself from them.

Back in the centre of Mersing the 2/20th had held their ground until 24 January, when the decision was taken to detonate the bridge. A couple of days later the battalion began their inevitable retreat towards Jemaluang.

Brigadier Taylor moved his headquarters back to the Nithsdale Estate, a rubber plantation a little over 12 miles (20 km) north of Jemaluang. The 2/18th Battalion, less one company, accompanied him, while the 2/10th Field Regiment were there to provide effective fire to make good their escape.

This was to be the 2/18th's first major action. In the early hours of 27 January the battalion lay in wait for the advancing Japanese and sprang an ambush involving three of its companies. The Japs were taken completely by surprise and suffered heavy casualties. But the Australian offensive did not go quite to plan. What had been devised as a daylight operation took place at night. Command broke down and the complex plan ended in confusion. Brigade Headquarters ordered a premature withdrawal, forcing the abandonment of D Company behind the massed ranks of the Japanese force. It wasn't the major triumph the Aussies had hoped for but they still dealt a severe blow to several hundred enemy soldiers.[25]

Once again the 8th Division had demonstrated its resolve in battle, but at the same time the catalogue of defeats over the past six weeks could not be ignored.

Then came a cable from General Archibald Wavell, Commander-in-Chief of ABDA, who was in overall regional control. It alluded to the possibility of what was once unthinkable: the Allied evacuation of the entire peninsula.

'You must think out the problem of how to withdraw from the mainland should withdrawal become necessary and how to prolong resistance on the island,' he wrote in a communication to General Percival. 'Let me have your plans as soon as possible. Your preparations must, of course, be kept entirely secret.'[26]

Wavell's demand for confidentiality was understandable. Had word got out that British military chiefs were seriously contemplating the evacuation of the mainland, it would have undermined any remaining public confidence in the Allies and instilled the enemy with an even greater determination to march on to Singapore.

But what else could be done to delay the Japanese at this late stage? Eastforce continued to demolish bridges along the way but it was not long before Batu Pahat, a small town about 62 miles (100 km) northwest of Johore Bahru, fell to the Japanese.

The 2/20th Battalion got its marching orders to move early on the morning of 29 January to Johore Bahru, the regional capital, which overlooked the narrow waterway dividing the mainland from Singapore. The town was to accommodate the outer bridgehead force, which would provide cover for all Allied troops on their way from the peninsula to the island. Time was of the essence, as General Percival noted in a message to General Wavell.

'A very critical situation has developed. The enemy has cut off and overrun the majority of the forces on the west coast . . . Unless we can stop him it will be difficult to get our own columns on other roads back in time, especially as they are both being pressed. In any case it looks as if we should not be able to hold Johore for more than another three or four days. We are going to be a bit thin on the island unless we can get the remaining troops back.'

It was a humiliating admission and one which had to be addressed now rather than later. Within hours battalions from both the 22nd and 27th Infantry Brigades, whose presence had exuded so much public confidence in the early days of the war and whose valiant efforts had done so much to slow the Japanese, were on their way to certain defeat.

Before returning to HQ, Bennett decided to make a final call on the Sultan of Johore, who was so upset that the mainland was about to be abandoned at one stage started to sob. But the commander was not there to offer a shoulder on which to cry. He was there on a personal mission to save his own skin.

Bennett told the Sultan that he had no intention of becoming a prisoner of war and requested his help in acquiring a boat should it be necessary to escape.[27] There is no record of the Sultan's response, but given their close relationship, he probably would have offered whatever assistance he could.

After packing his bags at the 8th Division's headquarters, Major-General Henry Gordon Bennett reflected on Johore Bahru's demise. Once the streets had been full of Malays and busy Chinese; now the roads were deserted, the place was more like a ghost town than the thriving community it had once been.

'I have never felt so sad and upset,' he confided to his diary. 'Words fail me. This defeat should not have been . . . There seems no justification for it. I always thought we would hold Johore. Its loss was never contemplated.'[28]

For Bennett the prospect of being vanquished was almost impossible to bear. The events of the past few days had been an emotional watershed for him and he was desperate to vent his spleen. But who to blame?

There was never any doubt in Bennett's book that the defeat of the Allies in Malaya had to be put fairly and squarely at the feet of the British. In a vitriolic letter to Frank Forde, Australia's Army Minister, he 'venomously attacked the British, accused the 45th Indian Brigade of having "scattered like schoolgirls", [and] rebuked Forde for not promoting him to lieutenant general.'[29]

He claimed the British were more interested in promotion than winning the war.

'These English officers respect rank and little more,' he observed. As for Lieutenant-General 'Piggy' Heath, commander of the Indian III Brigade, 'He should have been relieved of his command long ago.'

What rankled Bennett was Heath's 'hidden power of influence' and the ease with which he was able to sway Percival. 'I have objected strongly to being placed under his command and have given as my reason that I will not allow the AIF to be slaughtered on the altar of Heath's inefficiency,' he wrote.[30]

And just for good measure Bennett could not resist a dig at his old bête noire, Blamey.

> To restore the position here would require two good assault divisions. Australian Divisions would be required to provide the needed reliefs . . . [A]re you going to send a Corp Commander with them or are you going to give me command? I know local conditions. I have experience in fighting the Japanese. When the war commenced I was senior to both Blamey and Lavarack and was superseded, not on account of inefficiency, but merely because of jealousy. Also, certain people wanted to see a permanent soldier, not a citizen soldier at the head.[31]

Bennett's thunder ended with a not-so-veiled threat: 'If you want to bring anyone else here to command the Australian Corps when it arrives, I will ask to be relieved. I will take it as a note of lack of confidence in me. I was a

Major General when Lavarack was a Lieutenant Colonel,'
he reminded Forde.

Perhaps sensing that he might have overstepped himself,
Bennett concluded: 'Please pardon my directness. It is a fault
of mine.'[32]

How different the situation might have been if the Japanese
had followed their original plan to invade Mersing by sea,
as Colonel Masanobu Tsuji, who devised the invasion of
Malaya, was to concede after the war.

'If, as was first intended, we had made the attack by
landing on the beach with 18 Division it would have ended
in disaster,' he said. 'Thinking back it makes my hair stand on
end to imagine what might have happened.'[33]

In the final analysis it was the right decision for the enemy
to take the peninsula by road and move south, a strategic
move that proved to be the Allies' undoing.

———·——

By the end of January the last retreat was underway. January
30 was the fateful day when 2/20th Battalion moved in
precision and on time to complete the withdrawal to
Singapore.

The Australian battalions were among the final units to
march across the causeway linking Singapore to the mainland before it was blown up. The depth charges were due to
go off at 8 am but a few hours before the deadline a familiar
wailing tone wafted through the morning air. It was the swirl
of bagpipes coming from the Argylls, whose dramatically
depleted ranks were not going to allow such an historic occasion to pass without honouring the fallen and the survivors
who were determined to continue the fight.

To the sound of 'A Hundred Pipers' and 'Hielan Laddie' those members of the 8th Division who were gathered on the southern side of the causeway listened, heartbroken, as the last link with the mainland was severed. Few would admit it then, but the sense of foreboding was palpable.

How had it come to this? Seventy-five years later Bart Richardson reflected on the unfolding tragedy over lunch at the Diggers RSL near his home in Nelson Bay, north of Newcastle. It was a dazzling spring day and Bart was in no mood to garnish his memories with a nostalgic gloss. Too many good men died because of the poor judgement of a few.

'It's time the truth were told,' he declared.

Bart, who was still driving his nippy VW Golf around town until shortly before he died in March 2017 at the age of 97, still suffered nightmares. Like so many of his mates he endured captivity in Changi and the slave-like conditions on the Burma–Thai Railway and he had little time for those who got him into the mess that ended in the fall of Singapore.

He rattled off a list of mainly British names, including Winston Churchill, as the principal culprits for what happened.

'Singapore was never at any time an impregnable fortress despite Churchill and senior army officers declaring it so on many occasions. It's said that at a British Army officers' school in India in 1938 an exercise was set for the capture of Singapore and one bright young officer captured it just the way the Japs eventually did so – coming down from the north and from the sea. What a shemozzle!'[34]

Bart was in full stride. It was as though the war had never ended and in many ways it hadn't. The men of the 8th Division had always felt let down by the colonial powers which held sway in the Malaya campaign and effectively ruined their lives. And they will feel it until their dying day.

But was the perceived failure of British military policy a justified criticism? Or were there other elements at play?

As Bart completed those final few steps over the causeway to Singapore, he could not foresee the bitter recriminations that would echo down the decades. The claims and counter-claims, the outrageous allegations and the sheer lies that would haunt all those who gave service in the pursuit of freedom.

Chapter 8

A TERRIBLE REVENGE

By now the Japanese were making their presence felt right across South-East Asia and much of the Pacific. On the same day that the Allies completed their evacuation of the Malay Peninsula, the Japanese Navy was about to strike further south on the island of Ambon in the Dutch East Indies.

Gull Force had already got wind of the enemy when an RAAF reconnaissance plane from 13 Squadron spotted a fleet of Japanese warships off the coast of Celebes to the northwest of Ambon.

There were 22 ships in all, including 13 transport vessels, three light cruisers, a heavy cruiser and five destroyers. The convoy was headed in a southeasterly direction, which could mean only one thing – its destination was Ambon.

Lieutenant William Jinkins confirmed the news a couple of days later when he saw the Japanese fleet approaching from his position 1000 metres above sea level, high up on the Mount Nona plateau.

Jinkins and his 2/21st platoon had been placed there just in case enemy troops tried to occupy the high point and in so doing gain an advantage over those members of the 8th Division based further down the hill.

He would not have to wait long. Soon Lieutenant Jinkins spotted the enemy coming ashore in motorised landing craft.

Elsewhere on the island, Walter Hicks, who had been out mapping near Eri on the southern peninsula, couldn't believe his eyes when he walked down to the beach and saw ten Japanese transport ships sailing across the heads which separated the Hitu and Latimor peninsulas.

'I thought where the hell did they come from?'

Not hanging around, he raced up the hill to raise the alarm and told his mates the news.

Walter remembers one of his officers shouting, 'Oh my God, we're dead.'

Cool-headed Walter replied, 'We're not dead yet, but we soon will be.'[1]

The initial assault involved four Japanese vessels, the *Yamaura*, the *Africa*, the *Zenyo* and *Miike*, which anchored at the southeastern tip of the Latimore Peninsula in the early hours of 31 January. Within a few hours the Japanese had landed three battalions of men who were fanning out across the island along narrow overland trails towards the main towns.

They made such extraordinary progress that by dusk on the same day one unit had converged on Ambon city, driving a wedge between the Australians, who were effectively trapped in the south, and most of the Dutch troops who were supposed to secure the north.

At the same time the other side of the island was being invaded from the north. Some 850 men of the 1st Kure Special Naval Landing Force made for the beach at Hitu Lama, cutting away the barbed wire defences and quickly securing the area.

The *Nippon Times* recorded in breathless detail how there was no stopping the Japanese landing parties.

'Crawling across the beach and into the enemy's pill box positions, the first charge scattered the enemy. The village of Hiti-lama was taken without much effort. But the fighting had only just begun.

'Immediately plunging into the jungle and smashing the pill boxes holding the enemy at every point, the Japanese forces covered more than 30 kilometres [roughly 20 miles] of extremely difficult territory and at 4.30 p.m. engaged the enemy's main strength holding the Laha airfield.'

The *Nippon Times*' correspondent Genichi Yamamoto's prose knew no bounds. To achieve their goal, the Japanese had 'crawled up steep cliffs, pounded through dark jungles and whirled like the wind through the village of Hasale'.[2]

In fact the account was largely accurate, but how had the marines achieved so much so quickly? The answer lay with Lieutenant-Colonel J.R.L. Kapitz, Commander of the Royal Netherlands East Indies Army and the man who was officially in control of the island. Kapitz had decided to withdraw most of his men from Hitu Lama to reinforce the town of Paso, thereby leaving the north coast extremely vulnerable in the event of an enemy attack. It was yet another example of what Gordon Bennett would see as the Allies' major weakness: the eagerness to retreat whenever conditions got too hot for them.

This time it was the Dutch who were to cave in without much of a fight. While the details remain unclear there were several reports of the Dutch hoisting a white flag, but offers to surrender went unheeded by the enemy. The Japanese still had the Australians to contend with and were in no mood to countenance a ceasefire until the entire island had downed arms. In the end it was bad advice that finally prompted the Dutch to capitulate. The official account of the fighting, as reported by Lionel Wigmore in *The Japanese Thrust*, claimed Kapitz was under the impression that the situation was far worse than it was.

'He considered that they had been intimidated by the bold action of small numbers of Japanese who had penetrated the lines and [he] was ashamed that fighting had been given up so soon.'[3]

Wasn't this the same old story? That the Allied forces all too often assumed the enemy was stronger than it was and gave in without a struggle? Hadn't the same happened in Malaya? And wouldn't a carbon copy mentality herald the fall of Singapore?

Up to a point, although on Ambon the jury was still out. The Japanese were yet to confront the men of the 8th Division's 2/21st and this battalion was certainly not prepared to give up without a fight. The Australians had no idea the Dutch had surrendered. Lieutenant-Colonel William Scott, who had taken command only three weeks earlier after a disagreement with his predecessor, knew they were up against it but was in no mood to hand in the towel. Supremely confident that help was on its way, Scott was convinced that Australia would provide air and naval support to see the enemy off. It turned out to be little more than wishful thinking.

Even the men were beginning to ponder their fate as morale started to plummet. But they didn't show it. In fact there were some remarkable acts of bravery over the next few days. In Joan Beaumont's history of Gull Force she cites the case of Lieutenant Ron Green, commander of 17 Platoon, who offered his men the chance to take part in an almost suicidal raid on Ambon town. All agreed to participate without exception.

One soldier's determination to take on the Japs would go down in battalion history as probably the most heroic act of the entire campaign. Bill Doolan, a transport driver, was in a reconnaissance patrol when they were sent towards enemy lines. They devised a plan whereby Doolan would drive into town with such confidence that the Japanese would assume he was one of their own. It was a cheeky and potentially fatal manoeuvre but surprisingly it worked. Once behind enemy lines the party let rip, tossing grenades out of the truck and spraying the Jap headquarters with gunfire before beating a swift retreat. Stunned by the audacity of the Aussies, the Japanese replied with force but Irish-born Doolan, who loved a good fight, stayed behind to assist the patrol's withdrawal. For several minutes he kept the enemy at bay, his brave actions culminating in an heroic last stand from up a tree. One of those who lived to tell the tale was Doolan's washboy, who would describe how Doolan turned on his pursuers and showered them with machine-gun fire and grenades.

By the time he dropped dead from his lofty perch, Doolan had, by some estimates, killed or badly wounded as many as 80 infantrymen. Even the Japanese were astonished by his fearlessness and gallantry, allowing his body to be buried beneath the tree from which he had fallen. A simple wooden

cross marked his grave and hardly a day passed when the
native population would not deliver fresh flowers to the site
in honour of the man who had given his life to defend their
island paradise.[4]

Doolan's spirit of derring-do reflected many similar acts
of bravery by the 8th Division on Ambon. Facing seemingly insurmountable odds, they refused to make life easy
for the enemy, whose navy was by now pounding Australian
defences at point-blank range.

Philip Miskin was the 23-year-old captain of B Echelon,
which was positioned in the foothills of Mount Nona on
the outskirts of Ambon town. Hiding in a coconut grove,
the location offered an uninterrupted vista of the Japanese
navy as it sailed into Ambon Bay. Usually the boys from B
Echelon found themselves at the rear of the battalion but on
this occasion they were in the front line, about a third of
a mile (300 m) from the enemy's shipboard guns. It was a
classic case of the mouse that roared, as *People Magazine* would
relate in a post-war account of the clash: 'The odds and ends
of B Echelon fought back magnificently under the terrible
pounding of the naval barrage. They swept the decks of the
warships with rifle, machine gun and mortar fire. But the
exchange was unequal. In return for .303 and .5 inch bullets
and three inch mortar bombs, they got 4 and 6 inch shells.'[5]

By now the Australians were beginning to enjoy the
game of cat and mouse, particularly the way one of the
unit's Brownings had forced a Japanese minesweeper to
steam away from the machine gun's range. Unfortunately
for those on board, the ship's crab-like manoeuvre was to
no avail. Suddenly an almighty explosion sent a column of
smoke and wreckage some 430 yards (400 metres) skywards.

The minesweeper had hit a mine, killing most of the 100-strong crew.

Alex Hawkins, who fired the fatal round, was so elated he claimed it as a 'kill', prompting Miskin to promise he'd give him the Browning as a prize once the war was over. Unfortunately Hawkins did not survive to collect his trophy, and through his actions many of his colleagues would also die. The 8th Division didn't know it then, but the Japanese would exact a terrible revenge for the loss of the minesweeper. It would result in one of the biggest and most bloody massacres of the war in the Far East and cast a dark cloud over the history of the 2/21st Battalion.

The so-called Battle of Rabaul began on 4 January 1942, when the Japanese dropped its first bombs on the peacetime capital of the Australian Mandated Territory of New Guinea. The 2/22nd Battalion, which comprised 900 men and 38 officers, had been in place since Anzac Day 1941 and with the arrival of more troops in December totalled about 1400. With them were members of the 2/10th Field Ambulance, anti-tank and coastal artillery batteries and militia from the New Guinea Volunteer Rifles. There was also air cover provided by 24 Squadron, which sent ten Wirraways and four Hudsons to Rabaul.[6]

Back in December, five days after Japan declared war, the Australian Chiefs of Staff were asked to advise the War Cabinet what to do with Lark Force. Should they leave, stay or be reinforced? Foolishly they ordered them to remain, despite the fact the Australian government knew there was little hope of holding out against a much larger and better equipped Japanese invasion force. And so it was on 23 January, a week before Gordon Bennett and his men evacuated the Malay Peninsula, that their 8th Division comrades in arms were feeling the full force of the Japanese Navy. As enemy ships entered the harbour at Rabaul, Japanese troops were coming ashore at Blanche Bay near Kokopo, to the southeast.

On 20 January around 100 Japanese planes attacked the island in successive waves. The RAAF sent up eight of their Wirraways but it was a futile mission. Three of the Australian aircraft were shot down, two crash-landed and another was damaged. Of the Australian air crew, six died in action and five were injured. Only one of the Japanese bombers was shot down and that by anti-aircraft fire on the ground. Like the situation on Timor and Ambon, the Rabaul campaign was turning into a disaster. And no one had heeded the warnings.

The 2/22nd Battalion didn't stand a chance. Armed with a few anti-tank guns, mortars and Vickers machine guns, the Australians fought valiantly for a couple of hours but were no match for the enemy. The first of 20,000 Japanese troops began to land and although some faced fierce resistance many came ashore unopposed. It was no fault of Lark Force, who were simply overwhelmed and outnumbered.

There followed a series of noble attempts by the Australians to turn back the enemy, particularly around Simpson Harbour, Keravia Bay and Raluana Point, but they were to no avail.

At one stage Lieutenant-Colonel Kuwada Ishiro, who was in command of the 3rd Battalion, 144th Infantry Regiment, endured heavy resistance at Vulcan Beach thanks to the combined might of an Australian unit from the 2/22nd Battalion and the New Guinea Volunteer Rifles, but elsewhere on the island the Japanese were able to land on unguarded stretches of coastline.

By dawn the airfield was in enemy hands and Lark's commanding officer, Lieutenant-Colonel John Scanlan, had no alternative but to issue the order, 'Every man for himself.' Twenty-eight Australians, including two officers, died on the day Rabaul fell. Only the RAAF, who had organised an emergency airlift, managed to escape. The army had made no such plans and simply retreated into the jungle, for which they had no training. Inexperienced in the skills of guerilla warfare, most of the soldiers who fled were forced to surrender in the coming weeks. Short of food and supplies, they grew hungry and eventually succumbed to tropical ailments which in turn reduced their effectiveness as a fighting force.

Japanese aircraft dropped messages warning the Australians: 'You can find neither food nor way of escape in this island and you will only die of hunger unless you surrender.'[7]

The Battle of Rabaul was a debacle but worse was to follow. In the coming weeks more than 1000 Aussies from the 8th Division were captured. While most were held as prisoners of war, 150 were massacred in a series of atrocities which became well-documented after the war. In one incident small groups of Australians were marched into the jungle near Tol Plantation and bayoneted to death. At the nearby Waitavalo Plantation others were shot.

Thanks to the testimony of six men who survived, the man held responsible for these massacres, Masao Kusunose, commanding officer of the 144th Infantry Battalion, was eventually accused of war crimes. However, rather than face military justice he starved himself to death before standing trial.

Remarkably some Australians succeeded in escaping from New Britain. About 450 troops and civilians were evacuated from the island by sea thanks to the efforts of individual officers who mounted rescue missions from New Guinea. Similar to other escapes from Ambon, Timor and Malaya, they got away against all odds. Escape would become a recurring theme in the 8th Division, but for some it would not be without controversy.

Back in Singapore Major-General Gordon Bennett was already hatching plans to flee the island, but unlike others who managed to avoid capture, the Australian commander's excuse would have far-reaching consequences.

Chapter 9

'WE'LL BLOW THEM ALL AWAY'

And so the fall of mainland Malaya ended without a shot being fired across the causeway. Most of the Allied forces completed their withdrawal to Singapore safely, but not without the loss of the 22nd Indian Brigade and the British commander of the Indian 9th Infantry Division, Major-General Arthur 'Bustling Bill' Barstow. They were supposed to be following up behind but the Indians became isolated and Barstow was killed in an ambush near Johore. Only Major Charles Moses, the Australian liaison officer with the Indian Division, and Colonel Trott, the senior admin officer, made it back in one piece. Barstow, who was a popular officer among the Australians and widely respected for his reputation as a fearless frontline soldier, was found shot dead at the bottom of a railway embankment.

It had taken just 55 days for the Japanese to conquer the 550 mile-long (885 km) peninsula.

'Thus ended the retreat to the island,' Bennett recorded in

his diary entry for 31 January. 'The whole operation seems incredible . . . forced back by a small Japanese army of only two divisions, riding stolen bicycles and without military support. The Japanese sent patrols outside our resistance and sat on a road behind our troops. Thinking they were cut off, our troops retreated.'[1]

This was the Japanese military strategy in a nutshell. In essence it had been one big confidence trick and the Allies had fallen for it. Now only 600 yards (550 m) of water – the narrowest point across the Johore Strait – separated them from the enemy.

The blast which had partially demolished the causeway was still ringing in many ears. It was, as Lionel Wigmore was to acknowledge in his official history of the campaign, symbolic of the moment.

'The roar of the explosion seemed to express the frustration and fury of the forces which had been thrust back and penned up in "the island fortress",' as it was still regarded.[2]

The explosion had left a 70-foot (21 m) gap in the causeway but it would not remain that way for long. Still the army thought the island would offer them protection. It was Lieutenant-Colonel J.O.C. Hayes, the navy's liaison officer with the army, who saw the writing on the wall.

'It was the same sensation as after Dunkirk,' he would later say in a radio broadcast. 'We knew where we were. There could be no more retreat without calamity. But driving along the north shore that morning, back to the naval base, now an empty settlement, I doubted for the first time that Singapore was impregnable. Somehow it did not look its part.'[3]

Bennett had not taken long to acquire new quarters near Bukit Timah village, a strategically important location towards Singapore town on the south coast of the island.

'My home is in a delightfully furnished, comparatively new bungalow on a hill,' he described in his diary, much as a real estate agent might promote a property to potential occupants.

His staff did not fare quite so well: 'My headquarters officers are in a poky little place about a mile away, just off the Jurong road. The staff is very cramped. They are living in small cottages nearby, while some are in tents.'

It was a temporary hardship but far better than the conditions they would have to endure eventually.

As for the civilian population who had been left behind on the mainland, Bennett vowed to retake their homeland as quickly as he could.

'Our duty now is to recapture Malaya at the earliest possible opportunity. We owe it to the natives! We owe it to ourselves.'

At least that was what he promised in his diary, but as we now know his more immediate responsibility was to himself.

Casting an eye across the straits to Johore Bahru he saw a Japanese flag flying over the administrative buildings.

'Very soon the Malay inhabitants will be driven from their homes and possibly used by the Japanese, the men as workers and the women . . .! How will they be treated?' he wondered.[4]

Of course Bennett knew the answer but he was deluding himself if he thought the Allies would save the day. In the same way, many of his fellow officers also chose to ignore the inevitable. Back at Division HQ they had no conception of the seriousness of the situation facing the island.

As Don Wall revealed in his detailed history of the 2/20th Battalion: 'Orders began requesting details of leave arrangements for troops – a directive from Malaya Command informed officers that leave arrangements would commence on February 15th – and other matters concerning laundry.'

Were they living in a parallel universe? Maybe so. It certainly seemed that way. The mood was one of optimism. There was no consideration of defeat. Most of the mail sent home saw the men writing in glowing terms of their ability to hold Singapore. Though one letter – from Lieutenant-Colonel Charles Assheton to his family back in Australia – disclosed he had suffered many anxious moments.

'What the future holds it is impossible to predict, but there is no doubt that a stern struggle lies ahead, not only here but in other theatres of the war.'[5]

By now there were about 85,000 troops on Singapore Island, including most of the 18th British Division, who had disembarked on 29 January and had yet to acclimatise themselves. The fighting force was divided into 45 infantry battalions, which included 21 Indian, 13 British, six Australian, two Malay and three from the Straits Settlements Volunteer Force. There were also three machine-gun and one reconnaissance battalions.[6]

Nearly 2000 Australian reinforcements had also arrived but they were largely untrained and turned out to be more of a liability than an asset. Many hadn't even fired a weapon. Why these new recruits had been sent to fight and not some of the 87,000 militiamen on full-time duty in Australia, most of whom had received months of training, is a mystery.

Only the 2/4th Australian Machine Gun Battalion, comprising nearly 1000 men of all ranks, seemed up to the task when they sailed into Singapore. The rest of the reinforcements were mere boys in comparison. While the 2/4th Battalion were late arrivals, what they lacked in battlefield experience they made up for in training and esprit de corps. A largely West Australian battalion, they'd come by a most roundabout route to Singapore, first sailing from Darwin to Port Moresby then, because of a Japanese air attack on Rabaul, turning around to sail to Malaya via the southern route. It meant calling in on Sydney and Fremantle before heading north again.[7]

Given that many of the lads had family in the Fremantle area, there was no stopping some of them from disobeying orders and making an unofficial overnight stay ashore to catch up with wives and girlfriends. When the battalion's ship, the *Aquitania*, set sail the next day 94 men were left behind. Most were eventually picked up by the military police and held in custody for a fortnight, before being released and sent north on another ship, the *Marella*, to rejoin their mates.

In the meantime such was the Australian government's increasing panic over the deteriorating situation in Malaya, 150 partially trained reinforcements from the 2/4th's base in Perth were also despatched to Singapore. Truth be told, many of them lacked proper training and were ill-prepared for war.

It was frustrating for the 8th Division's 22nd and 27th Brigades, who had become hardened soldiers over the previous few months. The job of defending the northwestern sector of the island now rested on their shoulders.[8]

It was the 2/20th Battalion, numbering nearly 800, including 32 officers, that drew the shortest straw. They would be positioned along that section of coast immediately overlooking Johore Strait. None of them realised how difficult their task would be, until Captain Frank Gaven was taken down to the area adjoining the Kranji River.

'It was impenetrable, with all the streams coming in along the foreshore through the mangroves. I have never felt such a feeling of desperation in all my life,' he recalled. 'I then realised that forward defence in this situation was an impossible task. There were no defences or fortifications and no field of view of an enemy approach. It was a situation that would not offer the troops any glimmer of hope.'[9]

Singapore, which was about 30 miles (50 km) long from east to west and 16 miles (27 km) from north to south, had nearly 120 miles (200 km) of coastline. River banks and mangrove swamps dotted along the foreshore also made it difficult to access and patrol.

Percival, who was still undecided about Japan's plans to invade the island, had divided Singapore into three sections. The British and Indian divisions would guard the north and east; the Malays the south; and the 8th Division under Gordon Bennett the northwest.

The 22nd Brigade was allocated about ten miles (16 km) of water frontage, with the 2/20th responsible for half of it, from the Kranji to the Serumbun rivers. Alongside it was the 2/18th Battalion. The 27th Brigade was positioned to the west of the causeway but had only two-and-a-half miles (4 km) of frontage to cover.

As Don Wall put it: 'In effect the 2/20th Bn of 750 men had the impossible task of defending 8,000 yards, double the frontage of 27 Brigade.'

The unfairness was further compounded when the 2/20th discovered a main road ran right through their sector linking the straits to Tengah airfield, a few miles to the south. What's more there was a seawall down on the foreshore, providing an ideal landing spot for Japanese heavy equipment and tanks. How would a force of several hundred men defend such a long stretch of mudflats and marshy terrain? Not very well, if the Japs chose to invade at this point, which seemed the most obvious place to land.

Brigadier Simson, who was in charge of engineering and defence measures, was so convinced the Japanese would launch their main attack in this area that he had prepared numerous obstacles to be placed in the enemy's way. Percival, however, had now decided that the Japs would most likely invade from the northeast and promptly ordered Simson to move his obstructions to the other side of the island, together with large reserves of barbed wire and anti-tank weaponry. This left the Australians hideously unprotected. Even Bennett was alarmed when he saw how vulnerable his men would be in the event of an attack on the northwestern sector.

On 2 February Bennett dropped by on the 2/20th Battalion and had a detailed look across the straits to the Kulai River, which he could see was a likely place from which an invasion might be launched. He also had time to assess the division's strength along this part of the coast. His conclusions were not encouraging.

'The men are cheerful but the posts are lonely. The gaps between the posts are wide. The position is extremely weak.'[10]

Bennett also visited the 2/16th Battalion, which was positioned near the River Kranji.

'I gazed across the straits towards Johore Bahru with a sad heart and a full memory of my happy sojourn there,' he wrote in his diary. 'The place was very deserted. I saw a Japanese staff car driving along the waterfront. The occupant alighted and, from concealment in some shrubs, had a long gaze at the island.'[11]

Outwardly Bennett projected a brave and confident front, telling the troops 'We'll blow them all away', but privately his concerns were growing. On 4 February he toured northwestern positions on the island, where the 2/18th and 2/19th were stationed. The area was thickly covered with timber and had mangroves growing right down to the water's edge. When he saw the posts, which were many hundreds of yards apart and had a field of fire of roughly 200 yards, his heart fell.

'I am beginning to worry about the extreme weakness,' he wrote.[12]

Bennett cabled his concerns to Australia's Army Minister Frank Forde, pointing out that the western half of the island was only lightly held: 'Troops in excellent spirits but disturbed with negative policy apparent as result of demolition at naval base. Consider best policy is strong counter-offensive as soon as reinforcements of aircraft and quality troops can be arranged. Pure defensive policy cannot succeed but consider offensive cannot fail.' [13]

Was Bennett deluding himself about the imminent arrival of reinforcements? Perhaps, but it was worth a go. He had exerted all the pressure he could muster to encourage more military support and this was probably his last throw of the dice.

Back on the beach the men could also see their predicament with all the clarity of a condemned prisoner viewing the noose. If the Japanese attacked at this point, the 2/20th would be in the front line, facing the prospect of a quick and bloody end. It would be up to soldiers like Joe Byrne to keep the enemy at bay. Joe was happy to do his bit but as he looked across the waterway to Johore Bahru he knew the Japanese meant business.

'Right along the water's edge they went, about 70 or 80 bloody lorries and other heavy vehicles. It was obvious they were heading our way,' he recalled.[14]

Come February the northeastern front found itself under intense shelling from the Japanese. Reconnaissance planes circling ominously overhead only added to the sense of dread.

It was time to find out what was happening on the other side of the water so a platoon from C Company was ordered to send a night patrol across the straits on an intelligence-gathering exercise. Lieutenant Roy Homer was to head the mission and Snowy Collins, Henry Dietz and two others volunteered to join him. All five knew the dangers they were facing as they climbed into a canoe and paddled across the Johore Strait. If caught they would almost certainly be executed as spies.

With hearts thumping, they eventually came ashore on the west of the straits and hid themselves just beneath Japanese lines.

'They were so close you could hear them moving around giving orders,' said Snowy. 'We were up to our ears in mud in the mangrove swamps. Just as well the lieutenant knew where we were because we didn't have a clue.'[15]

Their brief during the 24-hour reconnaissance trip was to gauge the number of landing boats and gun emplacements in the area. It did not always go smoothly.

'We nearly ran into the Japs two or three times and we were certainly lucky to get back,' Henry told me.[16]

It was a hairy mission but worthwhile. Homer and his boys acquired valuable information about the Japanese war machine before making the perilous voyage back across the water. In fact it was the return journey that created the highest risk. A powerful searchlight shone across the water every 20 seconds. If they were illuminated by the beam the enemy would almost certainly open fire. Picking the exact time of departure was critical.

'All of a sudden Lt. Homer said, "We've got to take the risk." So I gave the canoe a push, we jumped in and away we paddled,' said Henry. 'It was touch and go. There were Japanese and British gunboats in the area and us trying to avoid being seen in our collapsible canoe – it was a nightmare.'[17]

Back in the island's northwest sector, there was growing concern over the fate of the platoon. So much so that they were drawing lots to send out a search party, when the five paddled back to their safe haven.

Homer's boys weren't the only ones to triumph against the odds. Merv Alchin's story was even more unbelievable. After escaping from his Japanese captors on the mainland and making his way across the Mersing River, he had teamed up with two British sailors who had managed to swim ashore after their ship was sunk. Both had badly injured feet, which Merv was able to treat with his limited knowledge of first aid, and soon they were able to walk.

One of the Brits decided to try to make his way to Singapore by land, but Merv and the other sailor reckoned they stood a better chance by sea. Ever the survivor, Merv managed to persuade the owner of a Chinese fishing boat to take them south and so, suitably disguised with Chinese coolie hats, they fooled Japanese pilots who swooped down low to check them out, and made it to Singapore.

Don Alchin couldn't believe his eyes when his brother turned up. Overjoyed at being reunited, their elation was overshadowed by the thought of the men Merv had left behind, including his old mate Donny. Should he have done more to encourage them to join him on his dash for freedom? Or would that have sealed his own fate? It was an almost impossible choice to make but one he would never forget. Their faces would be etched in his dreams and night-mares until his dying day.

While the men of the 2/20th remained on high alert along the northwest sector, some were employed on other duties in town. Conscious of the need to deprive the enemy of anything of value when they arrived, the governor, Shenton Thomas, had deemed it necessary to destroy every bottle of alcohol on the island. This made sense given the drunken scenes that had earlier played out when the Japanese occupied Hong Kong, but the Aussies, who were always partial to a drop of the hard stuff, must have considered it sacrilege to send so much grog down the drain.

Even more tempting was the money stashed away in a vault at the State Treasury Building. Five million Straits dollars and several other currencies were kept in the strong room. It would be worth the equivalent of tens of millions of Australian dollars today but that didn't stop the authorities from ordering the money to be incinerated.

George Daldry was among those sent along to build the bonfire and not unnaturally couldn't resist putting some of it in his back pocket.

'There was millions and the bonfire was as high as me,' George recalled in his later years. 'As the flames started licking the first few notes we all started grabbing bundles. The wads were tied up with rubber bands so it was easy to snatch a few thousand.'[18]

The story was corroborated by Don Alchin, who admitted the situation got out of control.

'You could take whatever you wanted and we did. When we all got back to camp we started playing two-up for bets of $1000 a time. We were just rolling in dough and because we had so much it became like Monopoly money.'[19]

But how would they spend it if they became POWs? One man who is believed to have pinched a few million dollars' worth of notes had the foresight to bury the cash, in the hope of collecting his jackpot at a later date. After the war fellow veterans were reliably informed that he retrieved his ill-gotten gains and was able to boost his pension.

Burying money and smashing bottles of booze may have taken their minds off the impending battle, but the boys of 8th Division were not oblivious to Japanese intentions. How could they, given the pounding the 22nd Brigade received over the next few days? Enemy aircraft and shells fired from Johore Bahru were making conditions distinctly uncomfortable in the northwest sector.

Gordon Bennett was not immune to it either. On the morning of 8 February, his headquarters at Bukit Timah was severely blitzed, killing one man. Half an hour of constant shelling followed, forcing the 8th Division's commander and his staff to seek refuge in slit trenches and shelters. A truck containing a stack of military documents was destroyed, though it did not seem to worry Bennett who reckoned 'a little less paper in this war will improve matters.' Such was his contempt for bureaucracy.[20]

Next day ten British Hurricane fighters from the RAF squadron based at Kallang in central Singapore took to the air to see off a force of Japanese divebombers. It made for an impressive aerial spectacle above Sarimbun Beach and inflicted considerable damage on the enemy but it would be the last time the British Air Force was seen in action on the western side of the island.

While the northwestern coast of Singapore was regarded by some, including Wavell, as the most likely invasion point because of its close proximity to the mainland, Percival continued to favour the eastern sector. The Japanese Imperial Guards did everything to reinforce this misguided view by doing little to camouflage their position on the eastern side of the causeway. On the night of 7 February they even landed 400 soldiers on Pulau Ubin, a tiny island off Singapore's northeastern coast, just opposite what is now Changi Airport. This was a deliberate feint by the enemy to attract attention away from the western sector, which was where they really intended to come ashore. Percival swallowed the deception hook, line and sinker, but he resisted the temptation to respond, even though enemy artillery was raining down on the 22nd Brigade's front. It was as though Percival and his cronies could not bring themselves to accept what they could see with their own eyes.

On top of this Percival seemed reluctant to go on the offensive. An observation balloon flying over Johore gave the Japanese an uninterrupted view over the Allies' positions on Singapore yet Percival refused to authorise attempts to shoot it down. Even the Sultan's palace, which was being used by the Japanese command, was off-limits to the artillery. When Captain Rod Richardson, sitting on top of his observation post on the roof of a bungalow near the foreshore, asked for permission to fire on the palace, the request was denied. What was going on?

Bennett had apparently agreed with Percival that his men could let loose on the enemy as much as they wished, but incredibly that message had not been conveyed to the right quarters, and the brigade held itself back from harassing the enemy with gunfire.

Back at Sarimbun Beach the 2/20th were getting restless. They could see enemy troops massing on the other side of the straits and were suffering continual enemy bombardment from artillery and mortar fire, aimed at softening them up.

Thankfully, so far, casualties had been few but there was a serious problem with communications. Lines had been badly damaged in the bombardment, preventing the scale of Japanese action being relayed to Malaya Command. It looked like Brigadier Harold Taylor's 22nd Infantry Brigade and the 2/4th Machine Gun Battalion were on their own.

Not so, it emerged. Another secret back-up force consisting of Chinese guerillas had been held in reserve and was ready to support D Company. It was named Dalforce, after the Commander of the Federated Malay States Volunteer Force, Lieutenant-Colonel John Dalley. His idea had been to train a force of Chinese communists with the prime intention of harassing the Japanese and their raiding parties. They were fervent supporters of the Allied cause and had already been formed into a number of companies under British officers.

There was just one last unforeseen problem and it threatened to result in utter confusion. Dalley's men did not have recognisable uniforms but were dressed in native garb with a white bandanna around their heads. Equipped with a variety of weapons, including machetes and shotguns, they could have easily been mistaken for Japanese. Most of the Brits and Aussies who had come face to face with the enemy on the mainland were hardly likely to differentiate the Chinese from their fellow north Asians.

The presence of Dalforce was notified to all platoons but unfortunately not everyone got the message. The last thing the Allies wanted was unnecessary confusion on the battle-field, especially as there was no doubt about the loyalty of the Chinese, who had every reason to hate the Japanese given recent experiences in China.

———————

By mid-evening on 8 February an inky blackness had settled on the very north of the 2/20th's D Company sector. The tropical night was unexpectedly quiet but it would not last for long. From a plantation bungalow on the foreshore a spotter group could hear the distant throb of Japanese landing craft setting off from Johore Bahru. This was it. The moment the men of the 8th Division had been waiting for. Let battle commence.

A prearranged gunshot to signal the imminent arrival of Japanese troops echoed along the beach. 'Turn on the searchlights,' someone shouted, but there was no response. Unlike the previous night, when Lieutenant Homer and his crew dodged around the beam on the way back from their intelligence-gathering mission, the searchlights weren't working.

Unable to locate the first thrust of the enemy's armada, the 2/4th Machine Gun platoon opened fire indiscrimi-nately in the hope they'd hit their target. More by luck than judgement they made immediate contact, sinking barges and killing enemy troops as they tried to wade ashore.

Private Walter Holding, who was born in Bassendean in the northern suburbs of Perth, was among several platoons which were split up and sent where they were most needed.

'When the Japanese started to cross the Johore Straits they had powered motor boats pulling half a dozen barges loaded with troops. The boys behind the Vickers gun had been trained for just such a show. After the firing started some of the barges caught fire and lit up the area.'[21]

The next day Private Holding found himself part of a composite battalion named the Australian Special Reserve Battalion, under Commander Major Saggers, a lay preacher and a champion pistol shot in the militia. In Holding's memoir he wrote that his new boss was a 'strange little bloke'. He added: 'Just not the sort of bloke one would expect to see in the position he was in, but he was a wonderful leader.'[22]

Walter's first contact with the Japs came when he was out on patrol. At first he didn't recognise them as the enemy because they were out of uniform and appeared to be coolies. That was until they saw the rifles.

'It was pretty lively for a couple of minutes . . . when two Japanese ran out of the front of the house and hid behind some scrub.'

Private Holding needed to get himself into the open and behind his Bren gun 'to get a bead on where they were'. He continued: 'Then I gave them a pretty good sort of a burst. It has always stuck in my mind when I see someone getting shot on TV, they nice and pleasantly fall over, but it doesn't happen like that. These blokes were behind the bushes and I think I chopped the bushes around pretty well – I could see arms and legs waving around.'[23]

Walter and his mates were certain of one thing. They had to get back to safety – and quickly. Unhappily, not every member of the platoon returned unscathed. Ern Munday, Ernie Thomsett and Syd Darby, who was known as 'The Kid', did not come back that day. They were the platoon's first casualties.[24]

There were 4000 enemy soldiers in that first wave, all men from Japan's 5th and 18th Divisions. The agonising screams of those Japanese caught in the volley of machine-gun fire was shocking in its intensity. The mud and water on the foreshore was blood red, yet still there was no easing of the advancing horde. Fierce fighting raged for much of the night. The Australians were hopelessly outnumbered.

Within a few hours of the initial assault on D Company sector, the situation facing the 2/20th was looking bleak. While the Aussies had inflicted considerable damage on the enemy, the Japs still kept coming. Backed up by seemingly endless support on the ground and superiority in the air, the Japanese were now taking advantage of gaps in the Allied lines – a risk Bennett had noted a few days earlier.

For George Daldry it was a night he would never forget. It would be the last time he saw his brother Charles, who was also in D Company. The brothers were exceptionally close and would do anything for each other. Charlie, who was on lookout duty down on the beach, was recovering from malaria, as was his close friend Spud Murphy. George felt sorry for his older brother and volunteered to take his place, but Charlie was having none of it, insisting he wanted to stay with Spud. It was a decision that cost him his life.

'Unfortunately the Japs landed shortly afterwards and he died a terrible death – we think he was bayoneted,' George recalled in later years.[25]

Moments of mateship and courage under fire were common that night. They were qualities that exemplified the spirit of the 8th Division, though not everyone covered themselves in glory.

Henry Dietz remembers how one officer was so scared he scarpered and left his men to it. 'We knew the Japs were coming,' said Henry. All of a sudden the officer shouted, 'Don't do anything until I give you the order to do it.'

Henry continued: 'I'm trying to pass this message down the line when I see this bloke of ours running away through the rubber plantation – he just cleared out and left us.'[26]

It wasn't an isolated incident. Courage was also in short supply when another officer deserted his troops near the Kranji River.

Scotsman Jimmy Houston was with a group of men who were suddenly confronted by Japanese on the river bank.

'About fifty of us lads who were surrounded by Japs were not strong enough to swim the river,' he recorded in his diary. 'Well, this officer, instead of helping them across the river, dived in and swam for his life, leaving them all to look after themselves.'[27]

Jimmy, a tough Glaswegian-born dock worker, survived but little is known about the fate of the others.

Was this cowardice or simply part of the natural human instinct to stay alive? Who knows how people will react to the threat of violent death until they face a similar situation?

While Jimmy Houston could look after himself, Henry Dietz sympathised with those who chose to run.

'You can't call it cowardice. It's what happens to a bloke when he can't control himself in action. I suppose we were all nearly at cracking point,' he told me. 'I don't care how good you are, there's nobody who could honestly tell you they weren't frightened then.'[28]

With the two Australian brigades out of contact with each other, the 22nd Brigade had no choice but to retreat. By dawn some units had been overrun, others were completely surrounded. Once again the Japanese pincer movement which had been so successful on the mainland was proving to be deadly effective during the assault of Singapore.

In the centre of the fight the 2/18th Australian Infantry Battalion had lost more than half of its men. The 2/20th Infantry Battalion had fared little better, with its right flank heavily committed. To the left the 2/19th Infantry Battalion was also in trouble as it became outflanked. Only B Company was left standing as it faced up to the enemy's initial landings, but it would not be long before it too was forced to join the withdrawal south.

It was an unedifying sight as the exhausted and walking wounded from the defeated Australian battalions made their way inland, some by road, others through the thick jungle. Those who were not capable of making the journey on foot were hoisted into trucks which would ferry them to hospital. At least that was the idea, but with the tide turning against the Allies nothing was assured.

As one convoy set off along Neo Tiew Road at dawn, it was ambushed. Only those fortunate enough to be in the trucks at the rear were able to escape into the jungle and avoid being massacred.

Among the fatalities that day was Lieutenant-Colonel Charles Assheton, the 2/20th Battalion's Kalgoorlie-born commanding officer. He had been instrumental in providing cover for the retreat of his men who were under fire from enemy units, and was making his way to Ama Keng to help others when he was hit by a blast of automatic gunfire. At precisely 11.30 am on the morning of 9 February 1942, the man whose bravery and honour was so respected by his men was dead. He was only 40.

Assheton had been a legend among the ranks of the 8th Division but his loss would be overshadowed by even worse to come.

The last act in the battle for Singapore was only just beginning. The question was, how long would it have to go? The enemy's rapid advance had already dealt the Allies a disastrous blow, and Major-General Gordon Bennett was in no mood to join them for the final curtain.

Chapter 10

'THE BATTLE MUST BE FOUGHT TO THE BITTER END'

Desperate though the situation appeared, the 8th Division was in no mood to give in. Although the 2/20th, 2/18th and 2/19th Battalions had suffered heavy losses overnight, they were already reorganising themselves and gathering together in defensive positions in readiness for further action.

The 2/18th, which was 330 strong, went into position in the Choa Chu Kang Road around Bulim village. The 2/29th was placed along Jurong Road. About 150 survivors of the 2/10th Field Company and a small party from the 2/20th joined forces and the 2/19th's A Company was placed in a reserve position at the rear of the 2/18th.[1]

Major-General Bennett ordered his artillery commander to support the 22nd and 27th Australian Infantry Brigades, as well as the 44th Indian Brigade. If they could make a stand along the so-called Bulim line, they might have half a chance of stalling the invaders.

About midnight on 10 February the plan was further

amended when Bennett decided to withdraw the 22nd Australian Infantry Brigade to a line between Kranji and Jurong. An hour later General Percival issued his final orders for the defence of Singapore. Bennett was to take complete responsibility for the western area northeast of Bukit Timah village.

As Brigadier Harold Taylor, commander of the 22nd Brigade, moved to carry out the plan, he got a bit ahead of himself. On his way to reconnoitre the new positions he called on Bennett, who tersely reproved him for implementing Percival's secret order before being instructed to do so.

Bombarded by orders from both Bennett and Percival, Taylor, ever the realist, concluded that Percival had set his battalions an almost impossible task. Not only would they have to occupy their first-stage positions in darkness in unknown territory, but they would have no opportunity of reconnoitering for their subsequent advance. In short it was a disaster waiting to happen.[2]

The military appeared to be running around in ever-decreasing circles, effectively making things up as they went along. It was obvious there were too many chiefs. General Archibald Wavell flew in to make a lightning-quick visit to Bennett's headquarters with General Percival, only to learn on arrival that the Kranji-Jurong defence line had already been lost. The commander-in-chief was not happy and immediately ordered the line be retaken. It was vital that the Kranji–Jurong line be used as a bulwark against the enemy thrust from the west, he insisted.

This was fine in theory but made no allowance for the facts. Much of the island was in chaos and the Allied troops were unsure which way to turn. Even Brigadier Taylor, who sensed a debacle in the making, protested in vain against Wavell's plan for a counterattack.

The top-level meeting between Wavell, Percival and Bennett was punctuated by a series of explosions. As if they needed any more convincing that the Japanese bombardment was getting nearer, their office in Western Command Headquarters was shaken by a bombing raid on the building.

Significantly Bennett was the only member of the group who wasn't fazed by the blasts. As the bombs fell thick and fast everybody else dived under the table and any other cover that was available.

It was an 'unedifying spectacle', wrote General Percival. 'There was a good deal of debris and a few casualties outside, but the party of VIPs escaped untouched, though I lost both my car and my field glasses,' he recalled.[3]

Once again Bennett had demonstrated his fearless response to mortal danger. Frank Legg, the war correspondent who went on to write a detailed biography of the 8th Division's commander, believes the episode did much to boost Bennett's image in the eyes of his men.

'What Bennett's staff remember of this incident was that, alone of the three, Gordon Bennett refused to seek cover and remained erect until he was joined, a little sheepishly, by the others,' he said. 'The story may be apocryphal. At least it shows the admiration the 8th Division entertained for its commander who, whatever the circumstances, refused to display the slightest sign of fear.'[4]

Bennett himself was more complimentary about his fellow officers' behaviour, claiming that Wavell and Percival had shown exemplary coolness. Nevertheless he agreed that it was a miracle they had all survived.[5]

Meanwhile, Japanese troops had reached the Kranji ammunition magazine, which Allied engineers should have destroyed earlier. The ammunition had been stored and kept in reserve in anticipation of a prolonged period of resistance. Now it was in enemy hands.

The last of the serviceable aircraft and their remaining crews on Singapore were also told to leave. They withdrew to the Dutch East Indies leaving the Allies devoid of all air support. The island had never been more exposed.

Yet on the ground, at least, the number of British, Indian and Australian troops far outweighed those of the enemy.

As General Wavell was to observe in his order of the day: 'It is certain that our troops on Singapore Island greatly outnumber any Japanese that have crossed the Straits. We must defeat them. Our whole fighting reputation is at stake and the honour of the British Empire.'[6]

It was impossible to disagree with the sentiments. In theory the Allies should have been in a strong position. If only they would send their entire force into action they might just, conceivably, stop the enemy in their tracks.

Recent history has only served to reinforce Wavell's view: 'The Americans have held out in the Bataan Peninsula against far greater odds, the Russians are turning back the picked strength of the Germans, the Chinese, with almost complete lack of modern equipment, have held the Japanese for four-and-a-half years. It will be disgraceful if we yield our boasted fortress of Singapore to inferior enemy forces.'[7]

General Percival was of the same mind as Wavell and noted that some troops were not showing 'the fighting spirit expected of men of the British Empire'. He went on: 'It will be a lasting disgrace if we are defeated by an army of clever gangsters many times inferior in numbers to our men. The spirit of aggression and determination to stick it out must be inculcated in all ranks. There must be no further withdrawals without orders. There are too many fighting men in the back areas. Every available man who is not doing essential work must be used to stop the invader.'[8]

Back in London, Churchill was quick to jump on the fact that the Allies had nearly 100,000 men in Singapore.

In a cable to Wavell he observed, 'It is doubtful whether the Japanese have as many in the whole Malaya peninsula. In these circumstances the defenders must greatly outnumber Japanese forces who have crossed the Straits and in a well-contested battle they should destroy them.'[9]

Churchill exhorted his regional commander not to countenance any thought of saving the troops or sparing the civilian population: 'The battle must be fought to the bitter end at all costs. Commanders and senior officers should die with their troops. I rely on you to show no mercy to weakness in any form . . . the whole reputation of our country and our race is involved.'[10]

This was stirring stuff but it conveniently ignored the reality of Britain's lack of planning and foresight. Given that the Malayan campaign had been virtually lost at sea and in the air within a few days of its start, one might also accuse Churchill of being wise after the event.[11]

Privately Wavell conceded that he was 'without much confidence in any prolonged resistance' and cabled the British prime minister accordingly, admitting that the battle for Singapore was not going well.[12]

But why? Was it simply a case of Japan being the far superior force or could the blame be put at the feet of the retreating Allies? Was there an essential weakness in their character, a fatal flaw in their fighting spirit?

Maybe the answer could be found in the back blocks of Singapore, where thousands of leaderless men were roaming the streets without any sense of purpose, except to avoid death or capture. Many were stragglers who had been separated from their units and did not know which way to turn. Confused and exhausted after weeks of battle, they searched for food and shelter in an increasingly anarchic atmosphere.

The Official Report of Operations of the 8th Australian Division in Malaya alluded to the crisis in what it described as a 'most disturbing report . . . to the effect that there were 2000 AIF troops in Singapore [town].

'The staff captain of the 22nd Australian Infantry Brigade was despatched without transport to collect these men and transfer them to their units. Some stragglers were found but the number originally stated seems an exaggeration.'

A check of units seemed to establish that all the artillery, signals and engineers were still at their posts and the 27th Brigade was intact. About 700 men who had been forced to retreat when the Japanese landed on the coast were found at Base Depot being reclothed and re-armed.

Yet undeniably an uncertain number had headed for the docks in search of some means of escape.

'There were many fighting men, Australian, British and Indians, wandering around the docks attempting to board ships, when their place was at the front,' the 8th Division's Official Operations report later confirmed.

There was no reason to disbelieve this account, coming as it did from Colonel Jim Thyer, Bennett's chief of staff, who compiled the report after the war from a narrative by Colonel Charles Kappe.

Once again it all came down to a lack of planning. In almost every case there had been a failure to establish collecting posts for those who were left behind and there were no unit representatives present to guide the men back to their HQs.[13]

General Bennett's immediate assessment of the problem revealed there were definitely men who were absent without leave. He described most of them as recent arrivals from Australia, where they had been hastily recruited and despatched. Most hadn't even fired a rifle, as if this excused their behaviour. Perhaps the 8th Division's commander chose to ignore the ill-discipline of some of his men, fearing it would taint the positive image won during the gritty battles of Gemas and Muar. Whatever his reasoning, further evidence would soon emerge of a more damning lack of order, one that would blur the distinction between straggler and deserter.

Not that most of the division hadn't risen to the occasion. Back on the front line individual units continued to defend the island, a third of which was now in Japanese hands. Over the previous 48 hours there had been countless examples of action beyond the call of duty. The 2/18th Battalion's carrier platoon was engaged in a bitter struggle which wiped out close to an entire company of Japanese around Tengah airfield. The 2/20th, who had already trekked their way through thick jungle during the withdrawal from the Kranji, were hoping to regroup at Bulim, to the south of Tengah airfield. This was a high-risk strategy and there were numerous near-misses and occasional tragedies in its prosecution.

Some higher power must have been watching over John
Cook that day. Still only 20, he'd given up his job as a driver
with Australian Glassworks in Sydney to join up. Now he
was lying next to his childhood mate Roger Mort in a field,
as enemy machine gun fire zipped overhead. The two C
Company men thought they were well-hidden until a stray
bullet hit Mort in the back.

Ever the loyal friend, Roger's first thought was for John.
'You okay?' he asked.

John muttered a reassuring 'yeah' before noticing the blood
pouring from his mate's upper body. The gaping wound in his
back was to prove fatal. John could do little but offer words
of comfort and Roger Charles Mort died soon afterwards.[14]

Mick McAuliffe, who before the war had worked in dairy
farming in northern New South Wales, also came under
fire as he made his way with other members of B Company
towards Bukit Timah, where he hoped to find sanctuary. He
was seeking to get a better picture of how the Allies were
going, but his more immediate concern was how to avoid an
enemy bullet. His mates were going down like skittles.

'Two of the blokes who came over with me on the *Aquitania*
got killed but I was lucky they missed me,' he told me. 'Before
we knew what was happening the Japs surrounded us. It was
uncanny. They were behind us and opened fire. It was like
all hell had broken loose – you didn't know whether it was
coming from east or west, but somehow I survived it.'[15]

John Chippendale, who was in the 8th Corps of Signals,
had several lucky escapes with five of his mates while on
patrol in the Bukit Timah area. They'd already been shelled
and bombed by Japanese aircraft and had dug a three-foot
(1-m) deep slit trench to shelter in.

'After the planes left us shaken but not hurt, that slit trench went down to six feet [2 m] deep very quickly,' he recalled.[16]

Sydney-born John, who was in his early twenties, scrounged sheets of corrugated iron and cut down some trees to cover the trench. 'We'd have had to have taken a direct hit to be hurt.'[17]

Later he had an even closer shave as he bent down to pick up a five-cent piece in the road when a bullet hit the tarmac just in front of him. Zigzagging across the road to avoid the sniper's fire, he found himself in the abandoned French Embassy, where he came across a fully loaded, automatic pistol. John seized the firearm and went outside to search for the person who'd nearly shot him.

'I saw a movement in one of the big trees and a Jap [sniper] strapped to a branch. While keeping another big tree between me and the Jap, I was just about to pull the trigger when there was a burst of machine gun fire from from Lt. Harrison that hit the Jap. We just left him there and went on with our mission.'[18]

The Allies were up against a formidable foe. With the so-called Kranji–Jurong line lost, the 2/20th Battalion was on the move again.

Around the same time X Battalion was formed, which comprised companies within the three 22nd Brigade units and was commanded by Lieutenant-Colonel Arthur Boyes, former CO of the 2/26th.

Bennett had got wind of a successful attack by the Indians, who had the Japanese on the run. Or so it was rumoured. On the basis of this flimsy military intelligence the 2/20th was ordered forward.

It was night as Captain Rod Richardson and his contingent made their way through the pitch black darkness. What they found along the way did not inspire them with confidence. Many of the Indians who were earlier reported to have launched a successful assault on the Japs were lying dead by the roadside.

X Battalion and its sundry units were practically on their knees by now and so the decision was taken to make camp.

Henry Dietz had loosened his belt and was settling down to a few hours of shut-eye when the night sky turned into day. The nearby fuel tanks had exploded, setting fire to factories and other buildings in the vicinity. Henry was only just beginning to take in the magnitude of the blast when a new and deadlier threat appeared. It came in the form of the Japanese 18th Division, who were about to launch a bloody assault on the camp.

The orgy of blood-letting that followed was so savage in its intensity that the men of X Battalion were completely overwhelmed. Some Australians were bayoneted as they woke up, while others were killed by small arms fire or grenades. Those who were able to do so rose from their blankets and engaged enemy troops in hand-to-hand fighting in a vain bid to defend themselves. The screams of shock and pain would never be forgotten by the survivors of that terrible night. The camp site was a slaughterhouse. Of the 200 diggers who'd made camp there, most would be dead or seriously wounded by dawn.

It seemed every attempt by the Allied forces to resist the invaders and fight back was to end in failure. But where to go? Singapore city was becoming increasingly isolated and safe havens were few and far between.

Lieutenant Harry Woods of the 2/20th found himself in what he believed was the relatively secure Reformatory Road. Right when they thought they were home and dry, Harry and his platoon were confronted by a large unit of Japanese, who immediately started shooting. With no shelter to protect him, he was shot in the thigh and shoulder.

'Both bullets missed the bones fortunately so I could still walk reasonably well. But I lost quite a lot of blood,' he said.[19]

He might not be able to run but Harry Woods had no intention of being captured either. Somehow he managed to hitch a lift on the pillion seat of a passing despatch rider who, after avoiding a hail of machine-gun fire from a Japanese fighter plane, was able to deliver the 24-year-old officer safely into the hands of a British medical orderly.

It was an extraordinarily lucky escape for Harry Woods but nothing compared with the near miracle that was to follow three days later. It happened after the young lieutenant was sent to Alexandra Military Hospital for further treatment. As he lay in bed recovering in a top-floor ward, a party of renegade Japanese soldiers arrived downstairs intent on violence. In one of the worst atrocities of World War II, hundreds of innocent nurses, doctors, patients and civilians were slaughtered as the troops ran riot. Despite pointing to the red cross on their uniforms and pleading for their lives, most were stabbed to death by bayonet. No one received any mercy, not even a patient about to undergo surgery on the operating table.

Because Harry Woods was upstairs, amazingly, he avoided the carnage. Another military patient, who could walk, went down to find out was happening, only to be executed on the spot a few minutes later. For whatever reason, the

Japanese never made it to the top floor. The screams and the horror of that day left an indelible impression on Harry's mind, burdening him until it was diminished in later life by a failing memory. All he could visualise of the scene was a sea of blood and family photographs and rosary beads dumped at random across the grounds of the Alexandra Hospital. For some, a black and white snap of a loved one or a crucifix on a chain had provided the only solace in those dying moments.

These were testing times and the future looked even worse. The 2/13th Australian General Hospital Battalion, which had been formed in Melbourne about six months earlier, was under intense pressure. Originally staffed by 18 officers and 44 nurses, most of its patients were victims of the AIF's battles in Johore. Now with the fighting getting closer by the hour, St Patrick's Boys School, which had been converted into a 700-bed hospital, was made into a large-scale casualty clearing station.

How the medical staff went about their work as bombs continued to rain down on them was a miracle in itself. The building, which sat on Singapore's largely exposed south coast, sustained hits to both its kitchen and a ward. At night the hospital was placed under a complete black-out and as the number of casualties increased, it soon became apparent that the hospital did not have the accommodation or facilities to nurse them. Many patients had no choice but to lie outside on the lawns as they awaited treatment.[20]

The 2/13th Australian General Hospital Battalion, whose love and care for the injured often exceeded what was expected of them, would have to be evacuated soon or risk falling into the hands of an enemy who had little respect for women, even those who might save lives. In view of the gravity of the situation the decision was made to evacuate the 2/13th's nursing sisters on three ships about to leave Singapore. The final contingent boarded the *Vyner Brooke* on 12 February.[21]

The British-registered vessel, which had been requisitioned by the Royal Navy for use as an armed trader, was usually equipped to carry 12 passengers but on that fateful day nearly 200 women and children were on board, including 65 Australian nurses. Among them was a nursing sister by the name of Vivian Bullwinkel, whose remarkable story of survival is firmly etched in the annals of the 8th Division's history.

After the *Vyner Brooke* was sunk by enemy aircraft, most of the passengers and crew made it safely to Banka Island, which had already been occupied by the Japanese. They would be shown no mercy. Twenty-two Australian nurses and one British woman civilian were ordered to wade into the sea, where they were mown down in a hail of gunfire by Japanese troops who were standing on the beach with loaded rifles. Only Vivian Bullwinkel lived to reveal this monstrous act of butchery.

Miraculously a bullet passed straight through her body without damaging her internal organs. Feigning death until the Japanese left, she hid for 12 days before being recaptured and allowed to live.

Out of the 65 Australians who left on the *Vyner Brooke*, 12 were killed during the attack by Japanese aircraft or drowned when the ship sank. Apart from those mown down in the water, the rest became internees or died as prisoners of war.[22]

Back on Singapore, Percival and Bennett were facing the inevitability of defeat, but they would not give up without a fight. A decision was made to establish a final defensive line around Singapore's urban centre. Bennett ordered all AIF personnel – 'no matter what duties they were engaged on' – to move into an area at Tanglin Barracks, about three miles (5 km) to the northwest of the city. This was to be the focus of the 8th Division's last stand 'where, if necessary, every man must be prepared to die,' Bennett declared.[23]

Some of the men were already close to collapse, among them Brigadier Taylor, who had been without sleep for some days and was overcome by fatigue. Relations between him and Bennett were now so fractious that the 8th Division's commander decided to relieve Taylor of his command. The brigadier had already asked the 2/18th's Lieutenant-Colonel Arthur Varley to take temporary command of the 22nd Brigade and Bennett decided to make it permanent. Taylor's condition was so bad that he was driven to hospital by his brigade major.[24]

General Percival had moved his advance HQ back from Sime Road to Fort Canning, the military stronghold known as the Battlebox. Entered through a door set in the side of a hill in Fort Canning Park, the wartime bunker was to be the nerve centre of Allied military operations during the final few days of the crisis.

Up to 500 staff crowded into the underground complex, which had 29 rooms and very little in the way of ventilation. With no airconditioning one can only imagine the stifling heat they were forced to endure as they fielded phone calls, deciphered encrypted signals and plotted the enemy's inexorable progress.

Only those with the strictest security clearance were allowed to enter the Battlebox. Even those who worked at Fort Canning were ignorant of the inner workings of the maze of tunnels and chambers that lay some 10 feet below ground level. This was Percival's kingdom, where the dying days of Britain's Far East empire would draw to a humiliating conclusion.

While all this was going on, chaos reigned in the surrounding countryside and on the roads and footpaths, which had become a battleground. Unlike today, Singapore was still rural then, with smallholdings and native villages dotting much of the landscape. As Allied troops tried to make their way back to base, many found the route cut off by the enemy. Dodging stray gunfire and forced to shelter from the continuous aerial bombardment, it was every man for himself.

The confusion of those last few days was probably best described by Major Charles Moses, one of Bennett's staff officers. In Frank Legg's account of the fall of Singapore, he quotes extensively from Moses's diary. In the early hours of 11 February the major found himself alone with his Webley automatic, crawling through deep scrub, with Japs everywhere.

'I began to feel I would never get through and I railed in my heart against the fate that let me live through the three ambushes up near Layang Layang two weeks before, only to be killed in this blackness alone,' he wrote.

'Why couldn't I have been killed cleanly that day instead of being saved up to be tortured like this? I prayed for a bullet through the head or heart – that would snuff me out like a candle. Yet behind it all was something which told me I was not meant to be killed like that.'

He stumbled into a Chinese cemetery and after about 330 yards (300 m) glimpsed the first light of dawn and the eerie outline of a deserted Reformatory Road. Now he was only a few hundred yards from Bukit Timah Road. There were British troops in the distance and the sound of Japanese machine-gun fire. Suddenly he spotted one of his own men, a Bren gun carrier, who took him to Malaya Command HQ.

Breathing a deep sigh of relief, Moses walked into General Percival's office and told him what he knew.

'What do you think we should do, Major?' Britain's GOC enquired.[25]

It was a very good question. If Percival didn't know the answer, what hope had the rest of them?

Chapter 11

SINGAPORE CRUMBLES –
THE GETAWAY BEGINS

For the men caught up in the mayhem that was enveloping Singapore, the memory of those final few days before surrender has become a kaleidoscope of random images.

Arthur 'Bluey' Kennedy knew the Malaya campaign was reaching a climax and inexplicably felt a moment of exhilaration.

As a member of the 2/15th Field Regiment he'd been guarding the northern sector just east of the causeway along with the 2/30th.

'I was too busy with the guns to worry about the Japanese. I was number two gun and there was an attack on the front of us and I had to go towards the west.'[1]

If Bluey was frightened he wasn't showing it. He was almost enjoying the moment and had to remind himself that all this was for real.

'You're here to fight a war, not play games,' he recalled his sergeant major bellowing. 'His training stood me in good stead.'[2]

Then came the order to pull out. He rolled his 25-pounder cannon into a ditch and took off.

'There I was standing with machine-gun bullets flying all about me, so I shot through along the road and jumped into a drain.'

What happened next took him completely by surprise.

'Suddenly I came face to face with a yellow-looking man who looked like a Jap with a rifle in his hand pointing at me.'

For a moment Arthur Kennedy thought his time was up, until he discovered to his relief that the man with the gun was actually Chinese.

'It was a ticklish moment,' he told me.[3]

Arthur, who had become separated from his unit, found himself tagging along with a convoy on the main thoroughfare from the causeway to Singapore town.

'At this time the enemy was working towards the west and continuing to attack the Indian troops. The Australian infantry had been outflanked and in some cases overwhelmed. It could not be expected that the three battalions could hold a front of around five miles [8 km].'[4]

The gunfire came from all directions. The Japanese seemed to be everywhere.

'After firing a number of rounds we came under fire from heavy machine guns.'[5]

It was too dangerous to continue so they were told to move back to Bukit Timah village and await further orders. The next morning Bluey and his mates were on the move again, this time to the racecourse a few miles away.

Although nowhere was safe, strangely there was an air of normality to the area, reinforced by the sight of several

Australian jockeys who invited them into their homes for a cup of tea and a shower. Only the distant wail of air raid sirens reminded those who might have momentarily forgotten that there was actually a war on.

After his wash and brush-up, Arthur took a truck to a nearby ordnance depot to pick up some ammunition. Someone else drove it back, and Kennedy got behind the wheel of a two-seater Packard that just happened to be parked nearby. Along the way he stopped off for a haircut – as you do when death might be only seconds away.

'During the operation an air raid sounded but I was able to persuade the Chinese barber to stay and finish it. He was so nervous that I decided not to have him shave me.'[6]

The day was to get even more bizarre as the Australians moved further towards the city. Despite the bombardment of the past weeks many palatial homes remained intact inside, even if they were silent and empty.

'We entered one and walked around. The house was full of beautiful furniture and valuable ornaments. It looked as if the owner would return at any minute and order us out.'[7]

Bluey Kennedy and his mates made themselves a meal in the well-stocked kitchen. As they tucked in an air raid siren sounded, followed by a heavy explosion which made a massive hole in the kitchen floor.

'Fortunately no-one was hurt and we continued on with the meal,' Arthur recalled, as if it happened all the time.[8]

Then it was on to the Orchard Road vicinity, now the glittering retail heart of Singapore but then a sedate residential area inhabited by wealthy Chinese. The troop took up position in a row of front gardens opposite the Goodwood

Park Hotel, a smart colonial-style building that continues to operate today.

A suspected fifth columnist opened fire on them from the hotel's tower, which offered a commanding view over the city, but a few shots in return put a stop to that.

Best to take shelter, they reasoned, in one of the many Chinese homes, which they duly did and they were stunned by the luxury. Bluey had seen nothing like this in the western suburbs of Sydney where he grew up. It was a standard of living far removed from the experience of most of the diggers gathered there that day.

'In one room there was an entire wall of built-in wardrobes filled with clothing and shoes. We took a number of frocks as they were suitable for pulling through the gun barrels. In another room there was a small safe which it was decided to open. The safe was tipped over on its face and the back cut out with an axe.'[9]

Disappointingly there was only a small amount of money and some jewellery inside, which was of little interest to them.

From the Orchard Road area they were moved to the Tanglin Barracks, where the guns were prepared for action. In the distance enemy troops could be clearly seen to the west and Japanese flags appeared to be just within firing range.

Yet the Allies' weaponry remained silent. Permission to fire could not be obtained because of concern about the enemy's response. Was the 8th Division in the same war? Hadn't it spent the last few days shooting and shelling the Japanese? So why the change in strategy?

'Permission to fire could not be obtained and no-one in close proximity was very happy for us to do so. They were worried about any action by the enemy to silence the guns,'

Bluey explained. 'This had always been a problem with the use of artillery in limited space. Everyone was happy to use the cover we could supply as long as we were some miles away.'[10]

The reasoning was that if the Japanese were able to pinpoint the guns, Bluey's troop would likely be attacked by mortars. And so it happened, even without the 2/15th Field Regiment firing a shot in anger. Somehow the Japs had got a bearing on them and blitzed the compound with divebombers and mortars.

'We were unlucky enough to have a shell explode on a gun killing an officer and injuring a number of the gunners. We received the orders to leave the guns and take cover in slit trenches.'[11]

Bluey stayed the night in a trench with an Indian officer who spent all his time moaning about his disorganised troops and the fact that he didn't even have a batman. Even the British refused to salute him, he complained, though he didn't expect the Australians to do so 'as they didn't appear to salute their own officers'.[12]

Such were the differing attitudes between the Allied fighting forces that day: the Indians were worried about being addressed with due etiquette; the British didn't seem to want to shoot in case the enemy returned fire and the Australians didn't give a damn about saluting as long as they could get on with the job.

But what was the point? When Bluey Kennedy heard rumours about a possible surrender and an officer ordered him to take as many gunners as possible under cover, he sensed the end was near.

As Lionel Wigmore wrote in his official history of the Malaya campaign: 'On Friday, February 13, whatever hope remained that Singapore might be saved was on its death bed.'[13]

A line of troops was spread along an arc between the enemy and Singapore town, but it was not tightly held or appropriately fortified. Most of the civilians who were sheltering behind the line were aware of their vulnerability. This was an area thick with shops and offices, schools and churches, houses and gardens. More importantly there were about a million refugees, many of them from the mainland.

As Wigmore noted: 'Most of the civilians, especially the Asians, were pitifully exposed to the effects of bombardment and without prospect of evacuation. In this densely congested area where there was now little room for discrimination by the enemy between what was or was not a legitimate military target, bombs and shells were blasting away the last essentials of resistance.'[14]

The 2/30th remained north of the defensive arc, though without its commanding officer, Black Jack Galleghan, who was in hospital receiving treatment for loss of hearing.

Slowly the men made their way along Thomson Road, which was like a parking lot. Those cars and transport vehicles which had the petrol headed towards Singapore town. The rest were simply abandoned. Occasionally there were cheers and bursts of laughter as the men recognised their mates in supporting units or passed through the long columns of British and Indian troops who were heading in the same direction.

It was roughly about this point they came across a sight to gladden the heart of any Australian who had been missing the creature comforts of home. On their way to the perimeter zone, the troops discovered the barracks store. And it was full!

'Without delay the troops began to help themselves to much needed stocks of clothing and, ignoring plain army rations, selected some choice lines of luxury foods which they had not seen for many a long day. There was also a fine collection of wines and spirits, together with a good supply of beer, which under the circumstances was not enjoyed to the full . . . It is unusual for Australian soldiers to deliberately pass up the opportunity of enjoying a glass of beer, particularly Australian beer. But there it was, in a very large barrel, by one of the barrack roads, and a stray soldier was imploring passers-by to come and drink with him. They passed him by, pre-occupied and only vaguely interested.'[15]

Why the sobriety? Perhaps the enormity of what was happening was only just beginning to sink in. Capitulation could not be far away. It is tempting to speculate that the men recognised their plight and made provision for the unknown.

Major-General Gordon Bennett was already considering his options and they did not include incarceration. However, he was keen to play the game and was concerned to ensure the immediate safety of his men inside the Australian perimeter, which was fully manned on all fronts in case the Japanese should penetrate it and attempt to attack the Australians on either flank or from the rear.

As a practical measure the Tanglin swimming pool had been filled with water, and fresh supplies of food had also been put in storage so the men of 8th Division would not go thirsty or hungry. It was sufficient to keep them going for some days at least.[16]

Jack Boardman was holed up in the Portuguese consul's residence, which had been providing a temporary head-quarters for the 22nd Infantry Brigade.

'The Japs had control of the skies and they used to come over and drop a few bombs but they didn't worry us too much.'[17]

From his suburban outpost he never gave up hope that the Allies would prevail. 'We felt that even though everything was against us the thing was to fight to the finish. That's what Churchill told us to do.'[18]

It was not a message that everybody was prepared to heed.

Even those in charge could see the writing on the wall as they gathered at Fort Canning for a further briefing on the latest situation. Governor Shenton and most of the military leaders were there, the likes of 'Piggy' Heath, Major-General 'Billy' Key, who was in charge of the 11th Indian Division, Bennett and of course Percival himself. Each spent a few minutes offering his considered opinion on the likelihood of defeat and they all concurred that the position was hopeless.

The decision was made to send a message to Wavell, who was nursing a badly injured back after falling down some steps while trying to board his Sunderland flying boat on the way out of Singapore. Their despatch was short and to the point, urging him to agree to surrender. Wavell was having none of it. Even at this, the eleventh hour, his response was clear and unequivocal: 'Continue to inflict the maximum damage on the enemy for as long as possible.'[19]

At least Wavell was taking Churchill's instructions seriously, but then he was safely out of the way.

Others were also attempting to beat a hasty retreat, some officially, but many were mere opportunists who were anxious to save their own skin.

Word got out that Rear-Admiral Ernest Spooner had

decided to sail all the remaining vessels and seagoing craft left in Singapore to Java. With estimated space for up to 3000 people, this would be the last chance to leave the island for civilians and those members of the military not deemed essential for defence. A hundred spaces were allotted to the Australian military, and Bennett decided that 'only those whose capabilities would help the ultimate war effort should be evacuated and that the proportion of officers should be one officer to fifteen other ranks'.[20]

Among those hoping to get away was Australia's official government representative to Singapore, Vivian Bowden, who cabled the Department of External Affairs to ask whether he and his commercial secretaries might also take the opportunity to leave.[21]

The reply he received from the War Cabinet expressed its deep appreciation for his services, but told him to stay: 'Otherwise we shall be deprived of independent information and effect on morale would be bad.'

Oh, and by the way, 'very best wishes' read the closing message.

The next day, realising its Singapore rep was in mortal peril, the Cabinet cabled to say if the worst came to the worst he should 'insist on receiving full diplomatic immunities, privileges and courtesies'.[22]

Were the bureaucrats at home out of their minds? As if the Japanese would take any notice of diplomatic niceties offered by 'our man in Singapore'. In the end it was thanks to Percival that Bowden and his secretary got away. The pair joined a party of senior officers and civil servants on a small launch called the *Osprey*, which had a total seating capacity of ten.

Before his departure Bowden drafted his final message to Australia. 'Our work completed,' it read. Ever hopeful, Bowden added: 'We will telegraph from another place at present unknown.'

Such was the state of telecommunications at this stage that the message was transmitted via a small handset operated at a point where the cable entered the water. Amazingly it worked and was duly delivered to the War Cabinet.

Bowden and his colleagues were due to set sail on the *Osprey* at 6.30 pm on 14 February but by the time they reached the vessel it was apparent that others had the same idea. A large group, including Australian soldiers, some armed with Tommy guns and hand grenades, threatened to open fire on the launch unless they were taken aboard.

As the evening progressed the mood became increasingly tense. By 11.30 pm there were 38 on board the *Osprey* as it moved away from the quayside. Among them was Lieutenant-Colonel John Dalley of Dalforce and some of his men.

Suddenly the sound of rifle fire echoed through the tropical night. In a last-ditch attempt to secure their escape some of those left behind had taken pot shots at the launch. Thankfully no one was hit and the vessel slowly made its way out to sea, where the passengers were transferred to a larger vessel named the *Mary Rose*.[23] But misfortune struck when the bigger ship was soon captured by the Japanese in the notorious Banka Strait, where many other Allied craft would be attacked.

Wrongly believing that his diplomatic status would offer him protection, Bowden demanded an interview with a senior officer, only to be executed on the spot.[24]

Unidentified 8th Division officers and nurses during a lifeboat drill on board the *Queen Mary* en route from Australia to Malaya, February 1941 (AWM 005506)

The governor of Singapore, Sir Shenton Thomas (*left*), and Lady Thomas (*centre*) were among a group of officers who greeted some 5750 Australians of the 8th Division, including the 22nd Brigade, on their arrival (AWM 005908)

Major-General Gordon Bennett (*right*) with Lieutenant-General Arthur Percival, Malaya 1941 (AWM 134877)

Bennett (*second from right*) at a cricket match with his aide-de-camp, Gordon Walker (JOAN BENNETT)

Bennett takes parade, 1941 (JOAN BENNETT)

Saluting parade (JOAN BENNETT)

The 8th Division's band (JOAN BENNETT)

Bennett with Lieutenant–General Sir Lewis 'Piggy' Heath (*far right*), 1941
(JOAN BENNETT)

8th Division parade with Bennett, March 1941 (JOAN BENNETT)

Australian soldiers of the 8th Division and the Sultan of Johore at Istanc
Bezar, the Sultan's palace. Bennett and his men were entertained by the
Sultan at his palace and later at his club, the Royal International Club,
1941 (AWM PO3358.001)

Bennett with the Sultan of Selangor in Malaya on Anzac Day, 1941 (AWM 007094)

Noel Harrison with his machine gun, 1941 (NOEL HARRISON)

Jack Boardman (in pith helmet) and Alan Gaudry (with his hand on his hip) in a photo Jack sent home (ROZ HOGAN AND JACK BOARDMAN'S FAMILY)

Field Marshal Archibald Wavell (PICTORIAL PRESS LTD / ALAMY STOCK PHOTO)

Lieutenant Colonel Frederick G. 'Black Jack' Galleghan, Commanding Officer of the 2/30th Battalion (*right*), examining a map with an intelligence sergeant outside the battalion command post in Gemas, Malaya, 1942
(AWM 011304/04)

Lieutenant-General Tomoyuki Yamashita, Commander-in-Chief of the
25th Japanese Army, which successfully carried out the Malayan campaign
(AWM 127911)

A Japanese patrol coming down through Malaya on bicycles, January 1942

General Percival (*far right*) and his surrender party, walking to the Ford Motor Company to meet with Japanese and British officers, February 1942

British troops surrender to the Japanese in the city area, after the unconditional surrender of all British forces following the successful invasion of Malaya and Singapore
(AWM 127902)

Bennett (*centre*) with General Sir Thomas Blamey (*saluting*) in Harvey, Western Australia to inspect 3 Australia Corps Training School, September 1943 (AWM052322)

POWs released from Changi prison camp were evacuated from Singapore by the Australian hospital ship *Manunda*, the first Australian ship to arrive at Singapore after the surrender of the Japanese. Here, the ex-POWs, members of 8th Division, line up to receive their embarkation cards, September 1945 (AWM 116039)

POWs arriving home, October 1945, showing their gratitude to Bennett
(AWM 122157)

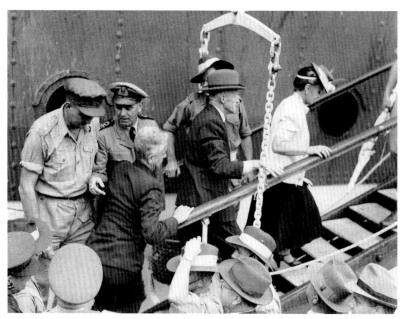

Bennett and his wife, Bess, board the *Manunda* at Woolloomooloo,
Sydney, October 1945 (AWM 122158)

A portrait of Major-General Bennett commissioned by MMI Insurance, of which he became chairman after the war, 1962. (AWM PO1461.002)

Arthur 'Bluey' Kennedy, September 2016, aged 99

Bart Richardson, October 2016, aged 98

Jack Boardman, August 2016, aged 96

Noel Harrison, September 2016, aged 98

Ron Ferguson (*left*), retiring secretary of the 8th Division Association, proudly carries the new banner during the Anzac Day march in Sydney in 2017

The Kranji Line
Memorial in what is
now the suburb of
Jurong West, Singapore
(MARK LAUDI)

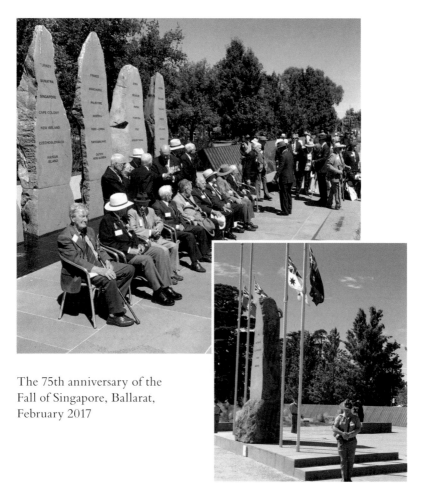

The 75th anniversary of the
Fall of Singapore, Ballarat,
February 2017

A good proportion of those on Bennett's list of one hundred failed to make it in time to board Rear-Admiral Spooner's escape flotilla. Given Bowden's fate, their failed departure may have been fortuitous.

Not that conditions on dry land were any better. Enemy gunshots were reported well behind British lines in the Botanic Gardens and Bennett ordered everyone who could be found to fill gaps in the AIF perimeter.

A lot of troops were still roaming the island, fearful of the future and dejected by their plight. Lee Kuan Yew, who was to become Singapore's first prime minister, was then a lowly medical auxillary. Cycling through the chaos one morning, he pedalled past a line of Australian soldiers who stood disconsolately by their vehicles. Lee paused for a moment to ask where the front was.

'It's over – here, take this,' one of the men replied before offering his rifle.[25]

Bennett suspected that many of the so-called battle stragglers were Indians, though he later amended this view, suggesting that because the British units had been given digger-style, slouch hats to wear, the Poms might have been mistaken for Australians, only adding to the confusion over who was where.

Whatever the true number of stragglers – or deserters as some were later described – there was no doubt they represented a significant problem. Bennett himself acknowledged that the situation had got out of hand. He maintained, however, that so far as the AIF was concerned the percentage of stragglers was small, consisting mainly of untrained reinforcements from the General Base Depot. This group included the 'bad hats', as he called them, 'the black sheep of the family'.[26] All units carried a small proportion of men who were constantly in trouble, drunk or absent without leave. Some were even drawn from the criminal class in civilian life, men who joined the military to avoid the police or a prison sentence.

Bennett viewed them as soldiers of moral weakness who invariably avoided the danger zone when fighting broke out. These 'problem cases' always caused trouble for unit commanders, he said.[27]

For the head of the 8th Division there were more pressing matters to deal with, including meetings with senior officers, as well as humanitarian concerns. Following an afternoon conference at Fort Canning, Bennett returned to his own headquarters in a sombre mood.

For a man who was used to the stench of battle and the death and bloodshed that accompanied it, Bennett could be surprisingly emotional at the sight of human suffering. On the way to the meeting he had realised how deserted the streets were. Everywhere was devastated. Churned up rubble was lying in great clods all around. Phone wires and power cables were strewn across the street in a tangled mess. The smell of cordite hung in the air and bombs continued to fall. On investigating the damage from a shell which had penetrated an air-raid shelter, he found a group of Australian soldiers and other nationalities shovelling away debris in the search for survivors. A Chinese man whose family was buried beneath the fallen masonry was desperately clawing away with the others when the top of the shelter was uncovered.

'Beneath lay a crushed mass of old men, women – young and old – and young children, some still living, others dead,' Bennett recalled.

'The little oriental never stopped his work and his sallow face showed signs of deepest anguish. His wife and four children were there. One by one he unearthed them all – all dead, but for one daughter. I last saw him holding his only surviving child, aged about ten, by the hand, watching others move away his family with the rest of the unfortunates who perished there. This was going on hour after hour, day after day; and the same stolidity and steadfastness was evident among the civilians in every quarter of the town.'[28]

Bennett's diary entry for 13 February suggested more considered prose, penned at a later date, than the notes he made at the time, but it also offered a rare insight into the softer side of a man who was often regarded as a martinet.

As dawn broke on 14 February the Allies' more immediate concern was for the living than the dead. While the AIF appeared to have enough food and water for a few more days, the civilian population faced a severe shortage of both. The water situation was particularly grave, with limited supplies only guaranteed for the next 24 hours. General Percival alerted Wavell, supreme commander for the region, to the deteriorating situation, and Wavell replied: 'In all places where sufficiency of water exists for troops they must go on fighting.'[29]

There were now roughly 4500 men within Bennett's newly established AIF perimeter, many of them untrained reinforcements. More pertinently some 3000 sick and wounded were in hospital.

Once again the 8th Division commander cabled Australia to advise the prime minister of the worsening crisis, advising him of the need to surrender to avoid unnecessary loss of life. In the absence of any sign from overseas that capitulation might be preferable, the fighting continued. The Japanese kept up their assault on the right and left flanks of the Australians, leaving many dead and injured.

Bennett was worried that the Japanese might have already infiltrated the area between the Australians and the troops on his right flank.[30] There appeared a very real possibility that the enemy might bomb, shoot and bayonet their way into the centre of town, risking carnage among the civilian population.

Only capitulation could stem the flow of further casualties, a point that General Tomoyuki Yamashita, Commander of Japanese forces in Malaya, had already spoken of in a message addressed to the British Army's high command. In a series of notes dropped in boxes from Japanese aircraft he wrote:

> My sincere respect is due to your army which, true to the traditional spirit of Great Britain, is bravely defending Singapore, which now stands isolated and unaided..
>
> Many fierce and gallant fights have been fought by your gallant men and officers, to the honour of British warrior-ship. But the developments of the general war situation has already sealed the fate of Singapore, and the continuation of futile resistance would only serve to inflict direct harm and injuries to thousands of non-combatants living in the city, throwing them into further miseries and horrors of war, but also would not add anything to the honour of your army . . . Give up this meaningless and desperate resistance and promptly order the entire front to cease hostilities.[31]

A group of Australian officers were now actively discussing the possibility of escape, among them Major Charles Moses, who was at this stage a liaison officer with Bennett's staff, and Lieutenant Gordon Walker, Bennett's aide-de-camp.

Moses spelled out his position in a diary note in which he spoke of the inevitability of capitulation. He recalled telling Walker that he, for one, was not prepared to be taken prisoner and intended to make a break for it when the time came.

Walker replied, 'Wouldn't it be marvellous if we could arrange to get the general away?'

The two men talked about arranging a boat and Walker said he would approach Bennett about the idea.

'A little later he said that the general was in favour of making an attempt if he found himself free to do so.'[32]

Although Bennett appeared to be keeping his cards close to his chest, he had effectively given a nod and a wink to the escape plan proposed by Walker and Moses. However, events were changing so rapidly that shortly afterwards Moses was promoted to brigade major of the 22nd Australian Brigade, effectively excluding him from the escape party. On hearing the news Walker realised he would need further volunteers and approached three more officers about the plan.

To add to the confusion Moses discovered that Lieutenant-Colonel Albert Varley had already been appointed the new brigade major. When Moses returned to the AIF HQ he found that the escape party had increased to six, including Brisbane-born Captain Harry Jessup, who was fluent in Dutch and Malay; Captain Adrian Curlewis, who as president of Surf Lifesaving Australia was a strong swimmer; and Lieutenant Vernon Baynes of the 2/30th, who was an experienced yachtsman. Everyone had the right credentials, but the larger the party the higher the chance of being spotted. Undeterred, the group set about acquiring a boat and obtaining equipment from Tanglin Barracks for the voyage.

Events were moving at a pace when they decided to divide into two parties: Moses, Walker and the general on one boat; and the rest on another.

Despite uncertainty about Bennett's plans, Moses reckoned the old man would not want to be left behind and decided to pack a large box of cigars for the commander. Then came confirmation of the 8th Division commander's intentions – he was determined to 'chance his luck', Walker reported. Although in anticipation of a last-minute conference at Fort Canning, Bennett realised it would not be easy to break out, especially if the Japanese were in Singapore town behind enemy lines.

There was also doubt about the other party and whether Captain Curlewis was committed to the escape attempt, even though they had apparently found a boat. Amid the growing pandemonium there was one piece of good news. Major Moses had managed to find a Chinese guide to help them infiltrate Japanese lines and make their way through the swamp to open water, where they might find means to sail away.

On the night of 14 February Moses wrote, optimistically: 'Feeling sure tomorrow will see the end of it and hoping that the end will give us a chance to make our getaway.'[33]

At this late stage Percival's military options were few. He could either launch a counterattack in a bid to regain control of the reservoirs and military food depots or surrender. He sought advice from area commanders, who agreed that any kind of counterassault was doomed to failure. Percival was undecided about the next step, but then came another message from Wavell that strengthened his resolve.

'So long as you are in a position to inflict heavy losses to enemy and your troops are physically capable of doing so, you must fight on,' he made clear. 'Time gained and damage to enemy of vital importance at this crisis.'

However, a follow-up message from Wavell gave Percival the validation to make the final decision himself:

When you are fully satisfied that this is no longer possible I give you discretion to cease resistance. Before doing so all arms, equipment, and transport of value to the enemy must of course be rendered useless. Also just before final cessation of fighting, opportunity should be given to any determined bodies of men or individuals to try and effect escape by any means possible. They must be armed. Inform me of intentions. Whatever happens I thank you and all troops for gallant efforts of last few days.[34]

This was the signal Percival had been waiting for. Of course the likes of Bennett did not need Wavell to tell them how to act. The 8th Division's commander and his trusted fellow officers had already orchestrated their escape.

Chapter 12

'I COULD NOT FALL INTO JAPANESE HANDS'

As the first light of day broke over Singapore on 15 February 1942, Henry Gordon Bennett was filled with despair. The dying city was writhing in agony. The 8th Division was falling back as the enemy's advance continued unchecked. Japanese troops were opposite the Australian front and the Allies realised there was nowhere else to go.

Bennett had one more meeting to attend: the last conference of senior Allied officers before the final curtain fell. It was in the Battlebox at Fort Canning, where the penultimate scene in this disastrous and humiliating struggle would be played out.

Eschewing his staff limo for fear of being spotted from the air, Bennett and his aide-de-camp climbed into a truck and headed for the heavily guarded underground nerve centre. After convincing the guards that he really was the head of 8th Division, Bennett was allowed to enter.

The imposing, solid-iron doors, installed in the event of

a gas attack, opened to reveal a set of ten steps down and another six up. Ahead was a long hallway with a series of doors at regular intervals. Each room was locked securely. The occupants usually remained inside for many hours, communicating with other staff inside the honeycomb of passages and adjoining chambers only by telephone. Wall signs prohibited staff from smoking, eating and talking loudly in order to prevent operations being disrupted.[1]

In reality the bunker was almost cut off from the outside world. The Fort Canning staff were virtually incommunicado. Because the operations room did not have an accurate update of developments outside, the lack of information was deafening.

As Romen Bose, whose meticulous research provides a graphic picture of life inside the building, would later write: 'Pleas for help and reinforcements as well as blood-curdling screams were heard over the radio as the hapless residents of the bunker tried in vain to communicate with units being destroyed by enemy shelling and attacks.'[2]

Away from the radio room and shut off from the electronic chatter in the background, was the anti-aircraft defence Room, where the conference of senior commanders was about to get underway. Today it was as quiet as a chapel of rest. Only the gentle murmur of the ventilation system broke the silence.

Bennett and Percival sat down with formation commanders and senior staffs of Malaya Command. A.H. Dickinson, the chief of police, was there, as well as Brigadier Ivan Simson, the army's chief engineer and military liaison officer, who had done so much to alleviate civilian suffering. Everyone knew the end was near and each offered tales of death and disaster to reinforce his point. Dickinson told how some of his men had been bombed by a group of inmates released from jail. Simson seemed 'very disturbed' by the rate at which civilisation seemed to be falling apart.

'No wonder,' noted Bennett. 'The city is rapidly becoming a shambles, buildings have collapsed on the occupants, bomb holes in the road are unrepaired and the destructive aerial bombing is continuing unmolested.'[3]

As they sat around the table that morning each officer urged a termination of hostilities. All, that is, except Bennett, who suddenly and quite unexpectedly suggested: 'How about a combined attack to recapture Bukit Timah?'

The interjection was met with a stunned silence. What was Bennett going on about? Had he momentarily lost his mind or was he anxious to show he was not as defeatist as the rest of them?

Major Cyril Wild, who was on 'Piggy' Heath's staff, favoured the latter interpretation. 'I formed the impression at the time that it was made not as a serious contribution but as something to quote afterwards.'[4]

The conversation resumed with a dire assessment of conditions on the ground. The civilian population was almost totally out of food and water, it was impossible to treat the huge number of casualties and there was no one left to rescue those who lay trapped and injured in the countless wrecked buildings. The situation in Singapore was verging on the apocalyptic. To continue the fight would be pointless, they argued, prompting Percival, who now had the final say, to produce General Yamashita's latest missive.

By now Bennett was back on message. 'Silently and sadly we decided to surrender,' he later wrote.[5]

With the unanimous agreement of those in the room, Percival decided to seek a cessation of hostilities in the middle of the afternoon and to invite a Japanese deputation to visit the city to negotiate the terms of capitulation. With this in mind it was further agreed that representatives of the military and civilian authorities should visit the enemy lines as soon as possible to discuss the proposed ceasefire.[6]

Brigadier T.K. Newbigging, the Colonial Secretary Hugh Fraser and Major Wild, who was fluent in Japanese, drew the short straw and were sent on their way. They would ask for hostilities to end at precisely 3.30 pm and that the surrender should be unconditional, allowing some Allied troops to remain under arms in the city to preserve order.[7]

As the small delegation drove up Bukit Timah Road they met an Allied roadblock that marked the frontline. Uncertain of who they were or where they were going, a British officer pushed a revolver into Newbigging's chest but quickly withdrew the gun when the situation was explained to him. The three men got out of the car, taking a white flag and a Union Jack with them, then proceeded to walk several hundred yards into enemy territory.[8]

After a Japanese patrol removed their pistols they were escorted to a small villa, where they delivered Percival's letter seeking a cessation of hostilities. Initially the senior Japanese officer, Colonel Ichiji Sugita, was taken aback by the arrival of the British representatives. Many years later he revealed in the British television series *The World At War* that the Japanese had almost run out of ammunition and were seriously considering pulling back their troops to the mainland.[9]

The Japanese were also unimpressed by the Allies' demand to see Yamashita himself and subsequently handed over their own typewritten document, which requested Percival's attendance at Bukit Timah at a time to be agreed to meet Lieutenant-General Yamashita personally.

There were also a number of demands in an accompanying appendix which required the Allied forces to lay down their arms and stay in their positions. Major Wild pointed this out to Newbigging, drawing his attention to the fact there was no reciprocal undertaking from the Japanese that they would also agree to a ceasefire.[10] Colonel Sugita, who was charged with communicating the Japanese terms, was not happy, reminding Wild that he was not the negotiator.

The meeting appeared to be deadlocked so Newbigging decided to leave the matter and return to Fort Canning. As the delegation moved to return to British lines, Colonel Sugita gave them a large Japanese flag, with the instructions to hang it from the top of the Cathay Building as a signal that Percival was prepared to accept the conditions.

At precisely 3.02 pm the GOC Malaya sent a message to Wavell confirming that the fighting was about to end.

'Owing to losses from enemy action, water, petrol, food and communication practically finished. Unable therefore to continue the fight any longer. All ranks have done their best and grateful for your help.'[11]

With Percival acknowledging that it was all but over, Wild was sent to the Cathay Building to display the Japanese flag. The time was 3.30 pm, and with Percival having agreed to stop fighting at 4 pm, they needed to move fast. In fact even as the deadline expired the two cars carrying the official British party had only just entered Bukit Timah Road.

Once again the delegation was halted at the frontline and ordered to walk through enemy territory. Percival's perambulation was to provide the key image of Britain's defeat. The white flag carried by a fellow officer as the party made their way down Bukit Timah Road was a propaganda masterstroke. The black and white photograph which went around the world symbolised the final nail in the Allies' coffin.

The meeting with Yamashita, the Japanese commander, eventually got underway at 5.15 pm in the staff canteen of the Ford Motor Company's assembly plant in Bukit Timah village. The building had been seized by the Japanese the day before for use as their advance headquarters.

There was only one copy of the surrender terms, which Percival was allowed to read but not to keep. The ceasefire would begin at 8.30 pm local time and all weapons, military equipment, ships, aircraft and secret documents were to be handed over to the Japanese intact. The Japanese made only one concession to the Allies, allowing them to keep a force of 1000 armed men in the city to prevent looting and other trouble breaking out during the temporary withdrawal of armed forces.

All that remained was for Percival to sign the surrender document and for the two generals to shake hands. Once again the cameras were on hand to milk the event for its propaganda potential, though the less-than-august surroundings of the works canteen may have detracted from the gravity of the occasion.

Thus in little more than seventy days the entire might of the British, Australian, Indian and Malay forces had been brought to their knees.

Clearly in need of a tipple to drown his sorrows, Percival headed for the Singapore Club to share a whisky and soda with Shenton Thomas, who was politely told he was no longer governor. A few hours later at 9 pm, hundreds of civilians and many wounded servicemen attended evening service at St Andrew's Cathedral in the centre of town. The first hymn to be sung was 'O God, our help in ages past'.

Bennett was not among them. He had more on his mind than asking for heavenly support, preferring the company of his own men to spiritual sustenance. Curiously, although he was aware of the official surrender, he had not been informed of an earlier message from Wavell expressing the view that opportunities should be given for escape.[13]

———•———

Of course the commander of the 8th Division did not need any encouragement in that direction, given his plans to join Moses and Walker on the first available boat out of Singapore.

Bennett discussed the question of escape with his senior commanders but issued an order to all units to remain at their posts and concentrate at 8.30 am the following day. The thinking behind this strategy was that any large-scale escape attempt could result in confusion and slaughter, so it was agreed that the Australians should be kept together and sentries posted.[14]

Perhaps Bennett's conscience was pricked, but for whatever reason he decided to address the welfare of his men. After talking to his lieutenant-colonels, he made arrangements for all his soldiers to be given fresh clothing, new boots and two days' rations. He also demanded that a complete nominal roll of every man be compiled and handed over to the enemy with instructions for it to be communicated to

Australia as soon as possible to ease the concerns of worried families back home.

Among the lower ranks Bennett met that night was Signalman John Chippendale, who had been talking to his company commander, Major Jacobs, when the commander called in.

'He said that the war was over, we were all prisoners of war and that he was trying to escape and go back to Australia to tell them how the Japs fought,' he recalled. 'He shook my hand and said he would see me back in Australia after the war.'[15]

Many years later they did meet up and Bennett remembered the bloke who was there the night he escaped.

The caring gestures shown by Bennett during his last few hours on Singapore helped to reinforce the view that he had his troops' best interests at heart. Whether this was done to enhance his image once his escape became known is impossible to say, but for whatever reason he was apparently keen to be seen to be doing the right thing.

Interestingly Bennett's written account of that final day in Singapore differs slightly, according to which version you read. There is his book, *Why Singapore Fell*, which was published in 1944. There is an arguably more embellished record given to his official biographer, Frank Legg, whose book was published in 1965. And there is the typewritten draft memoir produced by Bennett, which is held by the Mitchell Library in Sydney. Disappointingly this last document is not dated so it is impossible to say how soon after his escape it was written.

In this version, with its handwritten corrections and amendments, he writes more candidly about what he saw and discussed that day. He talks about passing through the unit lines, where he found the men still full of fight. When he mentioned the word surrender they took it badly.

'Some of these tall, manly men wept at the idea. It was a sad parting.'[16]

Later, in his draft memoir, Bennett revealed that he passed the word around that escape was permitted only after and not before the cessation of hostilities.

'Numbers of officers and men then organised them-selves into groups and were seen putting together packs containing food and water, clothing and equipment suitable for escape.'[17]

These comments conflict with the official view put forward in Lionel Wigmore's *The Japanese Thrust*, namely that large-scale escape was not to be permitted. Or was Bennett's unofficial approval merely directed at the officer class? Crucially, was he excusing his own actions in advance?

His initial version of events also makes no mention of the fact he was actively considering escape some days before capitulation. Instead he maintains that he called Charles Moses and Gordon Walker and told them it was his decision to escape under the cover of darkness 'after the surrender had been completed'. Significantly he crosses out the phrase 'all arrangements for' as in 'after all arrangements for the surrender had been completed', suggesting that he did not want to admit he had considered escaping before the surrender time itself.[18] This might be seen as a nit-picking observation, but given the subsequent legal debate, the inclusion of those three words could have had a bearing on his case.

In all three versions Bennett describes how he received

confirmation of the ceasefire time, which would be 8.30 pm, and how he then gave detailed instructions allocating assembly positions where arms could be dumped. At 8 pm, Bennett recorded, he received a message from one of his units that the enemy opposite the front was singing, cheering and shouting excitedly. What should they do if the enemy ran amok? The unit was told that as the ceasefire did not begin until 8.30 pm they could take severe action to check any Japanese advance.[19]

About this time Moses arrived on the scene to report that he was negotiating with a Chinese for a boat so that they could either make directly for Sumatra or move around the island and sail up the Malayan coast to Malacca.

'Meanwhile, I moved among my senior staff, telling them of my intentions to escape, so that I could get back to Australia and tell the detailed story, passing on lessons we had learned during the last few weeks and also making requests to help in the ultimate relief of our grand army of brave men,' he wrote. 'They realised the risk and the difficulties ahead of the venture.'[20]

In his own account of the escape in *Why Singapore Fell*, Bennett recalled he told Moses that he would be ready some time after 10.30 pm and that if the Japanese approached before he had finished his work he would hide himself so that he would not be captured. Was mention of the time designed to emphasise that he left well after the signing of the surrender document?

The timing of his escape is also recorded in Frank Legg's official biography, in which Bennett recalls how Moses and Walker returned with their Chinese guide to lead them to their boat.

'It was well after 10 p.m. that I said a sad farewell to all my friends, most of whom I had known well in civil life,' he stated.[21]

In a more reflective mood, Bennett would mull over in his wartime memoir how the hopes and optimistic ambitions of his men had been shattered.

'Our individual efforts had been successful. Yet for some unknown reason they had lost the fight. It was not unlike the case of a man in a race who has thought he was winning, leading all the way, but who finds the judge's decision against him.'

Though this extract from his diary is dated 15 February 1942, it is obvious from his contemplative style that it was written some time later:

> Their war was over. They were to become prisoners of the despised Japanese. They were to submit to the ignominious position of spending the rest of the war behind barbed wire – at the mercy of the Japanese who had a very bad reputation for the way in which they treated their prisoners.
>
> Their wives and children, their parents, their friends, their homes in Australia were suddenly cut off. None knew when they would see them again. Proud men accept such servility with bad grace.[22]

Bennett also went into detail about his discussions with senior officers regarding the possibility of escape, urging them to go ahead and make a run for it. He shared his own views and explained the best ways of doing it.

All agreed that it would be a hazardous journey, with the likelihood of heavy casualties, although a number had banded together into escape groups and equipped themselves accordingly.[23]

'I personally had made this decision some time previously, having decided that I would not fall into Japanese hands,' he stated plainly. 'My decision was fortified by the resolve that I must at all costs return to Australia to tell our people the story of our conflict with the Japanese, to warn them of the danger to Australia, and to advise them of the best means of defeating the Japanese tactics.'[24]

The fact that others had already left the island and got back to or were heading to Australia might not sit comfortably in the narrative of a leader who believed only he could provide the necessary insight. Come what may Bennett was eager to put his own spin on his escape.

———·•·———

Before his departure Bennett handed over the 8th Division to Brigadier Cecil Callaghan, his next senior officer. The two men had not always been on the best of terms and Callaghan was battling malaria when his commander called by to inform him of his intentions. Their farewell was short but emotional, according to Bennett, who asked his second-in-command to tell the Japanese he had left some days earlier if they enquired of his whereabouts. Callaghan would be formally appointed commander of the AIF in Malaya the following day, when Bennett's departure became known to Percival. After the war he claimed that he had not immediately informed Percival of Bennett's departure because he 'felt ashamed'.

Bennett also said goodbye to Jim Thyer, Kent Hughes, Lieutenant-Colonel (later to become Brigadier) Duncan Maxwell, and Colonel Frances Derham.

On returning to his room, Bennett packed for a jungle trek, assuming that he would have to tramp a few hundred miles north to Malacca or Port Dickson. Outside, Major Moses waited with Bennett's car, ready to make a swift getaway. Also there was Gordon Walker and the Chinese guide who was to lead them to a boat, or so they hoped. Bennett was now officially an escapee – or as many would later describe him as a deserter.

Later he described their dash for freedom to Frank Legg:

> Passing through the deserted streets, crashing in the darkness through shell holes, we made for the coast near Kallang Airport. On the way we were bailed up at the point of the bayonet by some men of the Gordon Highlanders, whom we told that the war was over. They quickly ran off to join their unit.
>
> Arriving at our destination we found the boat owner's residence destroyed by fire. The whole of the Chinese quarter in the vicinity had been destroyed. It consisted of a terrace of shops, each room upstairs accommodating a Chinese family.[25]

After much difficulty they reached the waterfront only to learn that several Japanese officers were nearby. More alarmingly they also discovered that the promised boat was nowhere to be found.

Bennett thanked the Chinaman for his efforts and gave him the keys to his car. He carefully removed the AIF registration plate and dropped it into the water.

What next, they pondered? Beyond the jetty there were several sampans tied up across the water. Gordon Walker instinctively knew it was their only chance to escape. Within seconds he had stripped off and dived in, swimming at least 200 yards (180 m) out to sea to secure one of the small craft. As it happened most of them were totally unsuitable for a lengthy voyage, given they could only be manipulated by one oar and a short paddle.

Then a breakthrough. Walker found a sampan that he could just about handle. He rowed it ashore with considerable difficulty against the lapping waves of a receding tide. The trio tossed in their packs, scrambled aboard and made their way out into the dark yonder, only to be surprised by the sound of shouting from the shore.

Standing on the jetty were eight men who had been serving in the Malayan Volunteers. They were all planters and could speak good English. Bennett couldn't turn his back on them so rowed around and picked them up.

There were now 11 people aboard the small sampan, which was so overcrowded there was no room to work the oars. 'Our progress was slow,' Bennett told Legg.

> After half an hour of this, the situation looked desperate. We realised that it would be impossible to make sufficient way to clear Singapore before daylight, for it was then about midnight. I visualised the prospect of returning to shore and attempting to be well away from the danger area before daybreak. Then one of the party said that he had heard someone say that day, that it would be possible to secure a tongkan [a large Chinese barge fitted with sails] to go to Sumatra.
>
> For some time we were bumping into other boats in the darkness; all tempers were frayed and there was much swearing and grumbling.[26]

Then, in what must have seemed like a mirage at the time, a light wooden boat floated towards them in the darkness. If any group of men deserved a miracle that night, there were no better candidates than Bennett and his shipmates. Could this really be happening? Yes. Amazingly they had found the only seaworthy tongkan remaining in Singapore Harbour.

'We scrambled aboard and kicked away the useless sampan with disgust to find the Chinese owner, who was smoking opium, and his crew of two, one Chinese and one Malay,' said Bennett.

Also on board were three exhausted British soldiers who had swum two miles (3.2 km) to reach it. Later they would be joined by four more.

One of the planters who could speak Chinese was elected to negotiate with the skipper to take them to Sumatra. But there was a problem. The captain did not want to go. Then we'll buy the boat from you, the planter suggested. But the skipper was adamant and refused to leave Singapore waters. If this was a serious negotiating ploy it was evidently working.

First they tried to haggle, lifting the price by small increments, and when that failed they threatened him.[27]

According to Bennett's personal recollection, what the captain wanted was more opium, and he could only acquire it in Singapore.

While negotiations continued, the Australians discovered a large cache of ammunition stored in metal boxes in the hold, which, Bennett observed later, were 'as level as a newly ploughed field and as hard as flint. But it was a safe refuge and – well, we were not prisoners of the Japanese.'[28]

In the end, rather than let the foreigners take the tongkan themselves, the skipper agreed to take them to Sumatra for an unspecified sum of money. Moses gave him $150 Straits dollars on account and promised him a further sum when they reached their destination.[29]

Negotiations over, the captain raised his anchor and pulled up his sail.

'We felt that our escape was almost complete,' said Bennett. 'A fair wind took us on our course to the southwest, passing close to an island which we knew was occupied by the Japs. It was 1 am, February 16. Singapore gradually faded into the distance, the only lights coming from several burning oil tanks. Tired out, we made ourselves as comfortable as we could under the awning that spanned the hold, lying awkwardly in hundreds of rounds of anti-aircraft ammunition.'[30]

The next morning a quick look at the prismatic compass revealed that they were sailing back towards Singapore. Frustrated by the owner and his poor navigational skills, the men forcibly dumped him and his crew in the hold and appointed an American gunner, who had, inexplicably, also joined their number, to sail the boat.

There were now a total of 19 people aboard the tongkan, excluding the crew. At last they were on their way to Sumatra. Or at least that was the plan until the Chinese owner shouted up from the hold that they were actually heading into a minefield.[31]

General Gordon Bennett's seaborne adventure was only just beginning.

Chapter 13

DESERTERS OR STRAGGLERS?

Gordon Bennett was not the only one to make good his escape from Singapore. During the week leading up to the surrender thousands of men and women, both civilians and servicemen, were contemplating their exit strategy. Many of them were legitimate evacuees who had been given clearance to leave the island, but a significant number were military personnel who were determined to avoid capture.

Australia's official record of what happened during the dying days of the British colony asserted that those attempting to escape fell into three categories: 'Those who had deserted or had become detached from their units during the hostilities; those officially evacuated; and those who escaped after Singapore fell.'[1]

Lionel Wigmore's account of the evacuation refers to a 'confused undertaking'. He wrote: 'For many of those chosen to leave — mostly women and children, nurses, specialists and representatives of various units to form experienced cadres elsewhere – the transport available could not be found when the parties had been organised.' The servicemen among them, according to Wigmore, were given the option of rejoining their units or making their own escape plans: 'The dividing line between desertion and escape was in some instances indefinite, particularly as a report that the ceasefire on Singapore Island was to take effect from 4.30 p.m. on February 15 had gained wide circulation and many acted on it in good faith.'[2]

It was an important distinction as it was deemed legitimate to escape after surrender but not before. Uncertainty about the timing of the ceasefire only added to the confusion and by this stage the rights and wrongs of escape were academic. In fear of their lives, a lot of men decided to make a personal judgement based on how they viewed their chances of success. Bolstered by the vocal bravado of their mates and with little to lose, they opted for escape.

'Some, as the plight of the city worsened, consciously deserted. Once the fighting had ceased, others felt free to get away if they could.'[3]

While Bennett had earlier cautioned against large-scale escape attempts, it is clear that thousands of men were determined to get away.

At a human level the behaviour of some of those who tried to escape was sickening. Drunk, violent and with little regard for their fellow man or woman, they fought their way aboard the few remaining vessels in a desperate bid to save their own skin.

'Some, generally regarded as being among the deserters, and including Australians, blackened the reputation of their fellow countrymen and prejudiced the chances of those who followed,' reported Wigmore.[4]

Much of the official postwar documentation about the fall of Singapore conveniently avoids reference to deserters, although it is evident that the issue was a major problem.

In a report written by General Wavell in June 1942, marked private and confidential and addressed to the War Office in London, he claims Australian troops were responsible for the fall of Singapore.

'Their presence in the town in disproportionately large numbers during the last days, coupled with the escape of large numbers on ships and in boats, has aroused great indignation,' he stated. Nonetheless while he did not excuse their behaviour he did add a note of understanding:

> Though it must be admitted that the behaviour of the Australian troops in the final phase was a very bad example, particularly to Indian troops, it is only fair to remember that they had been really heavily punished by shell fire on the night of the 8th/9th [of February] and were in fact the only troops in the whole campaign to come under heavy shell fire; secondly a rumour got about that they were to be evacuated, and, lastly, they were near home and that home was under imminent threat of invasion.
>
> While these are not justifications for desertion and indiscipline, they do explain that glancing over the shoulder.'[5]

Wavell's report was largely based on secondary sources, including interviews with younger British officers and some civilians whose memories, for whatever reason, may have been embellished or could have been the result of overheard gossip. In war the rumour mill is in overdrive so the 'evidence' might be viewed with caution.

Whatever the truth, the allegations levelled at the Australians were bound to cause resentment. Those who have written extensively about the poor behaviour of the military, particularly Australian personnel, were often the subject of vehement criticism. The British writer and historian Peter Elphick, whose epic account of the Malaya campaign, *Singapore: The Pregnable Fortress*, unearthed many unpalatable truths, received a torrent of abuse when he investigated the matter of deserters. He was stung by the criticism and, two decades on, is still smarting, especially as he has continued to uncover hitherto secret documents that reinforce the veracity of his claims. Indeed, given the additional information which has come his way since his book was published, he is even more convinced of the documents' accuracy.

'Over the past 20 years I have been sent a deal of additional small but relevant bits of information, of which the great majority support the main thrust of my thesis about the Singapore deserter situation,' he told me. 'In fact I have come to think that to some degree I may have underestimated the situation.'[6]

One of the few courteous letters he received came from a veteran of the 4th Anti-tank Regiment who was appalled by the misconduct he witnessed. I have chosen not to identify him because the note, which I have sighted, was written in confidence, but his words make compelling reading.

'We were all aware of the desertion of some of our troops from Singapore and that many of them were drunk and behaved disgracefully,' he said. 'We regarded them as very green and untrained men who should never have been sent there and who really had no leaders as such.'

Yet while the letter-writer did not condone their behaviour, he understood the men's plight and pitied them.

'At the time we did not distinguish much between desertion and duty to escape, feeling that if there was no clear role for a serviceman in the muddle that prevailed in Singapore, it was better for him to get off the island to some place where there was. We still showed respect for those who did escape and were returned to Changi. [But] we did not ask them the date they got off the island.'[7]

This was not an isolated observation. Hank Nelson, whose detailed study of POWs during World War II, *Prisoners of War, Australians Under Nippon*, is required reading, interviewed many Australians who were caught up in the mayhem.

'A minority of the troops decided that flight and the chance of a charge of desertion were preferable to staying on in Singapore,' he explained.

He quoted Patrick Levy, who reported that men were running into the water at Keppel Harbour 'throwing their weapons away. They were panicking, trying to commandeer boats.

'At the wharves Albert Coates found that his rising sun badge of the AIF placed him under suspicion. A group of Australians displaying the independence and aggression which in other circumstances made them great soldiers, had forced their way at gun point on to one of the last boats taking out civilians.'[8]

An even more authoritative assessment of what happened during those final days – and the weakness of some troops – came from newspaper publisher Sir Keith Murdoch, who was then the director general of the Australian Department of Information. In an article that appeared in the *Adelaide Advertiser* in August 1942, he spoke of the 'greatest surrender in British history':

> Why the island passed so quickly into Japanese hands is explicable only by researches into the intricate subjects of morale, tactics and leadership.
>
> There were fully 90,000 British troops to give battle; stores and ammunitions were ample; yet from the first the garrison had few chances, and except for some sections of officers who maintain to this day that if the Australians had held on the north-western beaches, we would still have the island, the feeling of hopelessness seems to be general. In a percentage of the troops it was so close to the crust of morale that it soon broke through into demoralization . . .
>
> There were of course, many heroic incidents, much brave fighting and counter-charging worthy of the best tradition . . . We had sad defections and it was notable that the men who did not stand were the 'boozy' tough men who had always had the wrong ideas of discipline and were noisy and boastful . . .[9]

Murdoch blamed much of the problem on 'a constant jarring and belittlement of our British and Indian comrades, by inadequate discipline and finally by the percentage of weak and undisciplined soldiers breaking down under the strain of battle . . .

'The worst trouble we were under was the indiscipline of small elements that were never thoroughly digested by the better men.'

Ever the patriot, Murdoch also conceded that the main part of the Australian force was magnificent: 'They were imbued with deep patriotic devotions and had prepared themselves for their soldier tasks until they were like steel.'[10]

This may well have been the case in the early days of the invasion when the 8th Division proved their worth in the battles of Gemas and Muar, but Peter Elphick's account of the withdrawal from Singapore paints a damning and depressing picture of Australian behaviour. He quotes a British Royal Airforce technician by the name of Eric Bott who had been given permission to leave on the *Empire Star* but faced a 'God awful melee' when he arrived at Keppel Harbour.

'There were nationalities of all kinds trying to get on board this one remaining ship, abandoned cars were every-where, with harassed officials at the gangplank and a mob of Australian soldiers clubbing their way on board.'[11]

Another RAF man, Steve Stephen, had a similar experi-ence as he tried to board the last big ship to leave the island.

'When we arrived at Keppel Harbour to board the *Empire Star* there were armed guards – British – every few yards. Drunken looting Australians were swarming up the mooring ropes trying to get on board. They had looted the dockland warehouses and were intent on getting away come hell or high water.'[12]

These were serious charges and were not isolated. A group of military police were so concerned that they considered rushing the ship to pull the deserters off, but aborted the plan for fear of a bloodbath.

Another airman, John Dodd, was pressed hard against the rail of the ship and looked down to see the pleading faces of a group of women and children who were desperate to get on board. 'He saw an angry and frightened young European woman clutching the hand of a boy, aged about three, and two suitcases. She was arguing with two officials on the gangway who were ordering her to leave the luggage behind. Then out of the crowd behind her surged a group of about 20 desperate and armed Australian soldiers. The officials who tried to stop them were knocked out of the way with rifle butts and the group marched up the gangway.'[13]

The reports got worse. Secret files that were kept under lock and key in the Public Records Office in London until 1993 quoted Major A. Hart Davies, who was in charge of operating No. 4 Water Transport Company in Keppel Harbour: 'Deserters from the Australian Army were looting the Singapore Harbour godowns [dockside storehouses] all the time during the last three days before the capitulation and as my unit was stationed on an island in the harbour these men kept up a running rifle fire at my men and boats, the Australians being unable to get to them for further desertions.'[14]

Another comment from the secret files caused a furore when it was made public in Australia. A British major in the Malayan Volunteer Forces, J.C.K. Marshall, claimed, 'The Australians were known as daffodils – beautiful to look at but yellow all through.'[15]

Such descriptions were excruciatingly bruising for those Australians who had done the right thing and defended the island to the last, paying the price with three-and-a-half years as prisoners of war. No wonder relations with the British had slumped to an all-time low. The Poms had got them into this mess, and now they were blaming the Aussies for letting them down. No matter that the men of the 8th Division had won four Military Crosses, a Distinguished Conduct Medal, four military medals, a Distinguished Service Order and the greatest honour of all, the Victoria Cross.

There was fierce criticism of their commander too. In a letter addressed personally to Winston Churchill, Captain Tufton Beamish, who was on the staff of 18th Division, questioned Gordon Bennett's character: 'Everything I know of General Gordon Bennett inclines me to think him a most ordinary soldier and perhaps an even more ordinary man. The general behaviour and attitude of the AIF on Singapore Island certainly reflects nothing but discredit on its Commander.'[16]

These were wounding words, which struck at the very heart of the 8th Division and its commander. And Beamish's tirade didn't end there:

> As for the battle itself . . . the AIF did not comply with their orders and many forward posts withdrew or were withdrawn. Their resistance as a whole can but have been feeble and half-hearted. Their casualties in the early stages were not heavy. Some localities may have fought gallantly. I know that several posts withdrew without firing a shot and before they had come under fire.
>
> In actual fact the AIF was in need of a rest and their morale was extremely low. I am not exaggerating when I say that many of them had no intention of doing any more fighting. Several hundred Australians were in the docks days before the capitulation looking for a boat home.[17]

If the 8th Division was roused to fury when they read this in the early 1990s, it was perhaps understandable. Their reputation as a fighting force had been severely tarnished. Thousands of men had given their lives in the Malaya campaign in defence of a British colony with which few had anything in common and in support of an empire that had let them down in terms of military preparedness.

On the other hand there is a general acceptance that many of the reports of attempted escape were accurate and that those who felt compelled to stay behind resented those men's actions. One of these was Jack Boardman, who recalled how two men from his own unit managed to get away and eventually make it back to Australia. 'They went down and brandished their rifles and forced their way on to a ship.'

And he had no hesitation in labelling them deserters. 'Yes, of course they were. Anybody who left before 8.30 p.m. and attempted to escape . . . they definitely deserted. They refused to do as they were told. They went into town and got themselves on a boat or a ship. They did give the Australians a bad name these people.'[18]

Bart Richardson, who spent the rest of the war in Changi and on the Burma-Thai Railway, shared Jack Boardman's view of those who escaped: 'Many of those who reached Australia could probably be classed as deserters for most of them would have left early. There are always a number of deserters in an army but many soldiers in Singapore city were there [because] there was a lot of confusion in the fighting areas.'

Stragglers or not, he believed they had no right to escape. 'Apart from anything else they were letting down their mates by reducing fighting numbers. Actually many of those who did desert were the malingering types and it was no surprise that they went.'[19]

In the final few days leading up to surrender, conditions

were so chaotic that often it was a matter of chance whether you became a deserter or a straggler.

When Noel Harrison got back to Singapore most of his mates became separated from their units. 'I was one of them,' he volunteered. He explained to me how, lost and exhausted, they were helped to relative safety by a group of Malayans whom they happened to encounter.

'They took us back to an ammunition store, fed us and found an empty house for us to camp in for the night,' he recalled.

It was at this point that one of Noel's party decided he'd had enough.

'One of our corporals said, "I'm not staying here, I'm going," so he just walked out and managed to get on a boat. He was taken to somewhere over there in Indonesia and got back to Australia.'[20]

Was this man wrong to take his chance while he could or did he have a duty to stay? For some, snatching the opportunity to escape seemed infinitely more preferable than an unpredictable future at the hands of the Japanese.

Although Noel took the latter option he did not hold it against those who tried their luck, and until recently did not view them as deserters.

'Actually I've never thought about that, but [technically] that's what you should call them, I suppose.'[21]

Deserter or not, James Illife, a corporal serving in a special ordnance unit attached to the 8th Division HQ, had no reservations about trying to escape.

'Nobody who was not there could describe the absolute chaos prevailing in those final days,' he reflected many years after those events. This is how he looked back on them:

'There were dozens of troops in Singapore city, cut off from their units and without ammunition or food. They were not deserters, they were innocent victims of a futile effort to halt the invasion of a small island against an enemy whose navy commanded the seas surrounding Singapore and whose super-efficient aircraft controlled the skies, protecting a well-trained and disciplined Japanese army of superior strength.'

Still only 19, and slightly injured by a shell fragment that struck his left ankle, Sydney-born Jimmy could not walk properly but was determined to escape. So he teamed up with several mates from his platoon to try to make a break for it by getting hold of a boat. They eventually found a 16-foot sailing skiff in Singapore harbour and climbed aboard. The next few weeks would provide one of the most dangerous yet exhilarating periods of his life as he dodged the Japanese Navy and sailed and hitched his way south towards Australia. Like Gordon Bennett he had no intention of becoming a POW.[22]

Others were not so lucky. One of those caught up in the madness of those final days got away, only to be captured later. Roydon Cornford, who had arrived in Malaya as one of the untrained reinforcements allotted to 2/19th Battalion, had found himself cut off from his unit's leaders and ended up traipsing through the jungle before reaching Singapore harbour.

The story of his escape came to national prominence, and was not without controversy. It first appeared in a 1979 book, *Return From the River Kwai*, and some readers reached the conclusion that Cornford and his mates were deserters.

Historian Peter Elphick then quoted the same source in *Singapore: The Pregnable Fortress*, and subsequently those allegations were aired on television – in a 2002 ABC *Four Corners* program – in which Cornford denied he was a deserter. He told reporter Chris Masters how they got into a little boat and paddled their way out: 'In the distance we saw . . . we could see two ships. But we made for the closest one and we could see hundreds or, we reckoned, hundreds of soldiers on it. And they lowered a scrambly net and pulled us on board.'[23]

The ship was the *Empire Star*, which left Singapore in the early hours of 12 February with more than 2000 people, although the actual figure may have been closer to 3500. Most of them were legitimate passengers.

Peter Elphick claims that Cornford told Joan and Clay Blair, the authors of *Return From the River Kwai*, that when the ship reached Batavia the captain reported that Cornford and his party had 'shot and forced their way on to the ship'. More pertinently Elphick described him in his book as 'a deserter by his own admission'.[24]

What Cornford told Chris Masters was that he was put to work defending the ship against attack by Japanese aircraft, and after being briefly detained in Java he volunteered to return to the line and was eventually captured by the Japanese.[25]

Perhaps unwisely, Peter Elphick did not speak to Roydon Cornford personally to check his story, but at least the old soldier was able to clear his name in later years.

Rightly or wrongly many people had their reputations sullied at the fall of Singapore as a result of malicious gossip or a misinterpretation of the facts. From young men who were keen to stay alive, to senior officers who did not want to blemish their war record, everyone had their own agenda.

In fairness the criticism was not entirely one way. British and Indian troops were also castigated for their perceived shortcomings. As mentioned earlier, some badly behaved

British stragglers had been given Australian-style slouch hats to wear, leading to confusion over their nationality, while a significant number of Indians had simply laid down their arms.

One or two postwar reports actually praised the Australians. For instance Lieutenant-Colonel Ian Stewart, Commanding Officer of the Second Battalion of the Argyll and Sutherland Highlanders, insisted they fought very well:

'It is true that a number straggled down into town and did make an early getaway, but that equally applies to British troops.'[26]

Peter Elphick also quoted Lieutenant-Colonel J.M. Spurling's covering letter to the War Office: 'In fairness to the Australian troops it must be remembered that they fought well in Johore,' he wrote. [27]

He was, however, less complimentary about Bennett, whom he damned with faint praise: 'It appears that from General Gordon Bennett downwards the majority of the Australian Division were of the opinion that it was useless to try to defend Singapore. Thus, being intensely individualistic, and lacking discipline, they just never tried. I do not think they necessarily funked it.'[28]

There are conflicting reports about the total number of deserters, taking into account British, Indian and Australian personnel. Estimates range from a few hundred to several thousand.

Australian official historian Lionel Wigmore put the figure somewhere in between. 'The extent of the movement from the island is indicated by the fact that although many who took part in it died and others were captured, about 3,000 reached Java, Ceylon and India through Sumatra.'

He did not analyse the nationalities involved but grouped all military personnel together. And he focused only on those who left the island who could be classified as deserters. What about the ones who tried to escape but, through lack of will or sailing prowess, or problems with the availability of shipping failed to do so? In that case reckons Peter Elphick, the total could be as high as 10,000, and many of them would have been captured in the process.

Regardless of how you run the numbers the worst of the speculation would forever stain the brave band of men who formed the 8th Division. Not for nothing would they be tagged 'scapegoats for the bloody empire'.[29]

Chapter 14

INSIDE CHANGI

'I have often been asked about the surrender. It was not like the American westerns – "Come out with your hands up."'

At least that was Bart Richardson's view of the Allies' defeat. Most of the 8th Division assembled at the Botanic Gardens, where the majority had been fighting until the ceasefire. They threw their weapons into a pile and tried to hide more valuable belongings.

'Many buried compasses, binoculars, pistols and such like in the grounds of the gardens for future reclaim and use if possible . . . and those things are probably still there.'[1]

Others tried to keep their weapons with them for protection. George Daldry from the 2/20th held on to his trusty .45 revolver; and Scottish migrant Jimmy Houston, who had worked on the Sydney wharves before the war, grabbed a pistol from the heap for himself. He reckoned the gun might come in handy if conditions deteriorated and it was every man for himself.

However, they would have second thoughts about that when told to line up. George, who could always look after himself in a fight, spotted a group of fearsome guards and decided they were more than even he could handle.

'They were a gruesome looking bunch and pretty rugged looking,' he remembered. George knew that if he was found with a firearm hidden down his shirt, he'd probably be shot.

'I had to lose them and the revolver, so I walked calmly to a piece of grass while their attentions were distracted and dropped the gun surreptitiously to the ground. I was lucky to get away with it because they would have shown no mercy.'[2]

Better safe than sorry, he reasoned, before joining his mates with a sense of relief. After all, this wasn't Friday night in the backstreets of Sydney, but a far more dangerous battleground.

The long march to Changi eventually got underway around midday on 17 February. Arthur Kennedy and his mates carried their personal possessions in kit bags which they'd found in Tanglin Barracks, where they had spent the previous night.

Acrid smoke from burning buildings filled the air as officers barked their commands. Strangely there were few Japanese soldiers around at first, although they would make their presence felt later as the men made their way along the debris-strewn streets.

Arthur had lost most of his clothing and didn't have much to carry; even so it wasn't long before his kit bag weighed him down.

'We had a small truck which had been piled with unit equipment, a large amount of which appeared to be officers' baggage. Some of those who were not well were put on the vehicle.'[3]

As the march got underway they saw the horrific results of the battering Singapore had suffered in the previous weeks.

'Large numbers of buildings had been destroyed in the city but the damage tapered off as we moved out to the suburbs. Damage to the road was being roughly repaired by conscripted locals filling the holes with dirt,' Arthur recalled.

The human damage was another matter. 'Numbers of trucks drove past us with burnt bodies piled in them. We had heard that a large number of civilians had been killed.'[4]

Corpses also littered the area. 'On the side of the road to Changi and lying half through a hedge I saw the body of a Sikh NCO. The body was already swelling from lying in the tropical heat for several days. With the turban still on, the colourful uniform with its red sash made a strong contrast with the green hibiscus hedge,' he noted.

Arthur was impressed by the generosity of the locals. 'As we moved along the street many Chinese people came out and offered us food and drink. They ignored the guards and a number were beaten but this made little difference.'[5]

Others had a different recollection of the locals' behaviour. Don Wall noticed that some of the Malays who had worked for the AIF were now waving Japanese flags.[6]

By now the men of the 8th Division were accompanied by Japanese guards who pushed and cajoled those who were slow of foot and weary of manner. A rumour went around that the Japs had already shot six men and that anybody else who fell behind would receive a single shot to the head.

Sergeant Kevin Timbs, a dinky-di Aussie who had worked as a drover in the Glenn Innes area of New South Wales after leaving school, wisely chose to avoid eye contact with his captors. He had got through a couple of months of carnage relatively unscathed and was not prepared to lose his life at this stage. If he needed further evidence of the fragility of human existence, a squelching noise from just beneath his boot acted as a reminder.

'I just felt something soft under my foot and glancing down I realised I'd stepped on a human hand.'[7]

Across the road he saw the wreckage of a blown-up truck with the body of the driver lying on the roadside. His hand was missing.

Pint-sized Arthur 'Snowy' Collins from the Hunter Valley had also got the message about what might happen if you failed to keep up. Suffering from a badly festered toenail, he was in agony during the 19-mile (30-km) march.

'I was dying to sit down and take my boot off, but I knew if I did they'd probably shoot me.'[8]

The men of the 8th Division reached Changi in the early hours of 18 February and most were pleasantly surprised by their new quarters in Selarang Barracks. The 2/20th even received a tot of rum with their steaming hot cuppa.

This wasn't as bad as they had feared and even the food rations were better than they had expected. Each POW got 0.11032 pounds (50 g) of meat, some flour, just over a pound (450 g) of rice, a quarter pound (110 g) of vegetables, nearly half a pound (225 g) of sugar, some milk and small quantities of tea, salt and cooking oil.[9]

Those who had hung on to their money were able to buy little luxuries, including the odd bottle of Tiger beer from the local village. And if you were able to relax, the barracks offered a spectacular view of the South China Sea from certain vantage points.

Come the fall of Singapore there were more than 50,000 troops on the island, including 14,972 Australians. In addition there were 8th Division men captured in other areas of South-East Asia and the Pacific, including 2736 in Java, 1137 in Timor, 1075 on the island of Ambon and 1049 in New Britain, bringing the grand total to almost 21,000.[10]

To begin with the Japanese were reasonably friendly, providing cigarettes to prisoners. But even at this early stage the level of discipline among POWs was low, with many of them blaming their officers for the drubbing they had suffered.

'The men were despondent and listless, uncertain of their position in the scheme of things and obeyed orders grudgingly. The bitterness of defeat and the prospect of indefinite captivity by an enemy of whose tradition, customs, outlook and language most of the Australians knew little or nothing made the future seem black indeed.'[11]

Changi was Britain's peacetime garrison before the war and the Selarang Barracks were large and airy. But they became grossly overcrowded when the AIF arrived, forcing men to sleep outdoors, although this was no great hardship in the hot and humid conditions.

Camp control was left in the hands of Australian officers; the Japanese administrator allowed the Allies to enforce their own discipline. Officers were not segregated from other ranks and for a time the 8th Division and the rest of the POWs at Changi operated as normal military units, with little or no interference from their captors. Indeed life as a POW was half decent in those early days, but it would not continue that way. Soon the varied diet would be replaced by a tasteless rice ball and a tiny lump of fetid fish. More rigid prison controls were also imposed, with each division ordered to erect wire fences around their particular area. Until then the men were at liberty to roam around Changi at will.

The Japanese were also beginning to recognise the value of their prisoners as an enormous pool of labour and within a week work parties were being assembled to send out to repair roads or rebuild damaged property. Some were employed on the wharves unloading ships while others collected scrap iron and furniture for transport to Japan. These labour gangs provided not unwelcome relief for those POWs bored with life behind barbed wire. They also offered ample opportunity to pilfer food from Japanese stores or buy supplies from Chinese traders. Although hard labour, the work duties outside camp became increasingly popular, with several thousand men a day leaving Changi to perform manual jobs.

But there was no denying that living conditions generally were starting to worsen, especially in the overcrowded barrack blocks, where hygiene had deteriorated and dysentery and other diseases were taking their toll. Despite attempts to keep the men active with sports tournaments and other activities such as arts and crafts, morale began to plummet.

Penrith-born Alan Gaudry, who had been with the 22nd Infantry Brigade's HQ, said food – or rather the lack of it – soon dominated his life.

'It became our major pre-occupation,' he said, recalling how food sparked a lot of trouble in the camp.

'Initially there were fights with the strong and the greedy who tried to get more than their fair share at meal times by lining up first in the queues, then backing up to be the first again when it came to serve out the leftovers. We soon sorted that out by establishing a system of allocating back-up numbers, which was worked in strict rotation and guaranteed fair shares for everyone.'

Hunger dominated the POWs' every waking hour.

'It is like trying to describe a toothache to a person who has never had one . . . We talked, thought and dreamed about food and the less we received the more we thought about it, the more we talked, thought and dreamed about it.

'The aim of the Japanese was to weaken us to the point of apathetic acceptance of our lot, [and] reduce our numbers by overwork, semi-starvation, illness and disease.'[12]

Alan Gaudry's best mate was Jack Boardman, who shared those grim days with him in Changi and whose musical skills would often provide a little light relief. Jack's reputation as a pianist had been firmly established from the time of his arrival in Malaya a year earlier, when he'd formed a concert party in Kuala Lumpur. Now the problem was obtaining a piano.

Somehow an old upright was found in the nearby British naval base and at considerable personal risk an attempt was made to liberate the piano and carry it to Selarang, a distance of just over a mile (2 km). Fellow concert party member Keith Stevens and a few mates found a way of sneaking it through a gap in the barbed-wire fencing one night.

'Fortunately they were not seen by any Japanese who might assume they were escaping – this was a very serious offence usually punishable by death,' Jack recounted in his diary.[13]

The Changi piano, as it became known, would be used for concerts and occasional church services until early 1945. Such was its fame that the instrument was eventually shipped back to Australia and ultimately donated to the Australian War Memorial.

While the Changi concert parties helped to lift the spirits of the men, their physical and emotional state did not bode well for the far harsher conditions ahead. Soon many of them would be despatched as slave labour to Thailand, Borneo and Japan, where the inadequate food, intense workload and the brutality of the guards would consign thousands to an early grave.

The men's resolve had already been severely weakened by months of suffering. Now they faced an even more uncertain future at the hands of the Japanese. How would they cope? More to the point, how long would their imprisonment last? Would they ever be free?

Not knowing was the most unsettling aspect of all. As prisoners of war they had few rights and little hope. And where was their commander? Word was going round that Bennett had disappeared but his fate was unknown. Had he been captured and imprisoned elsewhere? Or had he joined those other men who'd made a run for it? Surely not the latter? How could Gordon Bennett turn his back on them in their hour of need? These were questions which had no immediate answer but did little to boost the troops' confidence in their military masters in the months and years ahead.

While many would remain loyal to Bennett and respect his decision to escape, there were those who would never forgive him.

'It was wrong,' says Bart Richardson. 'Bennett issued an order that no one was to try to escape and then went himself, which was wrong. In doing so he deserted his troops and that is very much a "no, no" in the army. One of the first things that is impressed upon a newly commissioned officer is that the troops always come first. You feed your men before you feed yourself – and you have what's left over.'[14]

Noel Harrison took the opposite view. 'He was able to get back to Australia and reveal the Japs' tactics. Good luck to him.'[15]

Arthur Kennedy, in his heart still a loyal member of the 8th Division, would never criticise his commander.

'I have no opinion,' he insisted. 'Bennett was an officer and he did what he thought he had to do,' was as far as he would go.[16]

Such a range of opinions, even 75 years after the event, is typical of much of the public sentiment expressed at the time.

Whether the differing views bothered the man himself is another matter. Bennett clearly had no qualms about deserting his men, although he would have plenty of time to think about it as he made his way to freedom.

Chapter 15

ALL AT SEA

Gordon Bennett and his crewmates aboard their tongkan were all at sea, both literally and metaphorically. In order to avoid the cluster of minefields around Singapore, they decided to head south, although even this direction did not guarantee a safe passage. The Japanese Navy was already attacking Palembang in the south of Sumatra and controlled much of the waterway in between.

Apart from the prismatic compass, the group's only other navigational aid was a schoolboys' atlas with a scale of 450 miles to the inch (720 km to 2.5 cm). Bennett decided to set their course across the Malacca Straits for the Indragiri River, roughly halfway down Sumatra's easterly coast. Though still about four days' sailing away, it was the closest point to the Dutch East Indies and might offer a degree of sanctuary for the intrepid would-be sailors. On entering the Indragiri they could sail upriver to Rengat, which was known to have a Dutch civilian presence.

The voyage would not be without its risks. The Japanese Air Force made regular sorties overhead in the search for Westerners trying to escape from Singapore, but every time they spotted a plane Bennett and his shipmates would hide below the awning and order the Chinese crew on deck. It seemed to do the trick and they sailed on without incident.

With 22 people on the tongkan it was crucial to ration supplies of food and water. One of the party was elected quartermaster, in charge of distributing a small beaker of water to each man twice a day and a morsel of bully beef and biscuit once a day.[1]

At night when the wind got up they made good progress, nudging six knots despite the boat's heavy load. It was not easy keeping a straight course, given the vagaries of the Riau Archipelago and its countless islands. And then there were the pagars, the native fish-traps made out of bamboo stakes, which poked out of the water and provided an ever-present hazard. In the dark it was hopeless trying to avoid the occasional collision with a pagar or, worse still, running the risk of becoming shipwrecked or left high and dry on one of the many reefs or tiny islands. In the end they decided to reduce speed until dawn and set full sail in daylight. After all, they'd got this far so why push their luck?

It was thirst that plagued them now. Desperate for water, when they happened upon an island in the dead of night they decided to make landfall even though the Japanese might also be there. There were few precautionary measures on offer but they devised a series of torchlight signals to alert other members of the landing party if they came across the enemy. Then a group of them set off. Dame Fortune was still with them. Plentiful supplies of fresh water were found for drinking and to fill storage containers for the onward journey.

But danger was never far away. By daylight Japanese planes reappeared, forcing Bennett and his men to once more seek cover under the awning. It had worked so far but for how much longer?

As Charles Moses had already pointed out, they were sitting ducks if the Japanese Air Force decided to bomb or shoot them up. With umpteen crates of ammunition below deck, the tongkan would go up like a rocket, so they decided to dump about 50 containers overboard. Not that it made much difference to the load.[2]

Three days had passed since they had left Singapore and slowly the vague outline of Sumatra appeared on the horizon. They would try to hug the coast while searching for the mouth of the Indragiri.

Others, it seemed, had much the same idea. The Strait of Malacca was swarming with refugees intent on finding a safe haven and an onward passage to Australia or the Indian subcontinent. They passed small yachts with brightly painted sails and a launch that was floating aimlessly because of engine problems. All were packed to the gunwales. Another tongkan, much like their own but better equipped, hoved into view with more than 40 men aboard, including several wounded. Bennett had a snatched conversation with an Australian officer on board before sailing on.

At a speed of barely two knots they were making slow progress and everyone was tired and hungry. Food and water had to be further rationed if they were to survive the voyage. They spent the night at anchor until the morning breeze.

It was 19 February and once again Bennett's guardian angel was about to smile sweetly on him. In the distance he spotted a large motor launch, which he hailed down like a passing taxi. Bennett was never backward in coming forward and, given his high military office, was used to issuing orders. Moreover he expected to be obeyed. Within minutes he was aboard the faster vessel, along with Moses and Walker.

Their new mode of transport was the *Tern*, which had previously been the property of the Singapore Harbour Board. It was diesel driven and capable of up to 12 knots. Bennett counted 17 others on the craft, including a British sailor who had survived the sinking of the *Prince of Wales*. More significantly the *Tern* carried a good supply of water and a small quantity of food. Even more encouraging was the fuel tank, which contained enough diesel to get them another 150 miles (240 km). Not enough to reach Palembang – which was fortunate as it turned out, given that the Japanese had just captured it – but more than sufficient to reach Rengat further up the Indragiri.[3]

This was an isolated corner of Sumatra where the native population rarely saw a white man. They were timid and reserved but also warm and generous. About 15 miles (25 km) upstream, the *Tern* approached a timber mill. Gordon Walker, who knew a little Malay, volunteered to go ashore to try to buy some food. He was met by two cheerful native boys who offered him and the others a meal of biscuits and fresh coffee for no charge.

What could go wrong? Well, accurate navigation for a start. Apparently the *Tern* had taken a wrong turn and entered a different river, depleting its fuel stocks by several gallons. They had no choice but to go-about and head out to sea again. This was crazy. Bennett and his fellow travellers were going nowhere fast and time was running out if they were to make it to Sumatra's interior before the Japanese got there.

Soon they spotted an island with a village built on stakes over the sea. It was Singkep, which sat off the southern end of the Sumatran coast. At first they ran aground but managed to swing the boat free and enter a deepwater approach to the village under the direction of a group of helpful natives.

Once again the locals were happy to provide them with some pungent-smelling sun- dried fish and a large number of duck eggs. The food was not very appetising but it was enough to keep them going for the next few days.

It was fortunate the locals were hospitable as the *Tern* was forced to spend the night there when the tide went out and the boat became grounded. As dawn broke on 20 February the launch refloated but there were still problems. The engine wouldn't start. Mud had fouled the exhaust and the crew were forced to spend the next hour cleaning it out.

Eventually they got underway and, by fixing their position on a map, sailed out into the Berhala Strait which separated the island from the mainland. For most of the voyage they stayed out of sight of land but after several hours sailing south their curiosity got the better of them and they made for the distant coastline.

It was stinking hot and many of those on board were becoming badly blistered by the sun. They needed shelter and fresh water, but they were in the middle of nowhere and home comforts were few and far between. Suddenly they came across a 'decent looking house' but the sea was too shallow to approach it and they continued their voyage south.[4]

As those on board the good ship *Tern* kept a lookout for any further sign of human habitation, they slid past the entrance to a large river. The mouth was at least 1000 metres wide and the water deep. A native man who rowed out to meet them revealed it was the Djambi River. They were a few hundred miles south of their intended destination, Rengat, but there was another town some way upriver which offered the quickest route to civilisation.

There was much handshaking as the locals, many of them dressed in colourful sarongs, greeted the new arrivals, who were given a tin of biscuits and some coconuts. They asked for more and tried to negotiate the purchase of a few chickens. Communication was difficult at first as neither party spoke each other's language, but Moses and Walker eventually got their message across by crowing and flapping their arms. A price was agreed and a bundle of Straits dollars was handed over.

'As usual with all Malays, they were very friendly and hospitable and their faces were wreathed in smiles,' Bennett told Frank Legg. 'We returned to our boat after learning that Djambi was far up the river – many days' journey. They measured distances by the time it took to travel, their means of travel being by small sampan or on foot.'[5]

The crew of the *Tern* didn't want to risk any more delays by striking the snags that dotted the river, so decided to drop anchor and spend the night there. The following day, Bennett's fifth since leaving Singapore, dawned with constant rainfall but they were determined to reach their goal as soon as possible and carried on up the river. Along the way they passed many villages but there was no sign of Djambi. How much further? they asked the natives who came out of their huts to wave.

'A long way,' they invariably replied.

As lunchtime approached they came across a few young men in two sampans in the middle of the river. They were also going to Djambi and wanted a tow. The boys were taking their fish to market, beautiful specimens which they carried alive in water-filled tins to keep them fresh.

The crew of the *Tern* transferred the load and made the sampans secure before continuing the long voyage. It was becoming a seemingly endless journey but at least the young men on the sampans knew where they were going. Finally, at 6 pm on 21 February, they reached the town of Djambi. They had sailed more than 200 miles (320 km) up the winding river and tied up with just one gallon (4.5 litres) of fuel left in the tank.

Their arrival took the Dutch by surprise. They were already on high alert as a result of random Japanese bombing. Several buildings, including factories, had been destroyed and a couple of ships were also badly damaged. Word was that the enemy was close by after capturing Palembang and they were heading for Djambi. As a result the authorities had set fire to petrol dumps and other important facilities so they would not fall into Japanese hands.

In town the senior Dutch official invited Bennett and his aide-de-camp back to his home to wash and brush up. Here they enjoyed their first bath in nearly a fortnight. Oh, the joys of civilisation, they agreed.

Major Moses and the rest of the party were ferried to the local rest house for the night. What bliss to eat a hot meal and sleep between clean sheets, they thought.

Meanwhile, Bennett was anxious to keep on the move and the next morning made plans to drive to Padang, a journey of nearly 90 miles (150 km). He still hadn't made contact with Wavell or any other Allied brass, because the telephone, he discovered, was one luxury that Djambi did not boast. He was also aware the Japanese were too close for comfort and he did not want to give them the pleasure of arresting the commander of the 8th Division.

However, there was one other matter he had to deal with before leaving. The Dutch administrator wanted to know if any of the *Tern*'s party could manage a diesel-driven boat. A ship had been wrecked by Jap bombers off Singkep Island and some of the survivors who had reached shore were badly injured. Djambi had a doctor and a boat that was ready to go but no one to sail it. Could they provide the crew?

Bennett had a word with the British officer who had allowed them on board the *Tern*, Lieutenant L.A. Carty of the Royal Army Service Corps, to see if he was interested. Carty turned to the rest of his crew and after a short discussion they all volunteered to sail back. The kindness of these men, who had endured so much hardship over the previous few weeks, clearly impressed Gordon Bennett, and he praised their generosity of spirit in his memoir.

'These men had struggled for many days in their attempt to escape from the Japanese and had just reached safety. Yet they volunteered without hesitation to go back into the jaws of death to help these injured women and children. This incident gives the lie to those who even suggest that the men of Great Britain lack courage or that they are not willing to make any sacrifice to help humanity,' he wrote.[6]

Bennett's reference to the British may have been sincerely felt but was it also an attempt to find favour with them?

A cynical view maybe, but given the controversy he was about to face back home, he needed all the friends he could find.

Interestingly Carty would write to Bennett some months later to inform him that after accomplishing their mission at Singkep Island, his party escaped to Ceylon (now known as Sri Lanka), where they reported for duty. By then Carty had been promoted to the rank of captain.[7]

Bennett seemed sorry to leave Djambi, where he had managed to buy some emergency clothing to replace the rag-tag kit he'd been wearing since Singapore. He was taken with the community, who appeared overawed by the threat of the Japanese invasion.

'It seemed dreadful that these quiet, peace-loving people who were living in the backwash of humanity and who were so amiably disposed to all whom they met, should be subjected to the terrors and horrors of this Japanese war of aggression,' he observed.

'They were living quietly among themselves and were harming no one. They were very happy under Dutch rule and could never be happy under the domineering, cruel rule of the Japanese.'[8]

Was Bennett an old softy at heart or was it merely another attempt to curry favour with his hosts in a bid to enhance his wartime image? I cannot prove his motives one way or the other but I suspect his emotional attachment to the people of Djambi was genuine.

Bennett had to get away – and fast. A bus was provided to transport the remaining members of the party to Muaratebo, which entailed a lengthy drive along the banks of the beautiful Djambi River. Once again they arrived unexpectedly and were directed by the Dutch governor to the local rest-house for refreshments.

The one breakthrough at Muaratebo was the discovery of a telegraphic link with the outside world. Bennett couldn't wait to fire off a telegram to General Wavell advising him of his safe arrival in Sumatra and asking for a plane to be sent to Padang so he could continue his journey south.

There was no reply and after breakfast the following day they got back on the bus for the final stage of their drive across Sumatra to Padang. The road was busy, with many buses transporting native soldiers to do battle with the Japanese. Oddly, a lot of them seemed to be taking their wives and children along for the ride.

At one village they drew up alongside an ambulance that contained two British women who had been wounded when their ship was bombed in Singapore. They had eventually made it to the Riau Archipelago, where they were picked up and brought to a hospital in Sawahlunto on the road to Padang.

By now this part of Sumatra was resembling a refugee camp; hundreds of men and women from Singapore were being housed in makeshift accommodation. All the survivors had their identities recorded and Bennett recognised the names of a number of Australians who had been evacuated by ship from Singapore on 13 February.

The Dutch provided Bennett, Moses and Walker with a car, which reached Padang about 7 pm. On arrival it seemed half the British Army and Air Force were also there, most of them from Singapore. An office had been set up to handle all the refugees and Bennett took the opportunity to send another wire requesting air transport from Padang to Batavia, now known as Jakarta. This time General Wavell was quick to respond, eager to find out what had happened in the final few hours before the fall of Singapore. He especially wanted to know more about reports of stragglers and deserters.

'I told him that there was in fact a large number of battle stragglers in the streets of Singapore during the last few days and that the proportion of Australians was very small.'[9]

This latter claim may have been an exaggeration, but truth is always the first casualty of war.

Bennett, Moses and Walker spent a comfortable night in a hotel and assembled at the wharf before daylight to be ferried out to a waiting Catalina flying boat with a Dutch pilot and crew. It was an agreeable conclusion to their ten-day adventure on the high seas and travelling the back roads of Sumatra. Next stop Batavia. From there Australia was merely a hop, skip and a jump away.

The air-raid siren that greeted them on arrival in Java seemed ominous, but Bennett and his team had been through enough by then not to be fazed by such alarms. Apart from anything else there was lunch to consider. The party arranged to be driven to the Hotel des Indes, where they enjoyed a substantial meal in the restaurant. It appeared to be a favourite haunt of the military. Bennett had hardly sat down when he recognised an Australian friend at a neighbouring table.

Ramsay Ray was an Australian officer serving in Britain's RAF and had just managed to escape from Palembang before the Japs arrived. The two got on famously and when Ray offered Bennett and his men a lift to Bandoeng after lunch, they were quick to accept.

Bennett was keen to catch up with Wavell, who was staying there, but on arrival later that afternoon, he discovered that the general had closed his HQ and flown to India earlier in the day.

By this stage about 2000 troops had arrived in Java, including the 2/3rd Motor Transport Company from Malaya and an advance party of Australians from the Middle East. At the helm was General John Lavarack, head of I Corps, who had arrived ahead of men from 6th and 7th Divisions, who were being redeployed from Egypt to the Far East to fight the Japanese.[10] Bennett was on the lookout for a flight home and when he heard that 'Joe' Lavarack was in town and was about to fly to Australia himself, he decided to ask a favour.

However, to add to military tensions, a fierce power struggle was going on between senior officers of the AIF at the time and when Bennett telephoned Lavarack's office to enquire about air travel out of the country, the request went down like a lead balloon. Bennett, Lavarack and Blamey all had their eyes on the top job – commander-in-chief of Australian forces. Bennett was told there was no chance of joining the flight due to leave the next morning with Lavarack and two of his senior officers.[11]

The implications did not escape Bennett's attention: he was being effectively superseded by Lavarack as commander of the AIF in Malaya. Then again, why was the head of I Corps planning to leave for Australia at such a crucial time?

'I thought that Lavarack was deserting his men just before the battle and should not escape while there was fighting to be done,' Bennett wrote.[12]

Perhaps the delicious irony of Lavarack planning a carbon copy of Bennett's own flight to freedom had not occurred to the former commander of 8th Division, though he was quick to point out that a week later, the head of I Corps had joined in the chorus that condemned Bennett's escape.

For the record, Lavarack was made acting Commander-in-Chief of Australia's military forces in March, before Blamey assumed the appointment on his return from the Middle East. By that time Bennett was out of the running, his future under a cloud.[13]

Bennett's eventual departure from Java was dogged by incident. First Moses was knocked down by a taxi and had to be taken to hospital. (He and Walker subsequently made it back to Australia by boat in March.) Then Bennett attempted to thumb a lift to Tjilatjap, on Java's south coast, in the hope of securing a flight to Australia. Once again his luck held and he hitched a ride with a party of British officers. On completing the 150-mile (250-km) journey he found the seaport was teeming with refugees and military personnel, including American Army, Navy and Air Force servicemen.

On the local airstrip he found a Qantas plane that was scheduled to fly out the next day. Unfortunately it was a charter flight and the pilot couldn't sell him a ticket, but Bennett was undeterred. He simply stowed away on the plane the night before. [14]

At least this was the story he related to Frank Legg. In an earlier account that he wrote for his memoir, he claimed that he obtained a passage for himself and opted to sleep on the plane before it departed because he couldn't find a room in town.[15]

This wasn't the only story to conflict with later reports, which claimed the aircraft was a flying boat. What is not in doubt is that Bennett and his fellow passengers, all of them civilian refugees, took off at dawn on 27 February. As they made height over Tjilatjap they saw a convoy of ships preparing to leave port crowded with passengers. Most were heading for India but at least one was hoping to make it to Australia. They would be the last merchant vessels to depart before the Japanese took control of the Dutch East Indies, dooming the native population and those Dutch civilian and military personnel left behind, as well as thousands of POWs, to three-and-a-half years of servitude.

———·——

Bennett finally got back to Australia in the late afternoon, the *Catalina* cruising to a halt just off the coast of Broome at 5 pm. A pearling lugger came out to meet it and ferry the passengers ashore to the Governor Broome Hotel. It was a moment that would leave an indelible impression on Bennett.

'To me Broome will always have a sentimental attachment,' Bennett would say later. 'To the ordinary visitor, Broome is just Broome, a not very inviting place. To me it was Australia, home. What is more I had succeeded in escaping. How different I felt when I left Singapore 12 days ago. Then the prospects of coming through alive looked hopeless and almost impossible.'[16]

Bennett enjoyed every minute of his newfound freedom. He headed to a local hotel to tuck into a typical bush meal before retiring to the bar. Everybody congratulated him on his escape, which he found 'flattering' and reinforced his view that the decision to leave Singapore was the right one.

They were all worried about Japan's victory and the army's relentless drive south into Sumatra, which made him even more determined to head back to Melbourne and brief his fellow officers and the government about the enemy's tactics.

Bennett evidently wanted to put his own version on the record before anybody else had time to question his motives. He claimed he wanted to tell Prime Minister John Curtin and his ministers the full story of Malaya, how well the diggers had fought and how the lessons learned might place Australia in a much stronger position to meet an enemy invasion.

'That was the main object of my escape,' he made clear. And to further justify his position he pointed out that it was the first duty of every prisoner to avoid capture. 'Anyway I did not relish the idea of cooling my heels in a Japanese prisoner-of-war camp while fighting was to be done,' he added. 'I felt that I could give valuable service, especially now I had learned Japanese methods at first hand.'[17]

These were admirable sentiments on the face of it but were they merely a convenient pretence? Whatever the truth nothing was going to get in the way of Gordon Bennett's speedy return to Army HQ. The most direct route to Melbourne was via Perth but it turned out to be quicker to fly via Charleville in Queensland and then on to Sydney. A Dutch Douglas aircraft was available and Bennett booked himself a seat. He and his fellow passengers – a Dutch family – took off from Broome at first light and reached Alice Springs, nearly 900 miles (1500 km) away, by lunchtime.

During the refuelling stop he had time to send a wire to the Minister for the Army, Frank Forde, announcing his safe return and advising Forde that he expected to be in Sydney by the following day. Having hoped to surprise the authorities, Bennett had the wind taken out of his sails when he learned that the BBC had already broadcast news of his escape thanks to a tip-off from Charles Moses in Batavia.

Following another long flight from Alice, the travel

party arrived in Charleville soon after sunset. The town was bursting at the seams with hundreds of American airmen; the bars were packed with them. Once news leaked out of Bennett's presence he was warmly welcomed by the locals, many of whom wanted news of their relatives left behind in Singapore.

Bennett flew into Sydney's Mascot aerodrome at lunchtime on 1 March to be greeted by his wife, Bess, daughter, Joan, and dozens of press photographers. It was an exciting moment as he stepped onto the tarmac, but the emotion was mixed. He admitted later that the joy was dimmed by two factors – as the bearer of bad news to Australia and the fact he had left so many friends behind as POWs.[18]

Was Bennett's conscience pricking him again? If so there was little opportunity for second thoughts, given the clamour of reporters and admirers who descended on him at the Australia Hotel in Castlereagh Street in the city. Everyone wanted to congratulate him on his escape. Everyone, that is, except the military.

The first hint of a problem came when General Henry Wynter, who had met Bennett earlier at Sydney airport, took him aside and advised him not to make any public statements about the Malaya campaign and the Allies' defeat.

Bennett couldn't believe his ears. At Broome and every other stop, he had been besieged by anxious relatives who had expressed their concern for their loved ones and now he was being told to shut up. Surely they deserved reassurance, he reasoned. After all he was hardly going to reveal any state secrets the Japanese did not know already.

During the evening, as the beer and spirits flowed, Bennett was handed a message that he was expected in Melbourne the next day to meet the War Cabinet. A plane was put at his disposal and he flew into Essendon aerodrome the following morning.

Bennett, still in his makeshift army uniform, told the Cabinet the full story of the fall of Singapore and, to his relief, the prime minister and the rest of the government expressed their appreciation for his efforts. More specifically his escape also received their backing, a level of personal support that was then communicated to the media in a formal statement. The prime minister wrote:

> I desire to inform the nation that we are proud to pay tribute to the efficiency, gallantry and devotion of our forces throughout the struggle. We have expressed to Major-General Bennett our confidence in him. His leadership and conduct were in complete conformity with his duty to his men under his command and to his country. He remained with his men until the end, completed all formalities in connection with the surrender and then took the opportunity and risk of escaping.[19]

In a few sentences Henry Gordon Bennett had been exonerated by the Australian government. Unhappily for him, not everybody would share the Cabinet's view.

Chapter 16

BENNETT'S FALL FROM GRACE

On the same day he addressed the War Cabinet in Melbourne, Bennett called on Major-General Vernon Sturdee, at Victoria Barracks, which then housed the Department of Defence.

Anticipating a warm reception, the 8th Division commander entered the Chief of General Staff's office to find the conversation was formal and the atmosphere cold and hostile. Sturdee, whose rank for many years had been junior to Bennett's, told the commander that his escape from Singapore had been ill-advised.

You could have cut the air with a knife. During the excruciatingly uncomfortable silence that followed, Sturdee looked down and carried on working, while Bennett was left to stand there like a naughty schoolboy.

How had it come to this? Everyone else had been full of praise, except for the Military Board, who chose to ignore him.

Once again the Australian Staff Corps, who felt their long

and uninterrupted employment by the army gave them added rank and privilege over mere militia men, had shown Bennett who was boss. They were the military establishment. He was the Johnny-come-lately who had chosen a life in civvy street after his daring exploits in World War I.

Bennett was furious and returned to his hotel room 'white and shaking'.

'Let's pack,' he told his wife. 'We're going home in an hour.'[1]

On the flight back to Sydney he explained to Bess how shocked and shaken he was by Sturdee's reception. Hadn't he left his Singapore HQ and begun his dangerous escape *after* the surrender was signed? What more could he have done to help his men? Once the Japanese had found him they would almost certainly have marched him away, probably never to be seen again, he told her.

Bess may have provided a convenient shoulder to cry on at that moment, but Bennett was a fighting man and the Military Board's response only served to further convince him that he was right to escape. Now he was more determined than ever to prove the wisdom of his ways and to convince the authorities of the need for the kind of training which would prevent such disasters as the defeat of Malaya in the future.

Bennett was adamant that the most important reason for the Allies' failure was the rigid adherence to inappropriate textbook tactical methods. Military action had been based on experience gained in Europe and North Africa, and the jungles of the Far East demanded different thinking. Malaya had provided a prime example of poor military strategy, he claimed. Years later, when he collaborated with biographer Frank Legg, he articulated these ideas most succinctly:

In jungle country, particularly, an attacker can move around the flanks of a defensive position and cut off the defenders by establishing road blocks or some other obstacle in the rear.

Having isolated them he can continue his forward movement, leaving the defensive position miles behind his advancing troops. The psychological effect on the defender is superlatively depressing. This, together with a strong attack on the weak points in the defence, brings about victory for the attackers and defeat for the static defenders.[2]

Then there was the issue of war-like aggression. Bennett was highly critical of the British system's inability to develop the psychological side of a soldier's training. The Malayan campaign was different to the old days, when men fought shoulder to shoulder under the direct orders of officers who could see all their men.

'In modern war, especially in jungle warfare, officers can control only a few men who are within their sight or within range of their voices,' he pointed out. In the jungles of Malaya soldiers had to carry on fighting under their own initiative and often without the guidance provided by their leaders.

'To train a soldier how to use his weapons is not enough. He must be trained to be bold and determined and even to die,' he thundered.

Bennett preached his own brand of military strategy with almost evangelical fervour. Blessed with a professional certainty that rarely countenanced a change of heart, he believed that victory was only possible by adopting a superior fighting spirit.

'The only effective way to defend Malaya was to attack and destroy Japanese invaders on ground previously selected and reconnoitred by the troops detailed to protect the country. This demands, of course, an offensive spirit, which was absent in many of the units in Malaya,' he asserted.[3]

In the months and years following his dash from Singapore Bennett would become obsessed by tactical superiority. He detailed anything and everything connected to the Malaya campaign and the fall of Singapore in note form, in order for it to be collated and later printed in military training pamphlets.

The first few weeks after his return were a period of particularly intense activity for Bennett. Despite being granted brief leave he continued to write feverishly and took every opportunity to voice his concerns about the defeatist attitude he often came across. He despised talk about the so-called Brisbane Line, whereby Australia would cede the northern part of the country to the Japanese in the event of an invasion; it did little to boost national morale, and Japan's seemingly inexorable march across South-East Asia and the western Pacific further diminished public confidence in the Allies' ability to fight back.

It was during this time that Bennett, arguably, took his eye off the ball when it came to his own advancement. Obsessed by the need to record his training notes, which he believed were crucial to Australia's safety, he neglected to lobby the powers-that-be regarding his own military ambitions.

Rightly or wrongly there was a perception that Bennett had escaped from Singapore to secure the position of Australia's commander-in-chief. He always denied this, stating in his papers: 'I can truthfully say that the thought of securing a command in Australia on my return did not once enter my head. Of course the fabricators of the silly story that I should never have left Malaya when I did, could not understand that there are some people who give their service in war without any thought of self-aggrandisement or personal advancement.'[4]

Bennett's answer to his detractors in later years may or may not have reflected his true feelings, but his old adversary Blamey was never going to take the risk and couldn't wait to get back to Australia to throw his own hat into the ring for the position. The problem was that he was still in the Middle East and it wasn't until 7 March that he flew out of Cairo to Cape Town, where he intended to join the *Queen Mary*, which was en route to Fremantle. Air links between the Middle East and Australia were no longer possible due to the widening conflict across Asia.

To add to the sense of urgency Blamey had received a telegram from Prime Minister Curtin recalling him to Australia, but giving him no indication of his future role. Frustrated beyond belief, Blamey was desperate to outmanoeuvre Bennett – and Lavarack, who was also in the running – for the army's most senior post. With relations between the three men hardly cordial, the scene was set for a bitter struggle, especially between Blamey and Bennett, whose lifetime enmity was about to reach its climax. If successful, Blamey could take credit for engineering Bennett's final humiliation. If not, the old war horse's military career would be over.

But Bennett, for whatever reason, failed to exploit the personal advantage he enjoyed by being on the ground and by the time Blamey sailed into Fremantle the decision had already been made.

A letter handed to Blamey on his arrival informed him that the government proposed to appoint him commander-in-chief of the Australian military forces. Yet a shadow still hovered over Blamey: although he was the highest serving officer in the country, he would effectively be outranked by General Douglas MacArthur, the American five-star general who had just been appointed supreme commander in the South-West Pacific. In other words MacArthur would be in overall charge of the war against the Japanese and Blamey would have to accept playing second fiddle.

As for Bennett, he was appointed acting inspector general of training, a post in which he could make full use of his experience of the Japanese Army's tactics in Malaya and pass on his own strategies for dealing with them. While clearly disappointed at being overlooked for the top job, he would have taken pleasure from his promotion to the rank of lieutenant-general a month later and his appointment as commander of the 3rd Australian Corps in Western Australia, which had already been attacked by the Japanese. The catastrophic raid by enemy aircraft on Broome on the morning of 3 March, which claimed at least 40 lives and probably many more, had placed Australia's western seaboard on high alert and 3rd Corps was needed to play a key role in its future defence.

Gordon Bennett took to his new posting with characteristic verve and devotion to duty, using the opportunity to complete two detailed manuals on Japanese tactics which were to form the basis of an official Army Training Memorandum. These booklets, which contained a foreword by General Blamey requesting close scrutiny by all officers, were distributed to American and Australian troops in the South-West Pacific.[5]

It seemed the head of Australian forces had patched up his differences with his old adversary and recognised the value of Bennett's contribution to modern training techniques, but this was not to last. Soon Bennett was getting restless again, anxious to play a more challenging role as a commander in the field. While being in charge of the 3rd Corps was initially fulfilling, the fact was that he had been sidelined. At the age of 55 the man who believed his rightful place was commanding an active fighting force had been put out to pasture.

Several unpleasant incidents also occurred in which Bennett's courage in the field was questioned. They may have upset him though he would never admit it. White feathers were delivered to him in the post and on another occasion a pair of running shoes. Later his portrait, which hung in the Australian War Memorial, was slashed. Bennett believed members of the Staff Corps were responsible for the feathers and after a 'thorough search' claimed a high-ranking officer had sent the shoes.[6]

Later, in his draft memoir, he wrote, 'The receipt of white feathers did not worry me nor did the receipt of a dirty pair of old running shoes. These were easily traced to their source too close to my most bitter opponent at a certain Army Headquarters for anything but disgust. Such conduct would disgust the angels.'[7]

Bennett's relations with the Army Staff Corps continued to deteriorate. Repeated attempts to be moved to a command more in keeping with his experience as a fighting soldier fell on deaf ears. Blamey would not budge, preferring to keep his long-term rival at arm's length on the other side of the country, where he had little power to influence the way the war was being handled.

The extent to which Bennett was privately seething over his treatment after escaping from Singapore was later revealed in his draft memoir, in which he wrote of the 'Machiavellian intrigue of the Staff Corps and Blamey at the outset – and both can be grouped together – in their indecent scheming over the command of the AIF.'[8]

Bennett was equally scathing of the Federal Cabinet for appointing Blamey as head of the Army when they knew about his conduct as Victoria's chief police commissioner before the war. This was a reference to an attempt to cover up the shooting of a police officer, which led to Blamey's forced resignation in 1936, and a scandal over the discovery of his police badge in a Melbourne brothel.

Bennett accused the Cabinet of having no understanding of the 'great importance of selecting a leader in war who could command the respect of the men whom he was to lead'. And for good measure he added: 'That appointment submitted Australia to an indignity which it will take generations to forget. Had he been a brilliant general of the Monash standard, which he was not, the people could perhaps have overlooked his personal unfitness to command men.'[9]

These were harsh words which graphically exposed the fear and loathing that existed between Bennett and the military hierarchy, as well as the government. Of course these were sentiments which were yet to be made public but would, in retrospect, explain why Bennett decided to quit his post in April 1944.

Exasperated by Blamey's continued refusal to recommend him for operational command, he fired off an angry letter of resignation to the commander-in-chief of the AIF.

'It is not my desire to fill an administrative post gradually diminishing in importance . . . I therefore request to be relieved of my command and returned to civil life,' he wrote.

At a meeting between the two men prior to the resignation, Blamey had told Bennett that he had made a 'serious mistake' in escaping from Singapore and because of this he was associated with the failure in Malaya. As a result his appointment to any operational command would be unpopular with the public and at any rate there were other younger officers who now had the experience to take on the Japanese.[10]

Bennett was furious that his past record, seniority and experience could be so dismissed. In a press statement issued after his resignation was accepted, he insisted he had not wanted to retire from the army while the war was still on, but that he had been 'victimised' and 'frozen out'.[11]

The nature of Gordon Bennett's abrupt departure from military life did not go without comment in the newspapers. the *Examiner* described the decision as regrettable and did not mince words:

> General Bennett resigned because he could obtain no assurance that he would ever be granted an operational command. Apparently he felt this could be explained only by antipathy towards him in high places . . . Has Australia so many proved military leaders that we can allow one of them in the prime of life to go into retirement? . . .
>
> We know there are those who condemn General Bennett's action in escaping; they accuse him of deserting his men. But that is a foolish point of view and we hope that the Government has not been weak enough to allow the

attitude of itself or of the military chiefs to be influenced by
this section.[12]

By now Bennett was well into the final draft of his book,
Why Singapore Fell, which was based partly on his diary at the
time and subsequent reflections. When Blamey got to hear of
Bennett's plans to publish his own version of events – and in
particular a passage which criticised Australia's commander-
in-chief for not recognising the Japanese threat before the
invasion of Malaya – Blamey tried, unsuccessfully, to get it
censored. In the end Bennett's memoir was published in late
1944 and sold out within a few days, such was the level of
public fascination with his story.

Even when it was obvious that the end of the war was
near, closure was far from Bennett's mind. Come 1945 he
put his hand up to rescue the survivors of the 8th Division.
He wanted to supervise the repatriation of Australian POWs,
a move that received the overwhelming support of the
Returned Services League in New South Wales. But once
again the request was turned down, this time on the grounds
that he was too senior in rank. It was a job for a brigadier and
not a lieutenant-general was the military's response.

Bennett exploded, telling the newspapers that Blamey was
running Australia and not the government.

While the former commander of the 8th Division
continued to wage his personal vendetta against his critics
in the military, the debate over whether he was a deserter
or a legitimate escapee continued. The mood among other
ranks was largely supportive of the general, and public
opinion also seemed to be on his side. But his enemies
within the Staff Corps were still out to get him and in

August 1945 even bigger guns were assembled to destroy Bennett's reputation.

Brigadier 'Boots' Callaghan, the division's artillery commander, whom Bennett had appointed to take over from him after he left Singapore, was among the first of the POWs to return to Australia after being released from Chungking, then provisional capital of the Republic of China.

Among the documents he brought home was a letter from General Percival, which he had written in March 1943 while also in captivity. It was addressed to the secretary of the Military Board in Melbourne and made a serious allegation about Bennett's decision to escape.

'I have to report that Major-General H. Gordon Bennett, GOC AIF Malaya, voluntarily and without permission relinquished command of the AIF on February 15 1942 – the date on which capitulation of the British Forces in Malaya took place,' Percival wrote.[13]

The letter went on to praise Callaghan for his 'splendid work in holding the AIF together' and recommended he be promoted to the rank of major-general.

The opening paragraph went to the very heart of the charge against Bennett – that he escaped without permission. This assumed that Percival had command over the head of the 8th Division, which was not necessarily the case. While Australia was part of the Allied operation in Malaya, in the final analysis Bennett was answerable to Canberra and not to London. At least this was one interpretation of military law, though others begged to differ.

General Blamey could not believe his ears when he heard about Percival's condemnation of Bennett's action. It was just the sort of ammunition he needed to further prosecute his old foe and immediately he wrote to Forde, the Army Minister, drawing his attention to the serious allegation that Bennett had effectively deserted his troops.

The Minister replied that he was surprised at the letter's contents, as he had never heard about any claim that Bennett had deserted his men. Forde asked Blamey to elaborate and, if he was satisfied the allegation could be substantiated, what course of action he proposed to take. It was an offer too good to refuse for the commander-in-chief of the Australian Army, who promptly recommended that an official court of inquiry be held into Bennett's behaviour in Singapore.

Blamey placed further pressure on Forde in October when, in a note to the minister, he insisted the matter struck at the very core of military discipline and that he had already approached other senior officers to sit on an inquiry:

> A great deal of feeling [exists] amongst General Bennett's previous staff of the 8th Division and other senior officers who were prisoners of war in Malaya. I think it would be deplorable if political considerations should be permitted to interfere with a matter of such serious moment in the discipline of the Australian Army as an investigation into the conduct of one of its General Officers, when such is called into question by his immediate commander.
>
> As the preparations for the court are now in hand, I should be glad if any opposition to its assembly might be withdrawn.[14]

It seemed there were good grounds for supposing Blamey really was running the country, as Bennett had previously suggested.

Forde had no alternative but to accede to Blamey's demands and, after consulting Ben Chifley, who had recently taken over as prime minister following the death of John Curtin, agreed that the military court should be held at Victoria Barracks in Sydney from 26–31 October.[15]

———·——

As preparations got underway for the inquiry into Bennett's escape, troops from the 8th Division were already arriving home by ship. They had spent the past three-and-a-half years in captivity, often under conditions of extreme brutality. More than 1000 Australians died on the Burma-Thai Railway alone.[16]

Most of the survivors were lucky to be alive given the level of sickness and starvation in the camps and in the light of Japanese plans to execute their prisoners in the event of a US invasion. Only America's decision to drop the atom bomb on Hiroshima and Nagasaki saved them.

Among the men to have survived that ordeal were Jack Boardman and his lifelong friend Alan Gaudry. The two had been split up as POWs for much of the war and were only reunited on their return to Australia. While overjoyed to be back home, Alan took exception to some of the dockside well-wishers, specifically two soldiers from his unit who had escaped by boat at the fall of Singapore. He made no mention of it in his memoir, but Alan told Jack that he and his mates were singularly unimpressed by the behaviour of the men who got away.

'When he got into Sydney there were these two deserters to welcome him. Well, Alan and the rest wouldn't have anything to do with them,' Jack told me.[17]

Charles Moses, later to become boss of the ABC, also got the brush-off when he arrived at Sydney Harbour to greet his fellow officer Captain Adrian Curlewis, who had decided not to escape in 1942. Three-and-a-half years behind barbed wire had clearly left Curlewis with a degree of resentment towards those who had turned their backs on the men of the 8th Division at the fall of Singapore. As Moses spotted Curlewis on the wharf he went forward to offer him a friendly hand-shake, only to be rebuffed by the latter, who walked straight past him.

'You bastard,' muttered Moses. Curlewis probably didn't know at that stage, but after returning to Australia Moses had gone on to fight in Borneo and New Guinea.

Although the two men later made up, the incident symbol-ised the depth of feeling that existed between officers over the issue of escape.[18]

Bart Richardson sailed into Sydney's Darling Harbour just after breakfast on 4 October. He had been away for exactly four years, eight months and two days. From the deck he spotted two familiar faces. One was his old mate, known as 'Salvation Army' Woody, who had been repatriated much against his will before the fall of Singapore. The other was Gordon Bennett.

'Nobody took much notice of him for, after all, he had deserted his troops after ordering us not to try and escape but did do himself,' Bart observed.[19]

Woody greeted his pal as he walked down the gangplank but Bennett was nowhere to be seen.

Strangely the ostracism inflicted upon some perceived deserters was not suffered by all of them. Bennett still had many supporters, including a group of men on the hospital ship *Manunda*, who draped a banner over the side declaring, 'We Want Bennett.' This would have been of some comfort to the 8th Division's ex-commander, given the opprobrium he had endured at the hands of some of his brother officers in recent years.

Though the sign was confiscated by the authorities at the time, it later found its way into Bennett's car and remained one of his most prized possessions until his death.[20]

When the vessel docked in Sydney Harbour a reporter on the wharf spotted Bennett pacing up and down in a grey homburg, seemingly anxious about the response he'd get from returning soldiers.

'Inside the man's innermost mind was an unvoiced thought, "Are they going to be for me or against me?"'

'He need not have worried,' wrote Gilbert Mant, who had himself been a member of the 8th Division and had been a Reuters correspondent throughout the Malaya campaign. 'The men were for him. As they clustered around him and grasped his hand on the deck of the hospital ship, some said there were tears in the eyes of the tough, pugnacious General the Japs had tried so hard to kill.'[21]

Mant reported that the men from the 8th Division greeted Bennett with enthusiasm, crying out, 'Good on you, sir', and 'We are with you' as they crowded around their former chief.

'It was the vindication he wanted most of all: the faith of the rank and file. In the three years of frustration after his escape from Singapore, he had been the victim of a smear campaign and had developed almost a persecution complex. The knowledge that most of his men, who had had plenty of time to brood over the matter, were behind him, was a heart-warming experience,' Mant wrote.[22]

Although so many of the army staff had come out against Bennett, some senior officers who had been under his command remained stubbornly faithful, including Lieutenant-Colonel 'Black Jack' Galleghan, who had looked after the Australian POWs in Changi. He claimed to have never met a soldier who disagreed with Bennett's decision to escape.

'Whether a General in war is right or wrong . . . is determined by what his soldiers think and not by the opinions of his contemporaries. In the case of General Bennett there is no doubt what his soldiers thought,' he would later state.[23]

The groundswell of opinion in support of Gordon Bennett was in sharp contrast to the official position of the military, who wanted to exact retribution on the recalcitrant general once and for all.

The stage was set for his ritual humiliation on 26 October at Victoria Barracks, the stately edifice that sits between Oxford Street and Moore Park Road in Sydney's eastern suburbs. Much to the annoyance of the media it was to be a closed court, denying the press access to the proceedings and robbing the public of a comprehensive and impartial account of the evidence.

Bennett also objected to the private nature of the court, but as it was a military inquiry the army could write the rules. The arrangement also satisfied the government, which could distance itself from the investigation and any final ruling which went against public opinion.

But anybody who thought the inquiry would go to plan did not know Gordon Bennett and his propensity for fireworks.

Chapter 17

LIVING CADAVERS IN FILTHY RAGS

Today there are few old soldiers left to bear witness to the tragedy that enveloped Malaya, Thailand, Burma, Borneo, Indochina, the Dutch East Indies and New Guinea, but thanks to the testimony of those 8th Division members who spoke and wrote of their ordeal in later life, Australia has a detailed record of this dark period in history.

Alan Gaudry, who became enforced slave labour on the Burma-Thai Railway, would never forget the army doctors and medical orderlies whose heroic efforts helped to keep the death toll down.

'Denied the use of even the most basic drugs and medicines and using the most primitive of instruments for surgery, they performed prodigies of improvisation and saved many lives,' he wrote in his memoir.[1]

On one occasion he recalled seeing a doctor amputating an ulcerated leg on a bamboo platform out in the open, using butchers' knives and cleavers, a tenon saw and a needle and thread. The 'anaesthetic' was supplied by a former professional boxer, who knocked out the patient with a blow to the jaw.

Then there was the utter barbarity of the guards, both Japanese and Korean, who would inflict punishment for the slightest breach of the behaviour code.

'What we did not expect was the senseless violence which became part of our daily existence . . . the sheer pleasure of inflicting pain on others seemed to be the guiding motive behind the beatings and the ingenious tortures which they were so fond of devising.'[2]

What helps a man through such troubled times? Not religion in Alan's case. Few of the army chaplains impressed him with their integrity; least of all the padre who sold a full case of Bibles to the men: the pages were used for making cigarette papers. 'Most of them seemed to us concerned with looking after number one and carrying on their religious feuds to the point where representatives of one denomination would not preside over the burial of men of other denominations,' he claimed.

'Of course I can only speak of my own experience in this matter and things may well have been very different in other places,' he conceded.[3]

Without religious faith to sustain him, the only way Alan could cope with the death and suffering around him was to harden his heart against human emotions such as love and grief.

'I don't want to convey the impression that I had become indifferent to the horrors of war, only that I was able to bear these blows with the same kind of stoicism which enabled me to put up with physical punishment,' he explained.

'The only catch was that I was so successful in insulating myself against the possibility of feeling compassion for the suffering and death of others that, when peace came, I could not break down this wall that I had built around my emotions.'

Throughout his life luck was frequently on his side. Indeed the story of Alan Gaudry is not complete without reference to his remarkable salvation from a watery grave while on a ship to Japan in late 1944.

By now he had left the Burma-Thai Railway and had returned to Singapore, where he was placed on board a captured Dutch inter-island cargo vessel in readiness for further slave labour in Indochina. Fortunately he avoided boarding the *Rakuyo Maru* or the *Kachidoki Maru*, which were packed with Australian and British POWs and which were both sunk a few days later, with heavy loss of life. Instead he joined a convoy of seven large prefabricated merchant ships loaded with more than 30,000 Japanese troops and their equipment, including trucks, tanks and ammunition stores. In addition there were five naval escorts, a large destroyer, three frigates and an anti-aircraft sloop. The convoy would have been a prize target for any passing Allied bomber or submarine.

It was Christmas and Alan, who was also known as 'Butch', counted himself lucky to be allowed to stay on deck as the holds were already bulging with other prisoners.

The convoy sailed uneventfully in a northwesterly direction for the first few days and everybody soon settled into the routine of shipboard life. The sense of calm was not to last. At two o'clock in the morning of the fourth day all hell broke loose when a merchant ship on their port side was hit by one of two torpedoes. There was a massive explosion, which sent a tremendous column of sparks and flares into the sky. The vessel broke in two and sank within a few minutes.

Alan's eyewitness account of this devastating moment is as dramatic now as it would have been had the explosion happened just a few weeks ago.

> Those of us on deck could see shapes of bodies, crates, trucks and all manner of things whirling skywards, then falling as fiery debris back into the sea. The two halves of the stricken ship reared upwards and sank, one half bow first and the other half stern, amid more explosions and a great hissing of steam.
>
> Immediately pandemonium broke out. Every gun that could be brought to bear let fly at nothing in particular, naval guns firing across the water, anti-aircraft guns firing into the air, flares bursting to shed an eerie light over the scene, tracers flying from machine guns and depth charges being dropped by the naval escorts as they dashed around in their efforts to locate submarines. The gun crew on our deck managed to loose off one round in the darkness, whereupon the gun tore itself from the deck and jumped over the stern, taking with it the mounting and most of the gun crew. The machine gun set up on the deck rail above our heads gave us a warning burst, just in case we might have any ideas about taking advantage of the situation.[4]

Escape was the last thing on Alan's mind. He was more concerned about the possibility that his ship would be the next to be hit.

'Even though we were expecting something of this sort, the actual event came as a complete and terrifying surprise and when the same thing happened to the merchant ship on our starboard side an hour or so later we all thought that we would be the next to go.'

Yet again Butch Gaudry's run of luck held good. By dawn the convoy continued its zigzag course across the South China Sea but by night the American subs were back. Two more big merchant ships went down as well as one of the escorting sloops. Nearly every night that followed Butch would see two or three more vessels sunk by a torpedo. Tragically for the Japanese and POWs who went down with them, there was no attempt to pick up survivors.

'We reasoned that if the Japanese cared so little for their own countrymen they would have even less compunction for a shipload of the despised POWs,' he wrote.[5]

Butch Gaudry could not help but think it would be his turn next. It was around this time that his good mate Reg Sandon, from Wollongong, who had been a private attached to 22nd Brigade Headquarters, turned to him and said, 'Butch, I think we'd better start praying.'

Alan didn't need convincing. They knelt on the deck together and prayed 'very earnestly indeed to a God whose existence had not come into my calculations until now and promised to be one of his . . . a promise which I promptly forgot once we were on dry land again.'[6]

Whether by divine intervention or not, the little Dutch trading ship ploughed on undetected by the subs and within a few days Alan and the rest of the POWs on board sighted the mouth of the Saigon River. Even here they were not out of danger because the entrance was heavily mined and there were no charts to help them navigate around the obstacles.

The ship's captain ordered everybody on deck to act as spotters while they nosed their way through the minefield. Once again fortune favoured Alan and his mates, who made it safely upriver to a wharf just south of Saigon.

Along the way they passed more than 40 Japanese vessels, including large passenger liners loaded with about 200,000 Japanese troops and equipment, about to leave for a counter-attack on the Philippines. It was not to happen. At dawn the following day a large force of American bombers put the enemy airfield surrounding Saigon out of action and hit most of the anti–aircraft defences along the river. Soon afterwards a second wave of US divebombers swooped low overhead and destroyed the flotilla before it had any chance to respond.

Alan had a grandstand view of the attack, which left some 43 ships either sunk or burning. The whole counterattack force had been eliminated.

'Butch' Gaudry's war was nothing but action packed. He had escaped injury in the fall of Singapore, suffered hard labour building the Burma–Thai Railway, lost several stone in weight, endured malarial fever and miraculously avoided friendly fire from US submarines on the way to Indochina.

In later life Alan changed his mind about religion, becoming a devout Christian and forgiving his Japanese and Korean tormentors. Despite being told on his return to Australia that he would not make old bones, he took his soldier's settlement and bought a sugar plantation in northern New South Wales, living to the ripe old age of 94.

Many of Alan Gaudry's pals in the 8th Division had similar wartime experiences to his, though not all were lucky enough to survive.

Among those who perished as POWs were Rodney Breavington, who had been a police constable in Fairfield, Victoria, and Victor Gale, who had worked as a turner and fitter in Balwyn, Bennett's home town. Both were privates in the 8th Division who loathed prison life.[7]

In August 1942 there was a noticeable tightening of discipline in Changi when a new Japanese chief, Major-General Shimperi Fukuye, arrived to take command. Until then occasional excursions by POWs beyond the barbed wire had gone largely unpunished but on 30 August everything changed. The Japanese announced that all prisoners would have to sign a document promising not to escape.

This conflicted with the Allies' military code, enshrining the right of every man to try to evade his captors, and all refused to sign.[8]

The Japanese were furious and for the next five days all 20,000 Australian, British and Dutch troops were incarcerated in the barrack buildings and the square. Each man was given two pints of water a day and no one was allowed to leave. The Japs were determined to break their captives' spirit and in a bid to reinforce their message, on the third day announced the planned executions of Breavington, Gale and two British soldiers, Privates Harold Waters and Eric Fletcher. The four had escaped from a camp at Bukit Timah on 12 May and rowed a small boat some 200 miles (320 km) to the island of Colomba. In a ghastly twist of fate, they were re-arrested when they got there and sent back to Singapore. Now was Japan's moment of retribution.

As the Allied troops kicked their heels in the barracks square, creating a tremendous din, General Fukuye ordered the commanders of the British and Australian troops in Changi – Lieutenant-Colonel E.B. Holmes and his deputy, Lieutenant-Colonel 'Black Jack' Galleghan – to be present at the executions.

It was to be a grim but strangely defiant spectacle. As A.J. Sweeting described it in the official history of World War II:

At the execution ground Breavington, the older man, made an appeal to the Japanese to spare Gale. He said that he had ordered Gale to escape and that Gale had merely obeyed orders; this appeal was refused. As the Sikh firing party knelt before the doomed men, the British officers present saluted and the men returned the salute. Breavington walked to the others and shook hands with them. A Japanese lieutenant then came forward with a handkerchief and offered it to Breavington, who waved it aside with a smile, and the offer was refused by all men. Breavington then called to one of the padres present and asked for a New Testament, whence he read a short passage. Thereupon the order was given to fire.[9]

Even then it wasn't over. Whether by nervousness or design, the Indian National Army Guard's bullets failed to kill the poor men so they had to finish them off with a fresh volley.

Word of the executions travelled swiftly around the camp. So far only three soldiers had signed the 'no-escape pledge' but the rest steadfastly refused. After all, under the Geneva Convention every POW had the right to escape and should not be punished if recaptured. The problem was that Japan had not signed the Geneva Convention and Fukuye was infuriated by this mass revolt.

But the reality was that the prisoners could not hold out forever. There were sick and injured who desperately needed treatment and some were beginning to die. In the end the commanders decided to compromise. The troops would sign the pledge under duress. As the Japanese did not recognise English names, the British and the Aussies made them up, signing themselves as Donald Duck and Ned Kelly. It made a nonsense of the contract but it seemed to please the Japanese and life returned to normal.

Interestingly the barrack square incident seemed to cement a new bond between the British and Australians. As Black Jack Galleghan would later write: 'The most notable feature of this incident was the cohesion and the unity of British and Australian troops and the fine morale and spirit shown.'[10]

The order and comparative comfort that set Changi apart from other POW camps helped prisoners hold on to life in mind and body. Sure there was sickness, hunger and boredom, but if you kept your nose clean then Selarang Barracks was almost tolerable.

Pity the poor bastards then who ended up on the Burma–Thai Railway or in the mines and factories of Japan. This was slave labour in the extreme, consigning so many members of the 8th Division to an early death.

Arthur Kennedy found himself working near what would become known as the Bridge on the River Kwai, later to be immortalised in celluloid but in those days a symbol of Japanese oppression. Arthur's first task was to build an earthen embankment which was to rise to a height of 50 feet (15 m).

'Each day we were required to dig and move a cubic metre [35 cubic feet] of soil. The soil was dug out by one man and then two men carried it in stretchers, dumping it to form the embankment. During each carry the man in the hole dug out earth for the next load.'

It was back-breaking toil, digging, lifting and carrying huge piles of soil in high humidity and under a burning sun. Sometimes they had elephants to help them drag tree trunks up to the embankment but the animals often resisted working on steep slopes and the prisoners were forced to do the job themselves. This gave rise to the popular catch-cry from Japanese guards that one elephant equalled ten Australians.

'Ropes were used on big logs and there was always the danger that they would slip due to the greasy conditions. By the time a day had been spent on this work a team would be completely exhausted.'[11]

And no health and safety either – far from it. When the men slowed down the guards hit them with bamboo poles. When the Japs used explosives to shift the rock there was no warning and no shelter from the tumbling debris.

'Not everyone was lucky and one day a single rock reached the embankment and killed a man.'[12]

'Bluey' Kennedy protested but the complaints had no effect. The guards would merely laugh and increase the workload. Exhaustion, injury and sickness were no excuse: there was a bridge to build and they would have to stay there until it was finished.

'Soon we were completely exhausted by the lack of sleep. Completing the task was aided by the constant application by the Japanese of bamboo rods to the nearest body as a spur to greater effort. By the end of the raising of what looked like a mountain we could only crawl back to the camp. Without thinking of food or washing everybody collapsed into their tents and slept.'[13]

And so it went on, day after debilitating day, until the job was done and they were marched to the next section. This was conveyor-belt torture – toil without end – the work just kept coming. Only death could provide a blessed release.

The number of sick had increased dramatically and several men were already dead from malnutrition or disease. Cholera was also soon to take its toll. An isolation hut was built and two medical orderlies volunteered to look after the sick; a considerable act of courage as the slightest relaxation of personal hygiene might have infected them too. Thankfully the two survived but it was too late for those who had already contracted the disease. Within a few days 16 men in Arthur Kennedy's camp were dead.

It wasn't only the Japanese who inflicted pain upon the prisoners. John Chippendale claimed the Korean guards were even worse. They had names for these sadists such as Boy Bastard and BBC, which stood for Boy Bastard's Cobber, individuals whose cruelty knew no bounds.

'One of our sergeants went into the bush to relieve himself when a Korean guard shot him in the face and chest at close range – he thought he was escaping,' said John.[14]

Then there was the weather and the disease.

'I was on a working party that was sent out to repair a bridge which had been washed away, during the wet season when the rain fell day and night. We stayed on the job 72 hours without a break. After we finished I came down with dysentery, malaria and very bad beri beri,' John wrote.[15]

He survived thanks to the efforts of his old mate Ken Ducros, who was also with 8th Division Signals. The fellow Sydney boy nursed and spoon-fed John back to health in a makeshift hospital, but others were not so fortunate.

'At this camp were some of the worst leg ulcers that anyone can imagine. Colonel Coates, our senior surgeon, was taking off about six legs a day. No one could imagine the horrific conditions that they had to contend with.'[16]

Come December 1943 many of the Australians who had been sent to work on the Burma–Thai Railway returned to Changi. First word of their condition and impending arrival

came from Sydney-born Major Albert Saggers of the 2/4th
Machine Gun Battalion, who had escorted the body of an
Aussie soldier back to Singapore for burial. He immediately
informed Black Jack Galleghan, who was in charge of the
AIF in Changi and advised fellow officers that the news was
not encouraging. In fact that was an understatement.

As the trucks containing the POWs pulled up in the camp
in the early hours of 16 December, the men who had assembled on the roadside to welcome them back were so shocked
by the sight they beheld that many gasped in horror. Those
members of the 8th Division who had left earlier in the year
were barely recognisable.

As Stan Arneil described it in Galleghan's biography: 'It
was a slow and ghastly business, there were no leaps from the
back of trucks, no sounds of cheering, just a slow and stum-
bling movement as the skeletons helped one another to the
ground.'[17]

They were like living cadavers, clothed in filthy rags and
many near to death. Most were suffering from beri beri, their
legs like tree trunks. The majority could not stand upright;
others were so incapacitated they were forced to lie on the
ground. Yet despite their physical state, those who were able
to do so formed a straight line before their commander.

Galleghan was momentarily perplexed and enquired
where the rest of his battalion were.

'They're all here, sir,' replied Sergeant-Major Noel
Johnston.[18]

Were his eyes deceiving him? Galleghan was confounded.
Hadn't 651 men of his own unit originally left for Thailand?
A quick head count revealed only 459 had come back. There
could be only one conclusion. One hundred and ninety-two

of his own soldiers had died in the past seven months. Galleghan was speechless. He would later discover that more than half of the 7000 Australian and British troops who had been used as slave labour on the Burma-Thai Railway were dead.

———·——

Fortunately for Arthur Kennedy, whether by luck, will-power or a strong a constitution, he managed to survive the railway and eventually found himself en route for a new destination. Even today few people know that there were more than 100 prisoner-of-war camps in Japan, and that's where Kennedy was heading. Thousands of other Australians were also shipped to the land of the rising sun, where in many ways work, weather and living conditions were even more extreme.

Those members of the 8th Division who felt they'd already suffered enough in the jungles of Malaya and Thailand would be in for an even bigger shock on the Emperor's home soil. The 2/20th Battalion had been assured they were going on holiday when they sailed for the Japanese port city of Nagasaki. Nobody believed it but it broke the boredom. There were 550 Aussies aboard the *Kamakura Maru* but they would form two parties once on dry land. Three hundred would be chosen for the next stage of the journey – by rail to the coastal town of Naoetsu, roughly halfway up the west coast of Japan.

It was early December and bitingly cold when the train finally pulled in to the minor industrial town northwest of Tokyo. On the last stretch the POWs passed two factories – the Shin-Etsu Chemical Company and the Nippon

Stainless Steel plant – where they would labour for nearly three years in the most appalling conditions. When they weren't working they would be subject to another reign of terror, as civilian guards beat them into submission in the prison camp.

'They were a pretty vicious mob,' said George Daldry, the Sydney kid who was used to looking after himself. 'Sometimes the guards would work on the same person each shift until he could take it no longer.'[19]

Cruel and sadistic, the guards took immense pleasure in meting out their particular brand of bashing, which came in the form of a thick 3-foot (1 m) long stick known as the dog walloper.

More than six decades later Joe Byrne could remember every agonising detail.

'It was rounded hard wood and they used it like a baseball bat. They'd break arms, legs, ribs and anything else they could take a poke at. They just beat the hell out of you. You were always at the whim of the guards, which meant they could clobber you for no reason at all.'[20]

The jobs were exhausting and uncomfortable. Some men were made to work in scorching temperatures shovelling coal into furnaces, while others would unload coal from ships in the harbour. It was back-breaking labour, and all this was on measly rations that made the men susceptible to illness.

'Felt very weak today,' Signalman Don Fraser scribbled in his diary. 'Too weak to lift an empty shovel really. Food less than half of what we need. Little bit of horse in the stew but only as big as a sixpence. It was an old horse at that, but lovely to chew.'[21]

The extreme weather, which could be intensely hot in summer and bitterly cold in winter, didn't help matters. It was inevitable that sooner or later the lack of food and heavy workload in tough conditions would start to claim victims. More and more men were falling seriously ill because of lack of food. How long before they started dying?

Dudley Boughton, a carpenter from Manly, witnessed the slow disintegration of his mates after each day's work.

'Another chap carried home tonight which brings it up to five in a row. One had pleurisy and several have bronchitis. We're so terribly hungry it hurts.'[22]

Kevin Timbs was hit with a strain of pneumonia so severe that he could hardly get out of bed for morning parade. The guards showed no mercy, ordering him to work regardless. Only his pals were able to save him.

'The next morning I went out with one each side of me holding me up because my legs just wouldn't work. Eventually I got over it, but that's the sort of thing that happened.'[23]

By the middle of 1943 diseases like malaria and treatable conditions such as beri beri were also taking their toll. Diaries that the POWs kept were now recording almost a death a day. The passing of a mate was so normal that it was usually dismissed in one line.

The guards took particular delight in targeting those who were obviously sick, men who were suffering from dysentery or beri beri. To mark them apart they were made to pin red ribbons on their coats, ostensibly to identify them as members of the so-called light-duty party. The name had little effect on the way they were treated. It simply made the guards' job easier in selecting those who needed a little extra physical encouragement.

As they crawled to work, they would be struck by dog wallopers for falling behind the main group. Private John Cook, who was born in Sydney's Clovelly, remembered it vividly.

'As the men suffering from dysentery and severe diarrhoea were not allowed to stop on the way to the factory to go to the toilet, they had no choice other than to defecate in their trousers. This meant that the excreta would finish in their boots and remain there for the whole day, or in some cases, until they were allowed to have a bath under the furnace prior to returning to the camp.'[24]

All this and random bashings too. One man was so ill with diarrhoea that he dirtied his bed. Lance-Corporal John Magin was trying to clean up the mess when a young Japanese medical guard walked in, screaming abuse. Jimmy Houston reckoned it was the worst violence he'd seen.

'He made this chap take off his clothes then laid into him with a thick leather belt. His body was a mass of bruises. After he got tired of using the belt he kicked him a number of times in the stomach, then made the poor chap do press-ups for an hour. When he finished doing that he was told to stand to attention to 5 am. All this happened because he was sick. This guard is nothing but an animal.'[25]

If you were suffering from beri beri, which was caused by thiamine deficiency, the daily grind was even more painful. The whole body would bloat to enormous proportions.

'The face would be swollen so much that the eyes were just narrow slits,' recalled John Cook. 'Walking became very painful as the thighs used to rub together, causing the skin to rub off. The testicles would be the size of tennis balls and the penis looked like a white cucumber. Men with this complaint still had to go to work. You had to be almost completely immobilised before being allowed to stay in the sick room.'[26]

Much further south, in the Dutch East Indies, the 2/21st Battalion of the 8th Division was in a similar situation on the island of Ambon. Hunger, disease, brutality and low morale only added to the dire plight of Gull Force, who had been imprisoned there since February 1942.

The daily food ration was down to just shy of half a pound (200 g) and the ever-present threat of death by the sword hung over everyone from one minute to the next. And as if conditions weren't bad enough, the POWs' commanding officer was about to make it worse.

Within this bleak landscape Major George de Verdon Westley decided to impose his own home-grown brand of discipline on the men by building a cage – a barbed-wire encircled contraption – designed to hold petty thieves and malcontents. Just six-and-a-half feet (2 m) square, it was a box within a barracks, within a jail, within an island prison. Not surprisingly the fact that Aussies were being jailed by other Australians did not go down too well.

It was inside this uncomfortable holding pen that POWs found guilty of stealing another's food were kept overnight with minimum rations, the idea being that it was a convenient way of punishing men and to send a lesson to the rest of the camp.

It's possible to see both points of view here. Perhaps Westley's controversial prison was ultimately in the interests of the camp as a whole. But some of those imprisoned in the cage died after the experience and few could forgive Westley for his role in it.

As the war rolled on, there were countless random bashings from the captors. Anybody who attempted to escape was
beaten savagely and some were threatened with execution.
Significantly it did not deter everybody. Here was a group of
men imprisoned some 590 miles (950 km) north of Darwin,
stranded right in the middle of nowhere, yet they never gave
up hope of getting back to Australia.

Among them was Lieutenant William Jinkins, who used
a small outrigger to sail from Ambon, and along the way
hijacked a 40-foot motor cruiser. It was an epic voyage, which
took about seven weeks, but amazingly he made it home.[27]

But for the rest of the men the mental and physical torture
continued. As the period of imprisonment dragged on, even
the tradition of supporting and helping your mates was being
undermined.

Ralph Godfrey, who like most of the 2/21st Battalion came
from Victoria, told me: 'There was absolutely no Australian
mateship for 18 months – it was every man for himself. If he
got something, he kept it; he didn't share it with anybody.'[28]

To make matters worse, a terrible tragedy occurred on
25 February 1943, when Ambon was bombed by a squadron
of US Liberators. In their wisdom the Japanese had decided
to store all their arsenal – about 200,000 pounds of explosives – right by the side of the prison camp.

It was a disaster waiting to happen. The POWs were quick
to realise that if the camp was ever bombed they'd go up
with it. And so it happened. As a result, among the 30 people
killed were six Australian officers.

Meanwhile the starvation diet continued and death became
an almost daily occurrence.

One of the prisoners, Stuart Swanton, was an experienced

stenographer and kept a daily diary of his three-and-a-half years on Ambon, all of it written in tiny shorthand notes. Today they make grim but fascinating reading. On 11 August 1944 he wrote: 'Jim Harvey died last night. I carried about two barrow loads of soil to my garden during the day. Cooked some cassava, paw paws, greens and had them for tea, Also had a bit of salmon which was beautiful.'[29]

How sad that the passing of a dear friend was dismissed in one line, while what he had to eat was deemed to be much more important. But that was the reality of POW life.

Eventually, under Westley's tough leadership, a subtle change came about in the men's social behaviour. The mateship that had been so sadly absent in the early days of incarceration began to return and a new spirit of mutual cooperation evolved, with the POWs forming themselves into small syndicates of four to five men. If they were to survive, they realised, they'd have to help each other and the syndicates proved to be a lifesaving move. If anybody fell ill the others would look after them. If somebody needed food they would share their own rations.

What a turnaround from the dark days that had gone before. In a strange way the camp had come to symbolise all that was right and wrong in society. It proved there were no easy answers to mankind's problems and that only the love and care of one's fellow man really mattered.

Unhappily this was of little consolation to those who didn't make it. A total of 378 prisoners of war died on Ambon, including the 328 massacred at the Laha airbase in the early days of the invasion. Perhaps fortuitously, details of that atrocity did not emerge until 1945. Until then the other POWs who had been held in the main camp on Ambon remained unaware of their comrades' fate. One wonders how their mood might have changed had they known earlier.

Gull Force was eventually evacuated from Ambon in September 1945. Out of 528 Australians who had been left there on October 1942, following the departure of the rest of the battalion for the Chinese island of Hainan, only 121 were still alive. As they assembled on the wharf to be evacuated by the navy, they were a sorry sight. Those who were able to stand joked and chatted with the incapacitated lying on stretchers.

One of the first Australian ships to arrive was the *Latrobe*, whose captain, Lieutenant-Commander Windas Smith, was momentarily stunned by what he saw.

'When we did berth there were 20 to 30 skeletons on the jetty, as if they were standing in front of Buckingham Palace, and there wasn't a dry eye on the ship,' he said.[30]

How they succeeded in standing to attention on legs as 'thin as matchsticks and knees like oversized cricket balls' would haunt the skipper for the rest of his life.[31]

There was no time to waste. Of the 42 men on stretchers some needed to be evacuated immediately, such was their physical state. The most common complaints were malaria, dysentery, tropical ulcers and severe malnutrition.

Could this really be happening? Were they about to be rescued? As if to break the spell of years of captivity, a little homegrown sustenance was produced. Mugs of sweet tea and plates of Vegemite sandwiches suddenly appeared before the POWs were carried aboard.[32]

There were tears as the men sailed out of Ambon harbour on the four corvettes that had come to evacuate them.

They were bound for the island of Morotai, where there was a hospital and plenty of medical care. After a two-day voyage they were welcomed by a military band and a fleet of ambulances.

Melbourne boy Eddie 'Max' Gilbert looked at his watch and noted the time. It was exactly 8 am. After three-and-a-half years of hell, freedom beckoned.

'We were immediately transported and put to bed. The sight of Australian army sisters was wonderful. It's hard to express one's feelings at seeing civilisation, white men's food and sleeping between sheets,' he recalled.[33]

Heartbreakingly two men from Gull Force didn't make it. They were so weak and sick they died on Morotai, casting a cloud over the excitement and sense of relief that had engulfed the rest of the battalion.

Within a couple of weeks the survivors were sufficiently recovered to sail home aboard the hospital ship *Wanganella*. Like the rest of the 8th Division's men scattered across Asia, they were on their way back to Australia. Unlike Gordon Bennett they had endured the physical consequences of defeat and the subjugation that inevitably followed. But did it matter anymore? And did Australia really care?

By the end of October 1945, most of the men from the 8th Division were home. They'd had three-and-a-half years to ponder their plight; now they wanted to put it all behind them. Thrust back into civilian life, trying to adjust to their newfound freedom did not come easily. There were families, wives and girlfriends to get to know again. Some men were still suffering from the effects of disease and starvation. Others were emotional and mental wrecks. How could they explain what had happened to those who had never been there? No one could fully understand what it meant to have been a prisoner of war except other POWs.

The scale of their personal hell would silence many for the rest of their lives. Few would talk about it to loved ones. For some the only way of escaping the mental isolation was with booze. Others could only share their bitter memories with fellow veterans down at the RSL or on Anzac Day marches. Dressed in their neat, grey trousers and navy blue blazers, with medals proudly pinned, they would recall the hunger, the sickness and the brutality that haunted their lives on a daily basis, while also remembering the jokes, the gambling and the black humour that took their minds off the terrible conditions and helped to boost morale.

But for now these men were caught up in the drama of reaching Australia. For some the years away had been so intense that their country of birth had become a distant memory. Thousands more had made the ultimate sacrifice. Would they be remembered as well? No wonder so many soldiers of the 8th Division were apprehensive and consumed by trepidation as they sailed into Sydney Harbour.

When Alan 'Butch' Gaudry, who was so fortunate to have come through the war relatively unscathed, finally stepped back on home soil, his main concern was not what had happened before but what sort of reception he and his pals would get from the people of Australia, especially from the soldiers of other fighting divisions.

'After all, ours was the first Australian force of Divisional strength ever to have surrendered en-masse to an enemy. We thought that by not fighting to the bitter end we had left our country exposed to invasion and conquest by a ruthless foe. At least some of us would not have been surprised if we had been ostracised by a public unaware of the valiant show our men had put up in the battle for Malaya and Singapore,' he explained many years later.[34]

Alan need not have worried. His hero's welcome put an end to any lingering doubts.

Gordon Bennett could not be similarly assured as he waited for the court of inquiry to assemble in Sydney's Victoria Barracks. While he had put up a good fight during the Malaya campaign, he had not shared the suffering of the men he had left behind as prisoners of war. While he was escaping by sampan, his men were about to face an indefinite period of captivity in subhuman conditions. While he would spend the next three-and-a-half years a free man, those whom he had commanded would be doomed to a life of hunger, disease and random brutality at the hands of their new masters.

Would Bennett's argument that he needed to return to Australia in order to brief the government and the military on enemy tactics stand up to close examination? Would Australia's fair-go attitude give him the benefit of the doubt? Would the military forgive and forget? More specifically would the perception that he had cut and run be upheld by the officers who now sat in judgement on him?

Bennett's character was about to be tested in a manner he had never experienced in war. Finally his reputation was on the line and there was no one else to take the blame.

Chapter 18

BENNETT PLEADS HIS CASE

The *Concise Oxford Dictionary* defines the word 'surrender' as to 'hand over and to give in to another's power or control'. Whereas the word 'capitulation' also means surrender, but 'on stated conditions'.

This small but significant difference was to vex many legal and military minds in both the army's court of inquiry into Gordon Bennett and the Royal Commission which was to follow.

At the initial inquiry the terms of reference required the court to address the following issues:

- What was the precise time that the surrender and/or capitulation of the Allied forces took place?
- Was Bennett at any stage under Percival's command?
- Did Bennett relinquish his command of the 8th Division?
- If so, did Bennett have Percival's permission to stand down?
- Did he have a responsibility to stay with his men?

- Did he issue an order that all members of the 8th Division were to remain at their posts and officers with them?
- And could Bennett at any time be considered a prisoner of war?

This last question was the key to Bennett's guilt or innocence. Officially only a prisoner of war had a duty to escape, but when could that classification be made? After the ceasefire? After the surrender was signed? Or when the men entered the prison camp? Given that the surrender was to take effect from 8.30 pm on 15 February 1942, the timing of Bennett's escape soon after 10 pm could be crucial to his defence.

The prominent king's counsel Brian Clancy was to represent Gordon Bennett at the Victoria Barracks hearing, which got underway on 26 October 1945. And from the beginning it was clear that his client had instructed him to go on the attack, questioning the validity of the proceedings on several grounds.

Clancy argued that the court was not properly constituted and only a full judicial inquiry free from military affiliations was appropriate.

He also alleged that General Victor Stantke, who was one of the officers sitting in judgement, was biased against Bennett.[1]

From the outset of the hearing the atmosphere in the room was heated. Lieutenant-General Sir Leslie Morshead, who was president of the inquiry, overruled the lawyer's objections, at which point Bennett, on the advice of his counsel, refused to take part.

This placed Bennett in an invidious position. His withdrawal from the inquiry meant that he no longer had the right to defend himself in court or call witnesses. But while some might assume this would weaken his case, Bennett had a far more effective trick up his sleeve. He would wage his defence through the media, issuing a long and detailed statement to the newspapers addressing all the issues raised by the court.

A total of nine witnesses were called during the military inquiry:

- Brigadier Callaghan, 8th Division's artillery commander and the man who took over from Bennett after his escape.
- Colonel (later to become Brigadier) John Broadbent, who had been chosen by Bennett to evacuate from Singapore and sail back to Australia two days before the surrender.
- Colonel J.H. Thyer, from Natimuk in Victoria, who had been Bennett's chief staff officer in the 8th Division.
- Ballarat-born Brigadier Charles Kappe, who was the Division's Chief Signals Officer.
- Colonel Wilfred (later to become Sir) Kent Hughes, who succeeded Broadbent as Assistant Adjutant and Quartermaster-General.
- Lieutenant-Colonel I.J. O'Donnell, Chief Engineering Officer.
- Captains Adrian Curlewis and Harry Jessup, both of them general staff officers under Bennett.
- And finally Lieutenant-Colonel Charles Moses, who had accompanied Bennett on his escape but had eventually got back to Australia some weeks after his commander.

Of the nine, Moses and Kent Hughes were the most supportive of Bennett's decision to escape.

The early stages of the inquiry were dominated by questions designed to establish when news of the commander's intentions emerged.

Lieutenant-Colonel Kappe told the court that the general first revealed details of his plan as early as 29 January, in Johore Bahru. This was before the Allies had even fallen back across the causeway. If this were true then it suggested that Bennett had been formulating his escape plan more than a fortnight before the fall of Singapore.

On 14 February Kappe had heard rumours about the formation of a Headquarters escape party but it was not until the following day that Bennett told him directly that he was going to leave.

Kappe said he did not think too much about the General's comments at the time, given that the military position appeared so hopeless. But he did recall a general order on the day of surrender that all men were to remain at their positions. However, he told the court he could not remember if Bennett had ordered his officers to stay with them.[2]

Major-General Callaghan said he had heard rumours of the General's escape plans but had not taken them seriously. He understood that the commander had ordered the men to remain in their positions and that officers were to stay with them, a claim that was validated by the Royal Australian Artillery's war diary.[3]

Captain Curlewis confirmed that he had been told about Bennett's intentions four days before the capitulation. He remembered discussing the possibilities with Moses and Gordon Walker as they pored over maps for the best route back to Australia. Curlewis later questioned 'the ethics of this show' and conceded he had a vague memory of an order that there was to be no breakaway escape by any members of the AIF.[4]

Captain Jessup told the military inquiry that he had also considered escaping but gave up the idea when he heard that

Bennett had ordered his soldiers to stay in position. This view was reinforced in evidence given by O'Donnell and Thyer, the latter of whom insisted that Bennett had spelled it out during a meeting on the morning of 15 February that no one was to leave the perimeter.

What had Bennett been up to? Was he on a mission to confuse his colleagues, imparting the truth about his plans to some, while demanding strict adherence to military protocol from others? If this was his strategy, it appeared to have worked.

Only Kent Hughes had an accurate picture of the General's dangerous undertaking. He told the court that he was under the impression it was general knowledge at Divisional Headquarters and, more pertinently, that he intended to escape *after* the capitulation.

Hours after the surrender document had been signed Bennett took Kent Hughes into his confidence and sought his views on whether he should escape or not. Kent Hughes suggested only he could make such a decision. He told Bennett to consider his responsibility to his troops as a whole but also his responsibility to the Australian government.

According to the Colonel, Bennett replied, 'In respect of my responsibility to the Australian government I feel that I should try and get back if I can – I intend to have a go.'

Bennett said he was confident Kent Hughes, Thyer and Callaghan could handle the job if he left and was satisfied he could not make better arrangements for the men in his absence.

Kent Hughes, who went on to become a government minister in civilian life, replied that he would support his commander and never utter a word of criticism against him.[5] It was a promise he kept until the end.

Their final farewell in Singapore happened 20 minutes before the official ceasefire at 8.30 pm, when the two men took their leave and Bennett went off in search of Callaghan and Thyer to say goodbye.

The last witness, Lieutenant-Colonel Charles Moses, and one of Bennett's closest allies, confirmed details of the escape and pointed out that Major-General Callaghan had wished them good luck on their journey.

It was now left to the president of the court to assess the evidence and make his findings, which were handed down on 31 October 1945.

The outcome was not unexpected, given the army's influence in the investigation and the staff officers' antipathy towards Bennett.

The inquiry found against him on all counts but most significantly that he relinquished his command without the permission of Lieutenant-General Percival, who as Britain's General Officer Commanding in Malaya was in overall control.[6]

This was a severe blow to Bennett, who had believed that he was no longer answerable to Percival after the surrender.

The problem was that the surrender took place in phases. First came the ceasefire at 8.30 pm on 15 February. Secondly the stockpiling of weapons under Japanese supervision at 10 am the following morning. And thirdly the movement of Australian troops to Changi, which began on 17 February and did not conclude until 20 February. As a result of this lengthy process, Bennett did not become a prisoner of war at 8.30 pm on 15 February, the court decided.

So when did the surrender take place? Unfortunately the court was unable to determine this important fact. Although the ceasefire time had been common to all parties, there was no incontrovertible evidence to ascertain the exact time the British forces commenced their surrender.[7]

Bennett must have been dumbfounded by the court's interpretation of the facts. It was a muddle. But to cover up the haphazard manner of their findings, the inquiry believed it was important to make one thing clear. After the ceasefire order and until the conditions of the surrender had been implemented, command and control of the troops had to be maintained. And Bennett should have been responsible for this. If the Australian command structure had failed during this period, the repercussions could have been serious, the inquiry noted.

As a result the court concluded that it was Bennett's duty to remain at his post, unless relieved of his command by proper authority or held captive as a prisoner of war.[8]

Quoting Percival's words, the president, Lieutenant-General Morshead, found that Lieutenant-General Bennett had 'voluntarily and without permission relinquished command of the AIF on February 15, 1942.'

And to reinforce the point, he added: 'The court is of the opinion, on the evidence, that Lieutenant-General Henry Gordon Bennett was not justified in handing over his command or in leaving Singapore.'[9]

For the moment the military might have won the battle but they hadn't won the war. The question now facing the army hierarchy was how to deal with Bennett. Should he be charged with desertion or should the matter be laid to rest?

Blamey was left in no doubt that Bennett's actions

constituted a grave military offence and in normal circumstances he would be charged with desertion. But given the massive public and political interest in the case he realised that the government might not agree, so he suggested two other options. Either Bennett should be retired from the army or the government should hold a Royal Commission into his behaviour.

The commander's escape from Singapore had transfixed the nation. Newspapers were full of letters about the rights or wrongs of his actions. A readers' poll published in the *Sydney Sunday Telegraph* revealed that 123 people supported a full and open inquiry compared with 60 who believed the matter should be closed.[10]

Even the men from Bennett's own division weighed in to the debate and sent a telegram to the prime minister supporting their former commander. Not only did they want a public inquiry into the circumstances of their leader's escape but they also demanded an investigation into the entire ill-fated Malayan campaign. There was no doubt where their loyalties lay.

'Further this Association wholeheartedly supports General Bennett's actions in successfully escaping from Singapore,' the telegram concluded.[11]

The 6th Battalion Association also requested a Royal Commission 'to clear once and for all his reputation and that of 18,000 good Australian soldiers and satisfy over one million soldiers plus their dependents'.[12]

Under pressure from Blamey, the public and the men, the government had no alternative but to agree to an open inquiry under the auspices of a judge.

On the face of it Bennett was more than satisfied. Now

he could have his day in court and no one would be able to prevent his words from being reported.

'I welcome the inquiry and I want to have the whole matter cleared up as soon as possible,' he wrote in a telegram to the Minister for Defence.[13]

Was this a genuine response or was he merely putting on a brave face? Privately, Bennett must have had his reservations about further questioning of his motives and the events surrounding his departure from Singapore, given that many of the same witnesses would be called. The findings of the military court had gone against him. Why would a Royal Commission be any different?

This was to be an anxious period for the man who had led the 8th Division in Malaya and whose character and standing as a senior officer were on the line. Would Gordon Bennett go down in history as a deserter or a man of solid moral principles who always had the interests of Australia at heart?

The next few weeks would establish the truth one way or the other.

———·———

The Royal Commission got underway in Melbourne on 26 November 1945 and ran until 13 December. The judge appointed to investigate the issue was Mr Justice George Coutts Ligertwood of the South Australian Supreme Court. Fundamentally his brief was to establish the circumstances surrounding Bennett's decision to relinquish his command and his subsequent escape from Singapore. He would also try to ascertain whether Bennett had the necessary permission to do so from the appropriate authority and if he was at any time classified as a prisoner of war.

Finally the Commissioner had to decide whether, as the commander of the 8th Division and GOC of the AIF in Malaya, Bennett had a duty to remain with his troops or was justified in relinquishing his command and leaving Singapore.[14]

All this depended on the commissioner's interpretation of the rules governing the decision to surrender to an enemy. Essentially we were back to the same questions that had dominated the earlier military court. Did the document signed by Percival agree to an unconditional surrender at 8.30 pm on 15 February 1942 or did it amount to a capitulation? If it was the former then Bennett had every right under military law to attempt to escape. However, if it was a capitulation he could not be classed as a POW at that stage and would therefore not have had the automatic right to escape.

In the International Convention Concerning the Laws and Customs of War on Land, which was signed by 41 countries – including Japan and Britain – at the Hague in 1907, article 35 dealt with capitulation but, surprisingly, did not offer a precise meaning.

According to the military's general interpretation of capitulation it is a surrender, but on certain conditions. The 1941 Australian edition of the *Manual of Military Law* shines further light on the issue: 'Capitulations are agreements entered into between the commanders of armed forces of belligerents concerning the terms of surrender of a body of troops, a fortress or other defended places.'[15]

But other specialists in the interpretation of military law would later point out that there was no precise time that expressly confirmed when a soldier becomes a prisoner. As the eminent lawyer Thomas Fry wrote in the *University of Queensland Law Journal* in 1948: 'There is no treaty provision defining the moment at which a combatant becomes a prisoner-of-war. The change of status occurs when the over-riding power of control over him passes from his own commander to the enemy.'[16]

So did POW status occur when the surrender was signed or when the ceasefire took effect at 8.30 pm? Or could it have been any time between the laying down of arms at 10 am the following morning and the arrival of the last of the Allied troops at Changi on 20 February?

This was beginning to sound like the age-old philosophical question about how many angels could dance on the head of a pin. No one knew the answer, and outside this courtroom it didn't really matter anyway. The fact was that the Allies had thrown in the towel on 15 February and Gordon Bennett saw no further point in staying. Whether it amounted to an unconditional surrender or not was academic. Forget the niceties of military law. They were all now prisoners of war, like it or lump it.

Certainly the Japanese had no doubt about the situation. When Percival signed the surrender document at 5 pm on 15 February he came under General Yamashita's command and thereby gave up his own authority. This is unequivocally the case, judging by the report that appeared in the *Japan Times and Advertiser.* 'Finally at [5 pm Singapore time] on February 15, the enemy surrendered, although their military strength was several times that of our forces.'[17]

Even if one disputes the exact timing, there is a strong case to suggest that the surrender happened a few hours later, when the ceasefire came into force.

As the distinguished lawyer Mark Clisby explains in his own investigation of the case: 'The use of the phrase "cessation of hostilities" in the Bukit Timah memorandum indicated that the signatories intended a surrender to come into effect the moment the hostilities ceased at 8.30 pm. Hostilities were to cease permanently, which is characteristic of a surrender. This is in contrast to an armistice, which admits a mere suspension of hostilities.'[18]

Interestingly the Hague Convention of 1907, which was agreed to by Britain and Japan, was not signed by Australia, so the extent to which Canberra was bound by the provisions of that understanding is debatable.

Justice Ligertwood was only concerned with international law during the course of his inquiry and although Australia might have abided by the terms of the Convention it didn't have to, as Clisby makes clear.

'It may not have had a legal obligation to do so because there existed no express Australian legislation which incorporated the provisions of the Hague Convention into Australian municipal or military law. Moreover, a compelling argument can be presented that Mr Justice Ligertwood should have looked at the issues in the Gordon Bennett case from the viewpoint of Australian domestic law and Australian military law, rather than the rules of international law.'[19]

Be that as it may, the legal parameters were in place and the Royal Commission was determined to investigate every minute detail and analyse every grain of evidence in pursuit of the truth. In so doing, much of the hearing got bogged down in legal technicalities such as the accepted definitions for surrender, capitulation, ceasefire and armistice.

Understandably the army brought in two of their big guns as expert witnesses to offer their considered opinions of Bennett's status at the time of his escape. Major-General Charles Lloyd, who was Adjutant General of the Australian Army, and Major-General J.B. Wilson, the Judge Advocate General, left no doubt about their views on Bennett's conduct.

'A soldier becomes a prisoner-of-war when he is under the physical control of the enemy, when he is in the control of his captors,' said Lloyd.

By that definition, at no time after 8.30 pm on 15 February until 20 February could Bennett be described as a POW.

Asked again to comment on Bennett's view that he had become a prisoner of war at 8.30 pm, Lloyd replied, 'Rubbish!'

It wasn't the sort of expletive one would expect to hear in the rarified atmosphere of a Royal Commission, but it demonstrated the level of anti-Bennett sentiment among most of the witnesses. It was a perception that Brian Clancy, Bennett's lawyer, was to raise when during cross-examination he asked Lloyd if his answer had been 'tinged with spleen'.

Lloyd denied the claim but dug an even bigger hole for himself when he was asked to define the word 'unconditional'. Lloyd said that he would like to refer to a dictionary before replying, which was a surprising request given that he had been called as an expert witness on the interpretation of such matters as 'unconditional surrender'.

Wilson also took a hard line, insisting that the commander would not have become a prisoner of war until he physically handed himself over to the Japanese. In addition, the judge advocate general stated, Bennett was legally obliged to follow the Japanese surrender orders once Percival had signed the surrender document.

It would later emerge that the opinion of these two men, who did not waver in their certainty about the time Bennett became a POW, would have a significant influence on Justice Ligertwood's summing up.

But the man who really put the knife in was William Dovey, the counsel assisting the commissioner. In years to come, he would become father-in-law to a prime minister; his daughter Margaret married Gough Whitlam. For now, however, it was his brilliant legal mind that was to the fore; his relentless questioning made him sound like the chief prosecutor in a criminal trial. Over two days he used his ruthless forensic skills to cross-examine Bennett on his thoughts and motives for escape. The general would often give as good as he got but there were times when he appeared hopelessly outmanoeuvred, as on the occasion when he was asked to provide the name of any senior officer who supported his actions.

'You have been in the Army quite a long while, as you have told us?' enquired Dovey.

'Yes,' Bennett replied.

'And I suppose you know quite a number of or very many senior officers in the Australian Army?' he suggested, before listing no fewer than 16 names, including General Sturdee.

Bennett replied 'yes' to all of them.

It was time for Dovey to go in for the kill.

'Perhaps I have left out some . . . Could you name one General Officer in the Australian Military Forces that you think I might call, who would share your views as to the propriety of your actions on February 15?'[20]

All eyes were on Bennett. How would he get out of this one? He was like a bull led to slaughter. But he was about to get a reprieve.

It was Commissioner Ligertwood who unexpectedly broke the silence, telling Dovey that the question should not have been asked. 'I mean, that is the very thing I am enquiring into, is it not?' he said.

Bennett was off the hook, at least for the time being, but there were many other exchanges during which the commander must have felt under siege.

On one occasion Dovey asked Bennett why he had not told Percival about his escape plans.

Dovey: Did it occur to you that it would at any rate be the courteous thing to have acquainted General Percival with your belief that you were the one man who should come back to Australia? Did it occur to you?

Bennett: Yes or no is not the answer. I would like to qualify it.

Dovey: Answer it first and then qualify it.

Bennett: I will give the qualifications first. I had no intention of escaping before hostilities ceased. I was only under General Percival for operational purposes and when hostilities ceased at 8.30 p.m. there were no more operations we were handling under General Percival. From that moment on my duty was to Australia, to the Australian Government. Therefore I was not bound.

Under further questioning Bennett repeated his view that he was, by then, not legally or morally required to seek Percival's permission to escape.

Bennett: If I had done something it would have wrecked all chances I had of getting out.

Dovey: By that you mean that if you had asked him he would have forbidden you to go?

Bennett: I mean if after the Japs were at his headquarters, as I expected. If we had an enemy in the same way we would have taken charge of the signal office at once, and if I rang him up and they listened in, what chance would I have of going? None.

Dovey: Is that the reason you put forward?

Bennett: Partly. The main reason was I had no obligation or need to communicate with General Percival because from 8.30 p.m. on we were under the Japs for all purposes.[21]

For much of the 18-day hearing, the minutiae of military law and the recollections of those who were with Bennett during the dying days of the Malaya campaign were intricately examined, none more so than the man himself. Everyone had a view about Bennett's status and the events leading up to his departure. Had he broken the rule that no soldier should escape until he became a prisoner of war? Had he deliberately kept Percival ignorant of his intentions because he knew the GOC Malaya would forbid him from going? Had he ordered his officers and men to stay at their posts while he planned to escape? Or had he given a nod and a wink to his men that they should get the hell out of it, if they could?

There was no satisfactory answer to this final question, as many of the officers who gave evidence had only vague or contradictory recollections of Bennett's final orders.

While there is no doubt that there was tremendous concern about the dangers created by a mass exodus of Allied troops, Bennett denied that he had explicitly given an order prohibiting his men to escape.

'No, absolutely no. Never in my life have I issued an order that officers or men should not escape.'[22]

Both Major-General Callaghan and Kent Hughes made no mention of such an order being given but Brigadier McEachern, who had taken over as commander of the Australian artillery, was less certain, saying he might have heard of such an order but had never seen a copy of it.

Bennett admitted that he had made an order demanding that every man should stay at his post, but pointed out that after the 8.30 pm ceasefire, the order no longer applied.

Brigadier Duncan Maxwell recalled that Bennett had suggested an order be issued reminding the troops of their duty to escape and encouraging them to do so.[23]

But Maxwell had cautioned against escape, as he told Dovey during the Royal Commission:

'In my opinion, considering the difficulties of getting away at that time, which was different from Dunkirk, Greece and Crete, and with the shipping and that sort of thing, any organised attempt by a large body of troops would involve a loss of life out of proportion to the individuals that would succeed in getting away, and I think that I urged Gen. Bennett that it would be undesirable.'

Dovey: And eventually he agreed with your view and it was decided that you should not pass the word round to the men to escape, but it might be left to their own discretion.

Maxwell: Yes, left to their own discretion?'

Later Bennett stressed that he believed all officers had a duty
to escape after the ceasefire was declared at 8.30 pm, but that
he omitted to include his earlier point that a full-scale evacuation would also be exceedingly dangerous.

'If a thousand officers, a thousand men, or any number
like that by escaping could get back to Australia and help to
make sure that we could defeat the Japs that was their duty,
their primary duty, even more important than staying behind
and look after the men, although that is what every officer
desired to do.'[24]

Such sentiments sat comfortably with his own view that it
was legally acceptable to escape after the 8.30 pm deadline,
when he believed everyone became prisoners of war.

To say that the evidence before the Royal Commission
on this point was bewildering is an understatement. As
A.B. Lodge in his definitive account of the Bennett case
argued: 'Although there was a great deal of confusion about
the issue, it appears that Bennett did not issue a general
order that there would be no attempt to escape, although
he had made it clear to some officers that they were not to
do so.'[25]

All this might have been easier to settle had Bennett been
privy to a message from General Sir Archibald Wavell, now
Supreme Commander of ABDA, the American, British,
Dutch Australian area, that those who wished to escape from
Singapore should be entitled to do so. The instruction had
been sent to Percival but the GOC Malaya had failed to pass
it on to Bennett. Whether or not it would have played a part
in his decision to leave, we do not know, but had Bennett

been aware of the message, it might have further validated his thinking.

There was also the question of Bennett's professed motive for making good his escape and returning to Australia. Ostensibly this was based on his desire to brief the government and the army on Japanese tactics so that the military would be better equipped to deal with the enemy in future battles.

Given that he had already despatched Broadbent on a similar mission a few days before the surrender, did this rationale stand up to close examination? It seemed unlikely, and Dovey would milk this to his advantage as he cross-examined Bennett on the value of the information he had provided to the army and the extent to which his training notes had been adopted in the field.

Bennett had already claimed in his memoir that his suggestions had been put to use by Australian troops on the Kokoda track and that officers had freely stated they had used his information to good effect.

'My methods, based on Malayan experiences, were taught to the AIF units on their return to Australia. My escape therefore, was worthwhile. I achieved the object I set out to achieve when I ran the gauntlet from Singapore to Australia,' he had written.[26]

On the stand Dovey queried the accuracy of these claims, given there was also speculation that the 7th Division, who had fought the successful campaign on the Kokoda Track, had been trained on methods learned from the commander of the Argyll and Sutherland Highlanders, Lieutenant-Colonel Ian Stewart.

'I never heard that and I would challenge it,' Bennett replied.

'But do you know one way or the other, do you?' Dovey enquired.

'I do. These Australian officers who took part in the fighting came along and said that they used my book, and naturally that is sufficient,' Bennett said.[27]

Once again Bennett was digging himself a hole, and Dovey was relishing every moment.

'Would you mind telling us what was the rank or the command of the officer who told you that your book was used through the campaign?' Dovey asked.

Bennett: I think he was a brigadier.

Dovey: I just want to know the name of the officer concerned.

Bennett: It was mentioned to me by several that they used the book and they were company officers upwards, who came sometimes indirectly.

Dovey: Can you think of anybody's name?

Bennett: There is one document produced which gives a name.

Dovey: Do you mean Col. Wolfenden?

Bennett Yes.

Dovey: You know he had nothing to do with the 7th or the 6th Division? . . . Will you tell us the name of them [these officers]?

Bennett: No, I do not recollect them.

Dovey: Will you please pay heed to my question, if you can?

Bennett: I mentioned the name of Col. Wolfenden. He signed that document.

Dovey: You cannot think of any other name?

Bennett: No. I cannot.[28]

Under such a savage cross-examination, Bennett's reputation was in danger of being mortally wounded. The lack of evidence to back up his earlier claims about the importance of his training pamphlets had left him scarred and vulnerable. Yet he was not a man to show it. Bennett's absolute self-confidence did not allow for a glimmer of doubt during his two days in the witness box. Here was a man who was imbued with an inner strength and self-belief that would not countenance failure.

Indeed, in fairness to the former head of the 8th Division, no one doubted his bravery or his loyalty to his country. And his king's counsel, Brian Clancy, in his final address, asked the commissioner to acknowledge this: 'Not only was General Bennett justified in what he did but that his actions were those of a reasonable man, a most courageous and far-seeing man, purely motivated by a patriotic sense of his duty, and without any consideration of personal safety or personal interest, which never entered his mind.'[29]

While these were highly prized qualities in a man, the case against Gordon Bennett had to be based on law, not character, as William Dovey, counsel assisting the commissioner, was keen to emphasise in his own summing up:

I put to Your Honour the circumstances are that Gen. Bennett left Singapore with his companions on the night of February 15 at a time when he was under a duty as a soldier, and as officer commanding the AIF, to faithfully assist Gen. Percival, his GOC, in carrying out the terms of the capitulation and that he left Singapore, knowing that this was his duty, in deliberate breach of his duty, he believing that he was acting from high patriotic motives in that he conceived

himself to be the only one who could save his country, but
I suggest that a belief in no wise justifies him doing what he
did.[30]

This then was the essence of the case against Bennett: could
his departure be justified for any reason?

As Dovey pointed out, justified meant justified in fact and
not justified in Bennett's own opinion or that of anybody else
in the community.

'Indeed there will be very many of them in the community who might believe that he had the right to do it, but
justified in accordance with his obligations to his troops – his
obligations to the man under whose operational command he
was, and the consequential obligations to surrender himself
to his enemy in terms of the agreement that had been entered
into.'[31]

Justification under the law was what it all came down to
and Dovey's was a compelling argument. Gordon Bennett
must have sensed that the royal commission had not done
him any favours, but he would have to wait more than a fortnight before Justice Ligertwood handed down his findings.

As expected, the commissioner based his decision on
the timing of the surrender, which in turn would establish
the moment Bennett officially became a prisoner of war.
While the first part of Justice Ligertwood's report gave due
consideration to the professed motives for Bennett's escape,
as outlined by his lawyer, he was unable to accept Clancy's
contention that his client became a POW at 8.30 pm when
the ceasefire took effect.

It was not the interpretation that the former commander
of the 8th Division had been hoping to hear on that warm

early January day in 1946. Instead he was told in no uncertain terms that it was the commissioner's view that none of the Allied forces became prisoners of war until they were held captive in Changi jail.

'At the time General Bennett left Singapore he was not a prisoner-of-war in the sense of being a soldier who was under a duty to escape,' he explained. 'He was in the position of a soldier whose commanding officer had agreed to surrender him and to submit him to directions which would make him a prisoner-of-war.'

Justice Ligertwood said it was Bennett's duty to remain in command of the AIF until the surrender was complete.

'Having regards to the terms of the capitulation I find that General Bennett was not justified in relinquishing his command and leaving Singapore,' he stated.[32]

If Bennett felt things couldn't get any worse, he was wrong. Yet he would have been pleasantly surprised by the second part of Justice Ligertwood's report, which was much more sympathetic to his cause. On the subject of the escape, the commissioner found that the general was not conscious of committing a breach of his legal or military duty, neither was he driven by a desire to secure his own safety:

I think that he acted from a sense of high patriotism and according to what he conceived to be his duty to his country. The conviction hardened in his mind that it would be of great advantage to Australia if he himself could get back and acquaint the authorities with what he had learned. He nevertheless adhered to his primary duty as commander of the forces, and was determined that he would faithfully carry out that duty until the end of the campaign. He had no intention of escaping until the circumstances were such that he felt he was free to go.[33]

The commissioner listed eight reasons why Bennett had felt the way he did, all of which would have informed his thinking at the time:

1. He was the first Australian general to confront the Japanese in battle.

2. He had acquired valuable information and experience about Japanese tactics from his time in Malaya and had developed successful countermeasures.

3. He sincerely believed that Australia was at great risk and that it was of great importance for him to return home in order to take a leading part in his country's defence.

4. He genuinely – but in the commissioner's view – mistakenly believed that immediately hostilities ceased, that the whole of the British forces in Singapore were surrendered to the Japanese and that he therefore became a prisoner of war with a duty to escape.

5. He wholeheartedly felt that he had done all he could for his men and that if he remained he would be separated from his troops, preventing him from offering any assistance.

6. The escape was a hazardous enterprise and involved no reflection on Bennett's personal courage.

7. He did in fact bring back valuable information which the AIF was able to utilise for its training in jungle warfare.

8. His decision to escape was inspired by patriotism and by the belief that he was acting in the best interests of his country.

The commissioner said he had based these findings mainly on Bennett's own testimony in the witness box.

'One could not listen to his evidence without being impressed by his sincerity,' he went on. 'Having considered all the circumstances proved in evidence before me, I am fully convinced of General Bennett's good faith.'

For a moment it looked like Justice Ligertwood might find in favour of Bennett, but it was not to be.

'Whilst my findings as to General Bennett's reasons and motives establish his good faith, they cannot in my opinion affect the answers which I have given in Part 1 of this report,' he said.

'Those answers, although legal in character, are nevertheless based upon the word of a British General, given in an instrument of capitulation, which derives its legal sanction from the express terms of the Hague Convention, requiring the terms of a capitulation to be scrupulously observed.'[34]

So that was it. Major-General Gordon Bennett might have done the right thing by his own set of values, but not under international law.

Even so Bennett drew some comfort from the report. The next day his considered reaction was reported extensively in the Australian press.

'Now that I have digested the Judge's findings, I am elated with the result. The only adverse comment deals with a purely legal technicality, which most laymen would naturally debate.

'On the main point at issue, so far as I am concerned, the Judge decided that I acted on unselfish and high motives. It pleases me to know that he appreciated the fact that I was able to bring back useful information to my country.'

However, the fact remained that the Royal Commission had essentially reached much the same conclusion as the military inquiry – that he had relinquished his command without the permission to do so and was not at liberty to escape from Singapore.

Unless he was deluding himself, Bennett could not fail to see that both inquiries found that he had not met his duty as a senior officer.

No greater charge could be laid against a soldier of his rank. While his character was not under question, his decision-making certainly was. He had been humiliated by his peers and his career was in ruins.

On 7 January 1946 the Melbourne *Age* reckoned it was time to 'bring down the curtain on this episode'.

'Those who were emphatic in their support for or opposition to Lt. General Bennett's action probably will not be affected by the report; those who were open-minded will be grateful to Mr Justice Ligertwood for a very fair and lucid exposition of the law and the facts,' it declared.[35]

Yet the nation remained divided over the Bennett case, with newspaper correspondence pages and editorials debating the outcome for years afterwards. Clearly it was not going to be the last we would hear of the man who commanded the 8th Division.

Chapter 19

RALLYING TO BENNETT'S DEFENCE

With the war over, those officers and men who had fought for their country and endured three-and-a-half years of imprisonment under the brutal fist of a cruel and savage conqueror could now follow the Gordon Bennett case with interest. The 8th Division may have been disbanded but the veterans who had formed this fighting force continued to support their former leader and respect his legacy. In truth they had both been unfairly disparaged in the aftermath of the Malaya campaign. Critics had accused the troops of throwing in the towel too early and their commander of shooting through and abandoning his men.

A few days after Justice Ligertwood handed down his findings, the Melbourne *Sun* reminded its readers:

A blunder, whatever motives might have prompted it, remains a blunder. And the chief value of the report lies in its unequivocal finding that General Bennett's action was mistaken. Personalities and the attribution of unworthy motives have tended to obscure the main issue but the principle has now been clearly stated that while troops are carrying arms and are under the control of their officers, the place of a commanding officer is with his men. Should any similar emergency arise, the judge's findings should leave no no officer in doubt where his duty lies'[1]

Such was the level of antipathy to Bennett and his division that their achievements in battle and the bravery they so often displayed, especially at Gemas and Muar, were largely ignored. Their efforts to stop the enemy may have been unsuccessful, but Bennett had every right to be proud of his troops and the courage they showed under fire. Only in the dying days of the fall of Singapore did their esprit de corps begin to crumble and that was due in part to the island's poor defences and the inadequately trained reinforcements Australia sent to Malaya at the last minute. The occasional sideswipes fuelled the perception of failure, which subsequently dogged the 8th Division, but they also strengthened its resolve, unifying the men and their commander.

Bennett always tried to attend important ceremonies marking anniversaries such as the fall of Singapore. At one such gathering at the Shrine of Remembrance in Melbourne in 1952, he was cheered by members of the 8th Division as he made his way to the microphone. He told the men they had been treated like criminals after their capture and the anguish they had suffered would never be forgotten.

'Our men were guarded by sub-humans,' he declared. 'Before this holy shrine I proudly proclaim the heroism and the unconquerable spirit of our men against overwhelming odds. They were true in the finest traditions of our race.'[2]

The friendly reception that day dispelled any claim that Bennett was no longer respected. Here was an officer who commanded loyalty and affection from his men in equal parts.

As Brigadier Sir Frederick 'Black Jack' Galleghan was to comment in later years: 'In the case of Gordon Bennett there is no doubt as to what his soldiers thought – I have never met one who disagreed with his action in escaping.'[3]

For the rest of his life Bennett continued to enjoy widespread popularity, not only among his troops but also among the public. The support galvanised him in his attempts to clear his name, for although he had felt partly exonerated by the Royal Commission's findings, the fact remained that he had been found guilty, albeit on more of a legal technicality than the weight of evidence against him. He missed no opportunity to put the knife in, frequently lambasting politicians for their perceived inadequacies.

Just before one Anzac Day in the late 1940s he fired a broadside at parliamentarians for their hypocrisy:

On April 25 the cynical old men who govern us will take their pious platitudes out of mothballs, don their blue serge suits, and pay meaningless lip service to our gallant dead.

They will stand at the shrines and tell us how much they love the ex-servicemen; how deeply and truly they work for Australia. For one day they will move with gracious condescension among the men who fought to keep them free. Then back they will go to their petty bickering, their self-seeking and their completely cynical disregard for the welfare of ex-servicemen of Australia.[4]

Bennett might have been delivering a serious message but his words also sounded like they came from a sour and bitter old man. He knew he was past his use-by date and decided to turn his back on military life and buy a small orchard in the lower Blue Mountains. Any hope he had of settling down with his family and enjoying the countryside proved to be wishful thinking. Life on the land was gruelling, involving long hours and hard physical labour.

And being Bennett he could never quite forget the way he had been treated. Privately he was still spoiling for a fight and took every opportunity to have a dig at his critics. On the subject of British officers he claimed there were a minority who were 'strongly prejudiced against Australian soldiers'. In the draft of his memoir he wrote, 'The 1st AIF learned that in World War I and it was again so in World War II.'[5]

He proposed a full and public inquiry into the Malaya campaign, but the prime minister of the day, Ben Chifley dismissed the idea.

Bennett also tried to influence the official history of the war being compiled by Canberra, fearing that the content would show him in a bad light. On one occasion he wrote to his fellow officer and loyal friend Kent Hughes, who was by now in the Federal government, asking him to exert some influence in the matter.

'Surely the Minister for the Army should direct that the Australian history should be submitted to me for vetting,' he wrote.[6]

Kent Hughes was supportive and raised Bennett's concern with Gavin Long, general editor of the official history, but he also realised he was treading on dangerous ground. 'I have to be particularly careful that I do not give directions as to how the history should be written. At the same time, knowing the source of much of the material, I will feel much happier if people like yourself and two or three others are asked to comment on what is written before it reaches the final stage of publication,' Kent Hughes replied to Bennett.[7]

The relationship between Bennett and those charged with writing the official history of the Malaya campaign – Long and the journalist Lionel Wigmore – did not run smoothly. There were several angry outbursts from Bennett and, despite Long's diplomatic responses, the former commander of the 8th Division could not be assuaged.

'I am truly sorry that we cannot agree on the story of the Battle of Singapore Island and regret wasting your time discussing it with such persistence,' Bennett wrote on one occasion.

'We seem to be beating the air. Unfortunately I will be forced to submit my commentary as Commander and to see that it gains as much publicity as the history,' he warned.[8]

Bennett was sensitive to criticism and any potential threat to his reputation, so he would have been pleasantly surprised by the support he received from an unexpected quarter in 1948. The views of Queensland lawyer Tom Fry (mentioned in part in Chapter 18) were to provide much reassurance for the beleaguered general. Fry, himself an ex-military man who had served under Bennett in Western Australia, published a long and detailed analysis of the case in the *University of Queensland Law Journal*. Entitled 'Legal Aspects of the Departure of Major-General Gordon Bennett from Singapore', the study examined the circumstances of Bennett's escape and the terms of the Royal Commissioner's report 'in the light of relevant rules of international and military law'.[9]

It was clear Fry did not support all the Royal Commission's findings, asserting that they had 'dangerous implications which might nullify certain of the safeguards embodied in the Prisoners of War Convention and the 1907 Hague Convention'.[10]

He added: 'A soldier is taught to fight and, if captured or surrendered and therefore temporarily unable to fight any longer, to escape in order to be able to fight again some other day. If that honourable code is to lose its simplicity in a maze of legal subtlety, Australian soldiers will remember the alleged miscalculation made by General Bennett and hesitate in the early stages of capture or surrender, which, in the past, soldiers have always been advised is often the best time to escape.'[11]

Fry went on to insist that the material point was whether a conditional or unconditional surrender took place at 8.30 pm on February 15.

'If so, General Percival and his forces at that hour became prisoners of war and as such were each individually entitled to attempt to escape and any stipulation to the contrary would be inconsistent with the Prisoners of War Convention and customary laws of war and, therefore, invalid.'[12]

The lawyer pointed out that Justice Ligertwood believed the surrender did not take place at 8.30 pm on 15 February and seemed to base his decision on the view that the Bukit Timah memorandum, signed at the Ford motor plant, should be interpreted to mean the surrender was not to occur unless and until General Percival's forces were 'behind the wires' of prisoner-of-war camps.

'The Bukit Timah memorandum does not expressly say this, and his opinion does not seem to be supported by international practice, convention or text writers,' Fry pointed out.[13]

But what if the Royal Commissioner was correct in his interpretation of the time of surrender and Bennett was not a POW when he made his escape?

'What at that moment was his status, rights and duties?' Fry asked.

If Bennett was not a prisoner of war or a combatant, what was he?

'The idea that by means of a capitulation the victor can, by a simple device of postponing the moment of surrender, deprive enemy soldiers of their status as combatants without substituting for it that of prisoners of war, would seem to be without validity as a principle of international law, and capable of opening the flood gates to wholesale evasion of international safeguards,' the lawyer argued.[14]

However sound the commissioner's legal judgement and his findings, the fact remained that it was essential to remove any doubts for the future guidance of Australian soldiers, Fry wrote.

'It is suggested this can only now be done by the issue of clear, unequivocal instructions as to the precise time at which, in each possible set of governing circumstances, they are as soldiers obliged by the law of their country to attempt to escape. These instructions should make clear the circumstances in which international law and the customs of nations will afford them protection,' he concluded.[15]

For once the implications of the Royal Commission's findings, so far as they affected officers and men, had been made clear. And the law needed to be amended accordingly if only to ensure that henceforth all Australian soldiers knew exactly where they stood.

As Fry himself emphasised at the beginning of his report: 'The possibility of a courageous soldier being exposed to criticism and even punishment for making an alleged miscalculation of this kind points to the necessity of issuing clear instructions to all Australian soldiers in the future as to the governing circumstances and the precise time at which their duty to escape will arise.'

He went on: 'There is something wrong with the system of allocation of praise or punishment to a soldier for escaping, often on a sudden opportunity, usually in circumstances of great stress and strain, [if it] continues to depend upon legal points of great subtlety, which he cannot be expected to comprehend and about which legal experts themselves may differ profoundly, rather than upon the soldier's good faith and honest and faithful performance of what he conceives to be his duty to his country.'[16]

At last, it seemed, common sense had prevailed. So did the Royal Commission and the military inquiry get it wrong?

Certainly there are precedents which Fry believed supported his view about the timing of prisoner of war status. He cited the example of Italian soldiers who were captured during the Western Desert campaign of 1940–41 and subsequently marched to prison camps. 'Neither the Italians nor our troops ever questioned that these were prisoners of war and had to act and be treated as such.'[17]

Likewise, as Mark Clisby reminds us, during the Gulf War of February 1991, television cameras captured streams of prisoners marching from Iraq towards POW camps in Saudi Arabia well before the ceasefire was announced.

'These columns of troops certainly gave the indication that they had become prisoners of war and that there was no necessity to place them physically behind barbed wire before they assumed that status,' he wrote.[18]

Justice Ligertwood's ruling that the Allied forces in Singapore did not enjoy prisoner-of-war status, and therefore the right to escape, until they entered Changi, was clearly at odds with the experiences of soldiers in the Western Desert during World War II and Iraq some 50 years later. It also flew in the face of human instinct. Self-preservation is a powerful force, particularly in wartime, and if a man felt his only chance of avoiding capture and possible death was to flee, he could easily justify his actions.

However, in the case of Gordon Bennett, there were other considerations. He might well have decided it was essential that his knowledge of Japanese tactics should be shared with the authorities back home in order to defend his country. But did he not also have a responsibility to his troops? Like a captain who refuses to abandon his ship and goes down with his crew, did Bennett have a duty to stay with his soldiers until the end, in whatever form that might take? At least he might have been able to exert pressure on the Japanese over camp conditions and the cruel treatment of prisoners. If the men of the 8th Division knew their commander had not forsaken them but was still there fighting for their cause and aiding their welfare, imagine the impact on morale?

It was a point General Arthur Percival was to address in his memoirs when he alluded to arrangements to escape from Singapore in the last days of the battle.

'It was more than once suggested to me that arrangements should be made for the evacuation in the last resort of important personages and of as many others as the available transport would take,' he wrote.

'This I refused to countenance. Our job was to hold Singapore for as long as we could and not evacuate it, and any suggestion that arrangements for evacuation were being made would have had a most disastrous effect.'

Then, in what seemed to be a thinly veiled criticism of Bennett, he insisted: 'In my view the right place for an officer, and especially a senior officer, is with his men, unless of course he is ordered away, until it is quite certain that he can be of no further service to them.

'That may mean the ruin of a career and the end of personal ambitions, but one of the corner-stones in our military system is that an officer stands by his men, and that in the end will bring greater happiness.'[19]

There were no prizes for guessing to whom Percival was referring. It was a near-perfect assessment of the case of Major-General Gordon Bennett.

Percival made other more direct references to Bennett, such as his telegram to the Australian prime minister telling him that in the event of other formations falling back and allowing the enemy to enter the city behind him, it was his intention to surrender to avoid any further needless loss of life.

'That seems to be a most extraordinary procedure,' observed Percival. 'No doubt he was perfectly entitled to communicate with his own Prime Minister but surely not to inform him of an intention to surrender in certain circumstances when he had not even communicated that intention to his own superior officer [Percival].'

But there were kinder words for the 8th Division's officers as a whole: 'In the AIF also the officers were of a splendid type, but the nucleus of officers properly trained in the art of war, and especially of modern war, was very small. In jungle warfare it is more than ever the junior leader that matters, for small bodies so often get detached from the rest and have to act on their own initiative.'[20]

Was Percival damning the 8th with faint praise? For wasn't the point about the need for jungle training Bennett's constant cry? Only his division and the Argyll and Sutherland Highlanders had equipped themselves with the necessary jungle fighting skills. The rest of the Allied forces were singularly unprepared. No wonder Bennett could get so riled by those who dared to question his actions, and there was plenty of opportunity to dwell on long-held grudges as he pottered around his orchard.

Now in his late sixties, he continued to work hard but his physical health showed signs of strain. He was no longer a young powerhouse, and at the age of 68 he suffered a blockage in his coronary artery. Thankfully it wasn't fatal but it was enough of a warning sign to make him slow down.

Bennett swapped his life on the land for the semi-rural bliss of Dural in Sydney's northwest, but he continued to involve himself in military affairs, inevitably sparking controversy on occasion.

In the early 1960s he flew to Japan to meet some of the officers he had fought against two decades earlier. On his return he urged his fellow countrymen to foster closer peacetime links with their old enemy, a suggestion that was not entirely welcomed.[21]

By now Bennett had moved from Dural to a house in Turramurra on Sydney's north shore. On 1 August 1962, he had a massive heart attack while driving his car in neighbouring Pymble. He managed to pull over and slumped into the arms of his wife, Bess, who had shared so many of his highs and lows.

Henry Gordon Bennett was dead at the age of 75.

His funeral was held two days later in St Andrew's Cathedral in Sydney, where scores of men of the 8th Division formed a lane of honour through which the flag-draped casket passed slowly on a gun carriage.

If anybody doubted the high regard in which Bennett was held, they had only to be in George Street that day. Five thousand people crammed into the cathedral and its surrounds while an estimated 15,000 more lined the streets. The crowds extended for several hundred metres, as far as Grosvenor Street to the north.

Among the mourners were many men of the 8th Division, including Wilfred Kent Hughes, and several hundred more ex-servicemen who wore their decorations. A four-man army guard of honour with arms reversed stood either side of the coffin, which bore the general's cap and ceremonial sword alongside a bunch of red carnations.

'Australia has lost one of its most distinguished soldiers and revered citizens,' Canon A.B. Begbie, the Anglican Chaplain General, told the congregation.[22]

Speaking from a pulpit draped in a green banner bearing the insignia of the 8th Division, he said Gordon Bennett had spent his whole life believing his highest hope and ambition was to make a worthy contribution to the defence of the country he loved.

'The 49 years of his military career gave to the world one of its most colourful, yet controversial, military figures,' he added.

Turning to Bennett's escape from Singapore, Canon Begbie revealed that the general had maintained he had done the right thing until the day he died.

'Singapore was the greatest thing in General Bennett's life,' he said in closing.[23]

For a man who had been crucified by the military establishment, the funeral, the oration and the crowds who came to honour his memory were Bennett's vindication.

Eight pallbearers, including Brigadier Galleghan and seven generals, carried the casket from the cathedral, where it was escorted by three white-helmeted military policemen on motorcycles along George Street. Two hundred soldiers from the lst Battalion, Royal Australian Regiment followed the cortege and another escort of 200 troops met the procession at the Northern Suburbs Crematorium.

Following a brief ceremony, a bugler sounded 'The Last Post' and 'Reveille' and a 15-gun salute was fired from a battery of howitzers.[24]

One of the most extraordinary characters in Australian military history had fought his final battle.

EPILOGUE

It is 15 February 2017, the 75th anniversary of the fall of Singapore and nearly 130 years since the birth of Henry Gordon Bennett at Balwyn, in Melbourne's eastern suburbs. There is no tin-can band marching down the main road, only the distant rattle of a tram as it makes its way through the shopping parade on this warm summer's day. Balwyn is no longer the sleepy backwater where the future commander of the AIF's 8th Division spent his formative years, but a bustling middle-class community of people who would have little in common with the boy who led his school mates through the streets to celebrate the relief of Mafeking. These days few of the locals would be aware Bennett was born here on 15 April 1887, but 80 miles (130 km) away at Ballarat his name will be remembered by those surviving members of the force who served under him.

There is no reference to the controversial senior officer during the official service to commemorate the fall of

Singapore at the Australian Ex-Prisoners of War Memorial, but then this ceremony is in honour of the 15,000 Australian servicemen who were captured.

Governor-General Sir Peter Cosgrove, an ex-army man himself and a decorated veteran of the Vietnam War, is there to pay tribute to the men who sacrificed so much. He talks of the strategic defeat which brought such a terrible human cost, and declares:

> For thousands of Australians who surrendered along with so many others it marked the beginning of an ordeal of unimaginable horror and brutality at Changi, at Sandakan, on the Thai–Burma railway and beyond. A pain that should be visited on no human being, they suffered as no one should ever suffer. They were treated as slaves, degraded, starved and beaten, marched and worked to the brink of exhaustion, to the edge of death and beyond. It belies comprehension. There could be no justification.[1]

He praises their resilience, ingenuity, compassion and camaraderie. 'For those magnificent, gallant men and women, whether in uniform or not, theirs was not the explosive and immediate courage of the battlefield, on land or at sea or in the air. It was instead a form of slow-burn courage, stoic and enduring often until death, a courage of daily sacrifice and determination not to give in, not to despair.'

It was, he says, this unquenchable fortitude that got so many through those dark times, easing the suffering of those who did not survive and preserving the dignity and humanity that captivity and ill-treatment could not dampen or displace. The governor-general concludes: 'Three quarters of a century on, we remember the fall of Singapore – an event which led in so many ways to a further definition of our Australian spirit, of our fortitude and of our place in the world.'

There are several hundred people in the congregation, most of them relatives of long-gone prisoners of war, here to honour their loved ones. And to the side, beneath a marquee shielding them from the blistering sun, the few remaining old soldiers alive today who suffered the indignity of defeat and enjoyed the triumph of survival remember their comrades who didn't make it.

It is a historic moment but only the ABC and a few local commercial TV channels are there to record the occasion. There is little or no coverage of the commemoration in the metropolitan newspapers the next day. Such is the dwindling level of interest in events that were once of burning importance to Australia and the rest of the world.

A similar ceremony in Sydney's Martin Place is attended by nearly 500 people, including eight veterans, six of whom were POWs, and five widows. The governor of New South Wales, retired General David Hurley, is there, as is Lieutenant-Colonel Neil James, executive director of the Australia Defence Association.

After the governor delivers the epilogue, the 8th Division's old banner is officially retired, though a new one will still be carried in future Anzac Day parades. Given that this is the last ceremony of its kind to be held in Martin Place, there is an added poignancy to this historic occasion, but again there is scant coverage in the following day's newspapers. I have to turn to the *Straits Times* in Singapore to find a front-page story which does justice to the 75th anniversary.

Under the headline, 'Never forget darkest time of

Singapore's history', Prime Minister Lee Hsien Loong says the lessons learned from the Japanese occupation must never be forgotten. 'Singapore will always be small and vulnerable. No one owes us our sovereignty or security. These are truths we must never forget,' he says. It is a salutary reminder to the free world, as relevant today as it was three-quarters of a century earlier.

Back at the Australian Ex-Prisoners of War Memorial in Ballarat, the service is moving towards its climax. Wreaths are laid by local and visiting dignitaries, the 'Ode of Remembrance' is read and 'The Last Post' is delivered by a lone bugler, followed by a minute's silence. Nothing stirs. Only the distant squawk of birdlife permeates the peace.

The catafalque party dismounts, slowly making its way out of the memorial area into the parkland, and the 75th anniversary commemoration of the fall of Singapore is over. Those who have shared in this moving celebration rise and mingle with fellow guests for the next few minutes, recalling old times and the long-departed loved ones who are central to their story. And the few ageing POWs who remain remember what it was really like to be in Singapore on that fateful February day.

Only these men know the truth and, arguably, only they have the right to judge the behaviour of others. They are eager to talk and it takes only a few questions to rekindle their support for their former leader.

Among the POWs who have made this final pilgrimage is Leslie 'Bunny' Glover, aged 96 and late of the 2/26th Battalion. I ask him if he believes it was right for Gordon Bennett to escape when he did.

'Yes,' he replies without hesitation. 'The war was over and

he felt he would be able to give more back to Australia by escaping than being in a prison camp.'

Other old boys share his sentiments, including Jim Kerr, who was a member of the 4th Anti-tank Regiment. Did everybody feel that way about Bennett at the time, I enquire.

'Well, the troops did, although the higher-ups didn't. But he was the only one who had any idea of the Japanese tactics and why they inflicted such a defeat on the forces in Malaya,' he responds.

———··———

Given the fact that Jim and most of his mates feel the same today as they did then, I am curious to know whether the difference of opinion between the army brass and other ranks over Bennett's escape still exists. It is a sensitive issue which also raises questions about Australian military law and the extent to which any changes have been made relating to the rights and obligations of prisoners of war since 1945.

Amazingly my research suggests that if a carbon copy Gordon Bennett episode happened today, much the same rules would apply. Under the *Australian Defence Force Discipline Act* a member is guilty of an offence if he or she leaves their post, position or place while engaged on service without reasonable excuse for their conduct. More specifically, a member of the defence force is guilty of desertion if he or she departs from their place of duty to avoid active service without having a reasonable excuse for doing so. The maximum penalty is five years' imprisonment.

The important point here is whether Bennett had a 'reason-able excuse' by assuming the Allies had agreed to surrender at 8.30 pm. Unfortunately there appears to have been no legal clarification of what officially constitutes a surrender since Justice Ligertwood's Royal Commission found against the former commander of the 8th Division in 1945. And as Thomas Fry pointed out in the *University of Queensland Law Journal* in 1948, international law and the facts of the case 'provide reasonable grounds for an opinion contrary to the Royal Commissioner's findings'.

Fry's view is supported by Professor Anthony Cassimatis, who teaches public international law at the TC Beirne School of Law at the University of Queensland. He believes that the Royal Commission's suggestion that military personnel might cease to be combatants but might also not be prisoners of war, essentially at the whim of the opposing party to the conflict, is powerfully undermined by Fry's analysis.

He says the case law that Fry cites also undermines the Royal Commission's view that the establishment of prisoner-of-war status required Australian troops to have been moved behind barbed wire. 'Australian forces in Singapore became prisoners of war from the moment hostilities ceased,' he declares.[2]

What is clear is a soldier's obligation to escape once he or she is classified as a prisoner of war. The Third Geneva Convention provides numerous protections for POWs who escape or attempt to do so. Therefore there is no doubt that Bennett was in the right if the law regarded him as a prisoner of war at 8.30 pm on 15 February 1942.

While the same sort of legislation applies today, the reality is that modern warfare is substantially different from military conflicts of the past. These days the sort of war in which combatants might invoke their entitlement to prisoner-of-war status is rare. As Australian Army legal officer Colonel Jim Waddell points out:

By far the majority of armed conflicts in the world today are non-international in character, and the occasion for applying rules for the conduct of prisoners of war in inter-national armed conflict rarely arises. While there are certain rules for the taking and treatment of prisoners in modern conflicts involving non-state actors, most states in 2017 have little experience of dealing with prisoners of war. The laws relating to prisoners of war, while extant, seem quaint and almost belong to another age of warfare.[3]

Colonel Waddell, who co-wrote *Justice in Arms: Military Lawyers in the Australian Army's First Hundred Years*, rightly points out that nowadays rules relating to the duty of escape are probably more focused on surviving as a hostage or detainee than as a prisoner of war.

Lieutenant-Colonel Lachlan Mead suggests that the key issue of Bennett's escape from a modern perspective may not be so much about technical military law that applied to pris-oners of war at the time, as the friction between Coalition command authorities and national command prerogatives. In other words, was Bennett bound to obey an order given to him by a senior officer from another national military force, when countervailing action may have been required by Australian national interests or directives.[4]

Of course, there is one other factor in what is now a largely academic discussion and it applies to the morality of Bennett's decision. Regardless of military law, was he right to leave his men behind? I am indebted to Colonel Helen

Macpherson, who recently retired from the Royal Military College, Duntroon, for her considered analysis of Bennett's actions. She believes that he had a duty to remain with his division come what may. 'I base this on a moral imperative, in that having given the direction for his men not to abandon their posts, he indeed did,' she states. 'Regardless of the time in history, I feel it is the function of a leader to remain with their team, irrespective of the impending circumstances.

'It is worth considering the impact which may have occurred had every commander down to battalion commander elected the same option. From a command imperative Bennett was the GOC AIF Malaya. The GOC Malaya was Percival. At no time prior to his departure did Bennett seek permission from Percival to withdraw. He did so without permission and voluntarily relinquished command to Brigadier Callaghan on 15 February 1942. I cannot comment in detail as to whether Bennett was directly under command of Percival. However, if this wasn't the case, then it is worth noting that no such withdrawal permission was sought by Bennett from Australia either.

'So what if he had stayed? Did he consider the cause and effect of such an option? Bennett was a bombastic and dogmatic commander who possessed a universal dislike of the Staff Corps, which most of his senior officers were from. The relationship between him and his immediate subordinate commanders was always strained.

'Strangely, though, he was universally liked by his soldiers. I suspect this is because there was always a veneer of separation between the enmity he held for his senior commanders and the soldiers under their command.

I suspect the face of Bennett that the soldiers saw was significantly different to the one seen by his commanders and immediate staff.

'We will never know what went through Bennett's mind in electing to leave when he did. He said he had great knowledge of fighting in jungle conditions against the Japanese – this is without question. However, if we considered he'd stayed with his men what would have been the result? Of note, senior commanders were not removed from Changi until around August 1942. While the senior officers were separated from soldiers while at Changi, the compound was confined. I suspect Bennett's personality would not have changed in captivity and may have been more readily obvious to the soldiers under his command. Given his personality, it's reasonable to surmise he would have been a divisive influence in Changi, which may have exacerbated the lowering of morale within the Australian forces. Indeed, had they sensed discord, it wouldn't have surprised me if the Japanese then used this to their advantage.

'Bennett must have been aware of his personality. Did he realise that his manner may well have become a disruptive influence? If so then could this have in some measure informed part of his decision-making for his departure?

'I suspect unless you could directly ask Bennett this, then we will never know. He would never have offered this up at his Court of Inquiry for to do so would indicate a significant failing on his behalf.'[5]

These reflections are reinforced by a note to me from Brigadier Dianne Gallasch, Duntroon's first female commander, whose thoughts, it is fair to say, encapsulate modern Australian Army thinking.

'Hindsight is a wonderful thing and with this luxury and viewing the episode through today's contemporary lens and my own leadership style, I personally would not have left my men and I would have stayed in Singapore,' she says.

'Army's current values are courage, initiative, respect and teamwork. For me teamwork means you always place the team before self and in this case I would view my command as the team I had to place before myself or before the bigger army.'[6]

We can talk forever about the rights and wrongs of Bennett's decision, but in the final analysis it is his men who had to carry the can and therefore deserve the final word. With the 8th Division Association now no more, I turned to the few remaining old soldiers, whose memories I have recorded in this book, to reflect on those momentous days.

When asked about the experience of being a prisoner of war, Alan Gaudry answers the question by pointing out that the Australian soldiers were the bravest and toughest ever encountered by the Japanese:

We had delayed their planned advance, inflicted many casualties on their crack troops and wiped out some 800 of them in the ambush at Gemas.

While the Australian losses had been heavy and we had been reduced to filling the ranks with untrained reinforcements straight off the ships, we remained an effective fighting force, confident that we could meet the Japanese on their own terms at any time.

Consequently, news of the surrender of Singapore came as a terrible shock. Only the revelation of the slaughter of the civilian population in the ceaseless bombing and shelling of the final days and the certainty that this could go on as long as the war continued, was sufficient to persuade us not to fight on until the end. I cannot even attempt to describe the bitter despair and shame which possessed me when I learned that we had apparently fought in vain and that our beloved country was now at the mercy of the Nipponese.[7]

John Chippendale, who never thought he'd get back to Australia alive, remembers sailing through Sydney Heads, thinking of the mates he'd left behind. His final thoughts were for the medics who saved so many. 'I cannot end without saying that if it wasn't for all the doctors we had on the line, I don't think any of us would have survived. They were magnificent and they had it very bad. They were bashed and kicked as they tried to stop sick men being sent off to work. This story takes me back years, yet it seems like only yesterday.'[8]

Jack Boardman was haunted by the memory of the mass execution of Chinese on the beach near Changi. 'Some of us were ordered to bury the bodies which littered the beach. They were well-dressed and had good shoes on. They must have been on some hit list because the Japanese just rounded them up and machine gunned them.'

He suffered nightmares for years afterwards, often imagining there was a Jap soldier just up the hill 'and I had to go and knock him off'. When he got near the soldier in his dream he'd start to belt him, only to wake up and discover he'd been punching his wife, Barbara.[9]

Jack continued to love playing the piano and, until his death in 2017, regularly entertained fellow residents at his retirement home near Gosford. It was one of the few comforting reminders of life in Changi more than three-quarters of a century before.

Noel Harrison, who had always wanted to be a soldier, believed the army moulded his character as he endured the highs and lows of military life. There was mateship, heart-ache, hilarity and, surprisingly, optimism. 'The morale of the troops was always high as we knew we would be home for Christmas,' he recalled. 'Despite the fact we missed out on three, the carrot was always there – we made the fourth.'

Sadly Noel passed away at the age of 99, a few days after our meeting. His first wife, Laurel, whom he had met at the army training camp in Bathurst, had died of a heart attack some 30 years previously. He was survived by his second wife, Lois, who joined us for lunch. As Noel tucked into a glass of beer and a chicken curry he acknowledged his good fortune at having 'two bloody good women'. [10]

Then there is Arthur Kennedy, who surprised his family with his low-key return to Sydney in 1945. There was no welcoming party as he got off the train from Queensland; nobody knew he was coming. On arrival at Central Station he was given two weeks leave and an army car took him home. 'When I arrived there wasn't a soul there but I remembered you could lift the front window and crawl in.' And that's just what he did. Arthur slumped on the bed and promptly fell asleep, giving his family the shock of their lives when they got back from work.[11]

Later, he would write his life story for his children and grandchildren to read in years to come. His concluding paragraphs convey his characteristic feistiness.

'We were the victims of Allied propaganda about the impregnable fortress of Singapore, which was only an air-filled paper bag ready for the bursting,' he wrote.

'It seems clear, however, that only the destruction caused by the dropping of a single bomb on one town, killing and injuring hundreds of thousands of Japanese, saved thousands of prisoners and the troops who were committed to the invasion of Japan. I leave you to judge whether the ends justified the means.'[12]

Understandably many men remained deeply scarred by what happened all those years ago, and some of them have spent the rest of their lives in search of closure.

Bart Richardson confided that he had a lot of nightmares. 'No one can go through a POW experience without having some after-effects,' he said. 'I kept on dreaming I was lost and didn't know where I was going.'

When in 2011 the Returned Services League invited him on a trip to Japan as guests of the Japanese government, Bart declined. He said he wasn't interested in Japan or the Japanese and that 'Japan was the last place I would go to.'

Overnight, however, he had second thoughts, conceding that after so many years it was probably time for reconciliation.

Bart, accompanied by several other POWs, was stunned by the reception. 'We had an official welcome by the Foreign Minister, who gave us the first of three apologies we received for our treatment during the war.'

The experience was to have a considerable impact on his attitude to the old enemy. 'Reconciliation is a great thing. I can't forget and now there is no one to forgive, but there is no point in continually hating people, now dead, for something they did many years ago.'[13]

They are admirable sentiments which, in some small way, help to cushion the sadness and the loss of so many.

The official commemorations to mark the fall of Singapore and the imprisonment of 15,000 Australian troops will inevitably be fewer in number from now on, but the proud record of the men who fought under the 8th Division banner will survive for generations to come. Each year, starting from 15 February 2018, the plan is to pick one of the 8th Division members from the list of names on the Memorial Wall of the Australian War Memorial in Canberra to be recognised, as 'The Last Post' is played at the end of the day. It will be a fitting tribute to the men who sacrificed their lives and those who lost their freedom.

And what of the man who led and left them? Major-General, later to become Lieutenant-General, Henry Gordon Bennett was forced to fight his own battles for the rest of his life. Was this the punishment he deserved or was he unfairly treated by a military hierarchy bent on ruining his reputation as a soldier?

Perhaps the law of the day did suggest he was wrong to escape, but that verdict still rests on the interpretation of the Allies' surrender and the time it officially took place. Little has changed since then to provide a fresh perspective on what was once the most heated military controversy of the age.

You either support Bennett or you don't. I leave it to the men who were there to decide whether he was right or wrong. Almost with one voice they applauded his actions. To them the tragic defeat of the 8th Division was not of Gordon Bennett's doing and his decision to leave was largely justified.

Not surprisingly his family always stood by him, especially Joan, his only child. Joan was born on 4 February 1918 in Britain in the south-coast city of Southampton. Her mother, Bess, had gone to join her husband while he was serving in World War I.

When the family returned to Australia they settled in Sydney, and after Joan finished at Kambala School for Girls in Rose Bay she trained as a physical education teacher. She was employed in teaching jobs in Melbourne and Bathurst before joining the Voluntary Aid Detachment (VAD), which provided field nursing services. As a member of the VAD she was eligible to enlist in the Australian Army Nursing Service and eventually attended an officer training college in Victoria. Graduating as a lieutenant, she was sent to Japan with the occupation forces and demobbed in 1946. Bennett would have been proud of her.

After the war Joan returned to nursing, training as a midwife in Sydney before moving to Mudgee and ultimately Parkes, where she spent the rest of her career. In her spare time she ran the local Girl Guides Association. Joan bought a hobby farm about 19 miles (30 km) out of town, where she lived like a hermit in her retirement, though she formed a close friendship with Christine Curteis, her housekeeper.

Christine's husband, Alan, remembers Joan as tough and fiercely protective of her late father. 'Whenever his name came up she would always defend him,' he says.

She never married or had children and when Alan once asked her why she hadn't wed, she replied that it would have meant losing her independence.

'Joan was a very private person and could be very prickly, but once you got inside the gruff exterior and got to know her she was lovely,' Alan adds.

Other acquaintances in Parkes remember her as intensely patriotic, but she rarely discussed her father. If Joan was in any way embarrassed about the publicity surrounding her father's controversial past, she didn't show it. She preferred to keep herself to herself, while standing proud of his legacy.

As I wrote the final few sentences of this book I made a most unexpected discovery. Joan Bennett is still alive, although suffering from dementia. She manages to walk a few steps around her nursing home but is quite frail, which is not surprising considering her age.

Now almost 100 years old, she will take the memory of Gordon Bennett to her grave – not as a deserter, but as her hero and loving father.

ACKNOWLEDGEMENTS

Writing about something that happened more than three-quarters of a century ago inevitably requires much detailed research, the cooperation of a wide range of people and a lot of luck. Over the years I have found that the longer you spend on a story the more it opens up to you and that has certainly applied to the history of the 8th Division and Henry Gordon Bennett.

The following names merely touch the surface of all those who have offered their insight and guidance to me. My sincere thanks to them and anybody else I might have accidentally overlooked.

Roz Hogan, Jack Boardman's daughter, who also helped me to access the late Alan Gaudry's memoir; Jessie Webb and Jennie Norberry of the Australian War Memorial (AWM) research centre; Kerrie Leech, Curator, Private Records, AWM; Richard Wall, son of Don Wall; Sylvia Norton; Mark Clisby, author of *Guilty or Innocent? The Gordon Bennett Case*;

Robert Macklin; Peter Thompson, who generously allowed me to quote from his definitive work *The Battle for Singapore*; Wenona Byrne of Allen & Unwin; Stephanie Volkens and her dedicated colleagues at the Mitchell Library, Sydney; Chris Masters, formerly of the ABC, whose *Four Corners* documentary on the fall of Singapore was compelling viewing. Katherine Phillips, of the Imperial War Museum, London; James Keady, Secretary of the 2/20th Battalion, and Ron Ferguson, Secretary of the 8th Division Association, for help in locating veterans; Peter Elphick, author of *Singapore: The Pregnable Fortress*, who offered me so much background on his controversial findings. Bob Pink, Secretary of 2/19th Battalion. Lt. Col. Peter McGuinness, MBE, OAM RFD, ED (Rtd) President, NMAFCT, who provided me with a valuable copy of the 2/19th's detailed history, *Grim Glory*, which he edited. Captain Darryn Mullins, of the Asia Pacific Centre for Military Law. Jan Nelson, whose late husband Hank did so much to record the memories of prisoners of war; Col. Jim Waddell, co-author of *Justice in Arms* and Director of Operations and Security Law and Head of Corps for the Australian Army Legal Corps; Lieutenant Colonel Lachlan Mead, co-author of *Justice in Arms*. Air Chief Marshal M.D. Binskin, Chief of the Australian Defence Force; Brigadier Dianne Gallasch, Commander of the Royal Military College, Duntroon, and her retired colleague Colonel Helen Macpherson; Wendy Taylor of the Department of Veterans' Affairs; Mark Laudi for Singapore background and photographs; Tim Bowden for his encouragement; Robyn Matthews for providing her father John (Jack) Chippendale's memoir. Pauline O'Carolan at HarperCollins and Maggie Thompson at Allen & Unwin. Professors Anthony Cassimatis,

James Allan and John Devereux of the TC Beirne School of Law, University of Queensland. Richard Legg who granted me permission to access material from his late father Frank Legg's book, *The Gordon Bennett Story*, which was essential reading. Tighearnan Kelly, National Library of Australia.

Jim Kennedy and his family for helping to introduce me to his father, Arthur, whose memoir and recollections were so important. Henning and Pamela Nielsen, stepdaughter of Jimmy Houston, whose diary is one of the most detailed records of POW life I have come across. David Boughton and members of his family for sharing Dudley Boughton's diary. Jack Mudie's daughter, Jenny; Lindy Cooper, Don Alchin's daughter.

Bart Richardson, whose sharp memory revealed so much. Jack Boardman, whose recall was as fine-tuned as his piano skills. And Noel Harrison whose detailed thoughts of those dark days were as vivid a few days before he died as they were 75 years previously. Christine and Alan Curteis, without whose blessing I would have been unable to access so much of Gordon Bennett's material. Likewise, the *Sydney Morning Herald*'s, RSVP column, which helped me track down Joan Bennett.

My agent, Margaret Gee, who never gave up on the idea for this book. Alison Urquhart, my publisher at Penguin Random House, my editor, Catherine Hill, and copy-editor Anne Reilly.

And last but not least, Anthony and Dorothea Tom, who revealed to me that Joan Bennett was still alive at the age of 99 and thereby helped to bring this book to a fitting close.

Finally, my thanks to my wife, Vivienne, and my family, whose support and encouragement was invaluable.

ENDNOTES

Introduction

1   Bennett, H. Gordon, *Why Singapore Fell*, Angus & Robertson, Sydney, 1944.
2   Bennett Papers, Mitchell Library, Sydney, 807/10.

Chapter 1: The Early Days

1   Legg, Frank, *The Gordon Bennett Story*, Angus & Robertson, Sydney, 1965, p. 5.
2   Bennett Papers, Mitchell Library, Sydney, box 22, item 1.
3   Legg, Frank, *The Gordon Bennett Story*, Angus & Robertson, Sydney, 1965, p. 11.
4   Bean, C.E.W., *Official History of Australia in the War of 1914–1918*, vol. I, *The story of war to the end of the first phase of the Gallipoli Campaign*, 4 May, 1915, p. 416.
5   Ibid., p. 418.
6   Lodge, A.B., *The Fall of General Gordon Bennett*, Allen & Unwin, Sydney, 1986, p. 3.
7   Ibid.
8   Ibid., p. 140.
9   Bennett Papers, Mitchell Library, Sydney, box 22, item 1.

10 Wigmore, Lionel, *The Japanese Thrust*, Australian War Memorial, Canberra, 1957, chap. 3, pp. 33–4.

11 The *Sun*, 12 December 1937.

12 Wigmore, Lionel, *The Japanese Thrust*, Australian War Memorial, Canberra, chap. 3, p. 34.

13 Bennett papers, Mitchell Library, Sydney, 807/10.

Chapter 2: Readying for War

1 Wigmore, Lionel, *The Japanese Thrust*, Australian War Memorial, Canberra, 1957, chap. 3, p. 35.

2 Byrne, Joe, interview with author, Ramsgate, June 2006.

3 Daldry, George, interview with author, Bondi, August 2006.

4 Wall, Don, *Singapore and Beyond*, 2/20th Battalion Association, Cowra, NSW, 1985.

5 Maynard, Roger, *Hell's Heroes*, HarperCollins, Sydney, 2009.

6 Axis Alliance in World War II, www.ushmm.org/wlc/en/article. php?ModuleId=10005177

7 Gilbert, Max 'Eddie', interview with author, Melbourne, 8 June 2012.

8 Hicks, Walter, interview with author, November 2012.

9 Maynard, Roger, *Hell's Heroes*, HarperCollins, Sydney, 2009.

10 Mudie, Jack, interview with author, May 2006.

11 Wall, Don, *Singapore and Beyond*, 2/20th Battalion Association, Cowra, NSW, 1985.

12 Boardman, Jack, interview with author, August 2016.

13 Dietz, Henry, interview with author, June 2006.

14 Alchin, Don, interview with author, July 2006.

15 Boardman, Jack, interview with author, August 2016.

16 Mudie, Jack, interview with author, May 2006.

17 Wigmore, Lionel, *The Japanese Thrust*, Australian War Memorial, Canberra, chap 4, pp. 60–61.

18 Arneill, Stan, *Black Jack*, Macmillan, Melbourne, 1983, p. 76.

19 Maynard, Roger, *Hell's Heroes*, HarperCollins, Sydney, 2009.

Chapter 3: 'Give Us More Men'

1 Legg, Frank, *The Gordon Bennett Story*, Angus & Robertson, Sydney, 1965, pp. 166–67.

2   Bennett, H. Gordon, *Why Singapore Fell*, Angus & Robertson, Sydney, 1944, chap. 5, p. 19.
3   'Tactical Notes for Malaya', issued by General Staff, A.H.Q., Melbourne, 1940.
4   Wigmore, Lionel, *The Japanese Thrust*, Australian War Memorial, Canberra, 1957, chap 5, p. 67.
5   Ford, J.M., *Allies in a Bind: Australia and the Netherlands East Indies in World War II*, Australian Netherlands Ex-Servicemen and Women's Association, Loganholme, Qld, 1996.
6   Timbs, Kevin, interview with author, Dapto, May 2006.
7   Legg, Frank, *The Gordon Bennett Story*, Angus & Robertson, Sydney, 1965, p. 170.
8   Gilbert, Eddie, interview with author, May 2012.
9   Maynard, Roger, *Ambon*, Hachette, Sydney, 2014, p. 20.
10 Wigmore, Lionel, *The Japanese Thrust*, Australian War Memorial, Canberra, chap. 5, p. 72.
11 Thompson, Peter, *The Battle for Singapore*, Portrait, 2005, p. 81.
12 Ibid.
13 Newton, R.W., et al., *The Grim Glory of the 2/19 Battalion AIF, Part 1*, 2/19 Battalion AIF Association, 1st edn, 1975, p. 108.
14 Maynard, Roger, *Hell's Heroes*, HarperCollins, Sydney, 2009, p. 47.
15 Wigmore, Lionel, *The Japanese Thrust*, Australian War Memorial, Canberra, chap. 6, p. 102.
16 Gordon Bennett's diary and related papers, ML MSS 773. PRM520 AWM. Roll no. CY783.
17 Elphick, Peter, & Smith, Michael, *Odd Man Out: The Story of the Singapore Traitor*, Hodder & Stoughton, London, 1993.

Chapter 4: Attack, Attack, Attack

1   Bennett, H. Gordon, 'Report on Malayan Campaign Dec 7– February 15', Mitchell Library.
2   Bennett papers and diary, Mitchell Library, Sydney, MLMSS807
3   Ibid.
4   Manchester, William and Read, Paul, *The Last Lion: Vol 3, Defender of the Realm*, Pan Macmillan, London, 2015.
5   Thompson, Peter, *The Battle for Singapore*, Portrait, 2005, p. 105.

6 Gaynor, John, interview, IWM 008246/07.

7 Winston Churchill, *The Grand Alliance*, Cassell, London, 1949.

8 Wigmore, Lionel, *The Japanese Thrust*, Australian War Memorial, Canberra, 1957, chap 6, p. 100.

9 Bennett papers and diary, Mitchell Library, MLMSS807

10 Ibid.

11 Ibid.

12 Ibid.

13 Bennett, H. Gordon, *Why Singapore Fell*, Angus & Robertson, Sydney, 1944, p. 75.

14 Ibid., pp 75–7

15 Corfield, Justin, & Corfield, Robin, *The Fall of Singapore*, Hardie Grant Books, 2012.

16 Bennett, H. Gordon, *Why Singapore Fell*, Angus & Robertson, Sydney, 1944, p. 78.

17 Martin Gilbert, *The Churchill Documents, Testing Times, 1942*, College Press, Hillsdale, 2014, p. 211.

18 Maynard, Roger, *Hell's Heroes*, HarperCollins, Sydney, 2009, p. 70.

19 Lodge, A.B., *The Fall of General Gordon Bennett*, Allen & Unwin, Sydney, 1986, p. 75.

20 Bennett, H. Gordon, *Why Singapore Fell*, Angus & Robertson, Sydney, 1944, p. 83.

21 Maynard, Roger, *Ambon*, Hachette Australia, Sydney, 2014, p. 27.

22 Gilbert, Max 'Eddie', interview with author, Melbourne, May 2012.

Chapter 5: 'It Was a Bloody Show, I Can Tell You'

1 Wigmore, Lionel, *The Japanese Thrust*, Australian War Memorial, Canberra, 1957, chap. 11, p. 214.

2 Ibid.

3 Kearney, Des, report to 'Black Jack' Galleghan, February 1942.

4 Thyer. J.H., Report of Operations of 8th Division in Malaya based on narrative prepared by Col. C.H. Kappe; Kappe papers AWM MSS1393.

5 Wigmore, Lionel, *The Japanese Thrust*, Australian War Memorial, Canberra, chap. 11, p. 214.

6 Kennedy, Arthur 'Bluey' George, interview with author, 24 September 2016.

7   Penfold, A.W., et al., *Galleghan's Greyhounds, The Story of the 2/30th Infantry Battalion*, 2/30th Battalion AIF Association, Sydney, 1979.
8   Ibid., p. 89.
9   Kennedy, Arthur 'Bluey' George, interview with author, 24 September 2016; Kennedy, Arthur 'Bluey' George, *The Memoirs of Arthur George Kennedy*, unpublished, 1977.
10 Ibid.
11 Ibid.
12 Wigmore, Lionel, *The Japanese Thrust*, Australian War Memorial, Canberra, chap. 11, p. 218; Arneil, F., *Stand To*, 'Anderson's Company', 1954.
13 Kennedy, Arthur 'Bluey' George, interview with author, 24 September 2016.
14 Kennedy, Arthur 'Bluey' George, *The Memoirs of Arthur George Kennedy*, unpublished, 1977.
15 Arneil, Stan, *Black Jack*, Macmillan, Melbourne, 1983, p. 93.

Chapter 6: Kill or Be Killed

1   Newton, R.W., et al., *The Grim Glory: Official History of the 2/19th Battalion, Pt 1*, 2/19 Battalion AIF Association, 1st edn, 1975, p. 149.
2   Ibid.
3   Ibid.
4   Ibid., p. 189.
5   Ibid.
6   Ibid.
7   Ibid.
8   Ibid.
9   Ibid.
10 Wigmore, Lionel, *The Japanese Thrust*, Australian War Memorial, Canberra, 1957, chap. 11, p. 214.
11 Ibid., p. 244.
12 Ibid.
13 Hackney, Ben, *Dark Evening*, unpublished.
14 Ibid.
15 Ibid.
16 Ibid.
17 Percival, Arthur Ernest, *The War in Malaya*, Eyre & Spottiswoode, London, 1949, p. 233.

Chapter 7: 'If Anyone Tells You They Weren't Frightened They're a Bloody Liar'

1   Harrison, Noel, interview with author, September 2016.

2   Ibid.

3   Harrison, Noel, unpublished memoir, loaned to author, September 2016.

4   Wall, Don, *Singapore and Beyond*, 2/20th Battalion Association, Cowra, NSW, 1985, p. 26.

5   Harrison, Noel, interview with author, September 2016.

6   Mudie, Jack, interview with author, May 2006.

7   Dietz, Henry, interview with author, June 2006.

8   Wigmore, Lionel, *The Japanese Thrust*, Australian War Memorial, Canberra, 1957, chap. 13, p. 250.

9   Ibid.

10 Richardson, Bart, interview with author, 12 October 2016.

11 Dietz, Henry, interview with author, June 2006.

12 Maynard, Roger, *Hell's Heroes*, HarperCollins, Sydney, 2009, p. 62.

13 Wall, Don, *Singapore and Beyond*, 2/20th Battalion Association, Cowra, NSW, 1985, p. 47.

14 Ibid.

15 Mudie, Jack, interview with author, May 2006.

16 Dietz, Henry, interview with author, June 2006.

17 Collins, Arthur 'Snowy', interview with author, June 2006.

18 Ibid.

19 Wigmore, Lionel, *The Japanese Thrust*, Australian War Memorial, Canberra, , chap. 13, p. 251.

20 Alchin, Don, interview with author, July 2006.

21 Ibid.

22 Harrison, Noel, interview with author, September 2016.

23 Ibid.

24 Daldry, George, interview with author, Bondi, August 2006.

25 2/18th Australian Infantry Battalion, www.awm.gov.au/unit/U56061/

26 Wigmore, Lionel, *The Japanese Thrust*, Australian War Memorial, Canberra, p. 253.

27 Lodge, A.B., *The Fall of General Gordon Bennett*, Allen & Unwin, Sydney, 1986, p. 129.

28 Ibid.

29 Ibid.

30 Bennett, H. Gordon, letter to Forde, 27 January 1942, Forde Papers, AA 1974/398; Wigmore, Lionel, *The Japanese Thrust*, Australian War Memorial, Canberra, p. 272.

31 Ibid.

32 Ibid.

33 Tsuji, Masanobu, quoted in Wall, Don, *Singapore and Beyond*, 2/20th Battalion Association, Cowra, NSW, 1985, p. 47.

34 Richardson, Bart, interview with author, 12 October 2016.

Chapter 8: A Terrible Revenge

1   Hicks, Walter, interview with author, June 2012.

2   Yamamoto, Genichi, *Nippon Times*, 31 January 1943.

3   Wigmore, Lionel, *The Japanese Thrust*, Australian War Memorial, Canberra, 1957, chap. 19.

4   Mcilraith, Shaun, 'The Ambon Battle', *People Magazine*, 6 April 1955; 'Gull Force Ambon', *Reveille*, 1 July 1962.

5   Roger Maynard, *Ambon*, Hachette, Sydney, p. 54.

6   Fall of Rabaul, www.ww2australia.gov.au/japadvance/rabaul.html

7   'Rabaul, 1942', Campaign History, Australian War Memorial.

Chapter 9: 'We'll Blow Them All Away'

1   Bennett, H. Gordon, *Why Singapore Fell*, Angus & Robertson, Sydney, 1944, p. 163.

2   Wigmore, Lionel, The *Japanese Thrust*, Australian War Memorial, Canberra, 1957, chap. 13, p. 283.

3   Ibid.

4   Bennett, H. Gordon, *Why Singapore Fell*, Angus & Robertson, Sydney, 1944, p. 164.

5   Wall, Don, *Singapore and Beyond*, 2/20th Battalion Association, Cowra, NSW, 1985, p. 53.

6   Lodge, A.B., *The Fall of General Gordon Bennett*, Allen & Unwin, Sydney, 1986, p. 134.

7   History of 2/18th Australian Infantry Battalion, www.awm.gov.au/unit/U56173/

8   Lodge, A.B., *The Fall of General Gordon Bennett*, Allen & Unwin,

Sydney, 1986; p. 115; Wigmore, Lionel, *The Japanese Thrust*, chap. 13, p. 258.

9 Wall, Don, *Singapore and Beyond*, 2/20th Battalion Association, Cowra, NSW, 1st edn, 1985, p. 52.

10 Bennett, H. Gordon, *Why Singapore Fell*, Angus & Robertson, Sydney, 1944, p. 166.

11 Ibid.

12 Ibid., p. 167.

13 Lodge, A.B., *The Fall of General Gordon Bennett*, Allen & Unwin, Sydney, 1986 p. 141; Bennett to Minister for the Army, 4 February 1942, AB 106/153, PRO.

14 Byrne, Joe, interview with author, Ramsgate, June 2006.

15 Collins, Arthur 'Snowy', interview with author, June 2006.

16 Dietz, Henry, interview with author, June 2006.

17 Ibid.

18 Daldry, George, interview with author, Bondi, August 2006.

19 Alchin, Don, interview with author, July 2006.

20 Bennett, H. Gordon, *Why Singapore Fell*, Angus & Robertson, Sydney, 1944, p. 173.

21 *World War II Experiences of W. Holding*, www.anzac.dpc.wa.gov.au/ Resources/Stories/holding_w_pte_20050225.pdf

22 Holding, Walter, unpublished memoir.

23 Ibid.

24 *World War II Experiences of W. Holding*, www.anzac.dpc.wa.gov.au/ Resources/Stories/holding_w_pte_20050225.pdf

25 Daldry, George, interview with author, Bondi, August 2006.

26 Dietz, Henry, interview with author, June 2006.

27 Houston, Jimmy, unpublished diary courtesy Pamela and Henning Nielsen.

28 Dietz, Henry, interview with author, June 2006.

Chapter 10: 'The Battle Must Be Fought to the Bitter End'

1 Newton R.W., et al., *The Grim Glory: Official History of the 2/19th Battalion, Pt 1*, 2/19 Battalion AIF Association, 1st edn, 1975, p. 269.

2 Ibid.

3 Legg, Frank, *The Gordon Bennett Story*, Angus & Robertson, Sydney, 1965, p. 237.

4 Ibid.

5 Ibid.

6 Wigmore, Lionel, *The Japanese Thrust*, Australian War Memorial, Canberra, chap. 16, p. 341.

7 Ibid.

8 Peter Thompson, *The Battle for Singapore*, Portrait, 2005, p. 316.

9 Churchill, W., *The Second World War*, vol. IV, *The Hinge of Fate*, Houghton-Mifflin, London, 1950, pp. 87–88.

10 Ibid.

11 Wigmore, Lionel, *The Japanese Thrust*, Australian War Memorial, Canberra, chap. 16, p. 342.

12 Wavell, Archibald, Despatch on the Operations in the South West Pacific, 15 January to 25 February 1942, para 27.

13 Thyer. J.H., Report of Operations of 8th Division in Malaya based on narrative prepared by Col. C.H. Kappe; Kappe papers AWM MSS1393, p. 125.

14 Cook, John, interview with author, April 2006.

15 McAuliffe, Mick, interview with author, June 2006.

16 Chippendale, John, unpublished memoir, December 1997.

17 Ibid.

18 Ibid.

19 Woods, Harry, interview with author, May 2006.

20 History of 2/13 General Hospital, www.awm.gov.au/unit/U57200/

21 The Sinking of the *Vyner Brooke*, www.awm.gov.au/military-event/E302/

22 Ibid.

23 Thyer. J.H., report of operations of 8th Division in Malaya based on narrative prepared by Col. C.H. Kappe; Kappe papers AWM MSS1393, p. 163.

24 Corfield, Justin, & Corfield, Robin, *The Fall of Singapore*, Hardie Grant, Melbourne, 2012, p. 243.

25 Ibid., p. 241.

Chapter 11: Singapore Crumbles – The Getaway Begins

1 Kennedy, Arthur 'Bluey' George, interview with author, 24 September 2016.

2 Ibid.

3 Ibid.

4 Kennedy, Arthur 'Bluey' George, *The Memoirs of Arthur George Kennedy*, unpublished, 1977.

5 Ibid.

6 Ibid.

7 Ibid.

8 Ibid.

9 Ibid.

10 Ibid.

11 Ibid.

12 Ibid.

13 Wigmore, Lionel, *The Japanese Thrust*, Australian War Memorial, Canberra, 1957, chap. 17, p. 368.

14 Ibid.

15 Penfold, A.W., et al., *Galleghan's Greyhounds: The Story of the 2/30th Infantry Battalion*, 2/30th Battalion AIF Association, Sydney, 1979, p. 216.

16 Wigmore, Lionel, *The Japanese Thrust*, Australian War Memorial, Canberra, chap. 17, p. 369.

17 Boardman, Jack, interview with author, August 2016.

18 Ibid.

19 Wigmore, Lionel, *The Japanese Thrust*, Australian War Memorial, Canberra, chap. 17, p. 372.

20 Corfield, Justin, & Corfield, Robin, *The Fall of Singapore*, Hardie Grant, Melbourne, 2012, pp. 243–4.

21 Bowden, Vivian Gordon, Australian Dictionary of Biography, http://adb.anu.edu.au/biography/bowden-vivian-gordon-9552

22 Ibid.

23 Ibid.

24 Wigmore, Lionel, *The Japanese Thrust*, Australian War Memorial, Canberra, chap. 17, pp. 376–77.

25 Corfield, Justin, & Corfield, Robin, *The Fall of Singapore*, Hardie Grant, Melbourne, 2012, p. 244.

26 Lee Kuan Yew, *The Singapore Story: Memoirs of Lee Kuan Yew*, Marshall Cavendish, Singapore, 1998, p. 46.

27 Bennett, H. Gordon, *Why Singapore Fell*, Angus & Robertson, Sydney, 1944, p. 213.

28 Ibid.

29 Corfield, Justin, & Corfield, Robin, *The Fall of Singapore*, Hardie Grant, Melbourne, 2012, p. 245.

30 *The Percival Report*, 1948, www.pows-of-japan.net/articles/107.html

31 Bennett, H. Gordon, *Why Singapore Fell*, Angus & Robertson, Sydney, 1944, p. 246.

32 Ibid.

33 Hall, Timothy, *The Fall of Singapore 1942*, Methuen Australia, 1983.

34 Legg, Frank, *The Gordon Bennett Story*, Angus & Robertson, Sydney, 1965, p. 252.

35 Ibid.

36 Leasor, James, *Singapore: The Battle that Changed the World*, House of Stratus, Cornwall, 2nd edn, 2001, p. 264.

Chapter 12: 'I Could Not Fall Into Japanese Hands'

1 Bose, Romen, *Secrets of the Battlebox*, Marshall Cavendish, Singapore, 2005, p. 43.

2 Ibid.

3 Bennett, H. Gordon, *Why Singapore Fell*, Angus & Robertson, Sydney, 1944, p. 191.

4 Smith, Colin, *Singapore Burning: Heroism and Surrender in World War II*, Penguin Books, Melbourne 2005, p. 546.

5 Bennett, H. Gordon, *Why Singapore Fell*, Angus & Robertson, Sydney, 1944, p. 192.

6 Wigmore, Lionel, *The Japanese Thrust*, Australian War Memorial, Canberra, 1957, chap. 17, p. 378.

7 Ibid.

8 Thompson, Peter, *The Battle for Singapore*, Portrait, 2005, p. 341.

9 Corfield, Justin, & Corfield, Robin, *The Fall of Singapore*, Hardie Grant, Melbourne, 2012, p. 656.

10 Ibid.

11 Wigmore, Lionel, *The Japanese Thrust*, Australian War Memorial, Canberra, chap. 17, p. 379.

12 Ibid.

13 Ibid., p. 378.

14 Ibid.

15 Chippendale, John, unpublished memoir, December 1997, p. 4.

16 Bennett, H. Gordon, miscellaneous drafts and notes, Mitchell Library, box 22, item 1.
17 Ibid.
18 Ibid.
19 Bennett, H. Gordon, *Why Singapore Fell*, Angus & Robertson, Sydney, 1944, p. 195.
20 Bennett, H. Gordon, miscellaneous drafts and notes, Mitchell Library, box 22, item 1.
21 Legg, Frank, *The Gordon Bennett Story*, Angus & Robertson, Sydney, 1965, p. 255.
22 Bennett, H. Gordon, *Why Singapore Fell*, Angus & Robertson, Sydney, 1944, p. 195.
23 Ibid., pp. 197, 198.
24 Ibid.
25 Legg, Frank, *The Gordon Bennett Story*, Angus & Robertson, Sydney, 1965, p. 255.
26 Ibid.
27 Ibid.
28 Bennett, H. Gordon, *Why Singapore Fell*, Angus & Robertson, Sydney, 1944, p. 201.
29 Ibid.
30 Legg, Frank, *The Gordon Bennett Story*, Angus & Robertson, Sydney, 1965, p. 257.
31 Ibid., p. 256.

Chapter 13: Deserters or Stragglers?

1 Wigmore, Lionel, *The Japanese Thrust*, Australian War Memorial, Canberra, 1957, chap. 17, p. 387.
2 Ibid.
3 Ibid.
4 Ibid.
5 Wavell, A.P., Commander-in-Chief, India Command, letter to British War Cabinet, 1 June 1942.
6 Elphick, Peter, letter to author, 9 October 2016.
7 Anonymous, letter to Peter Elphick from member of 4th Anti-tank Regiment.

8   Nelson, Hank, *Prisoners of War: Australians under Nippon*, ABC Enterprises, Sydney, 1985, p. 18.

9   Murdoch, Keith, *Adelaide Advertiser*, August 1942.

10   Ibid.

11   Bott, Eric, letter to Peter Elphick, January 1993.

12   Stephen, S., letter to Peter Elphick, 12 January 1993.

13   Elphick, Peter, *Singapore: The Pregnable Fortress*, Coronet Books, London, 1995, p. 449.

14   Ibid., p. 475.

15   Ibid.

16   Elphick, Peter, *Singapore: The Pregnable Fortress*, Coronet Books, London, 1995, p. 476; PREM 3/168/7 PRO.

17   Ibid.

18   Boardman, Jack, interview with author, 11 August 2016.

19   Richardson, Bart, interview by author, 12 October 2016.

20   Harrison, Noel, interview with author, 27 September 2016.

21   Ibid.

22   Iliffe, James, interviewed for *Australians at War*, May 2002.

23   Cornford, Roydon, interview with Chris Masters, ABC *Four Corners*, March 2002.

24   Elphick, Peter, *Singapore: The Pregnable Fortress*, Coronet Books, London, 1995, p. 454.

25   ABC *Four Corners*, March 2002.

26   Elphick, Peter, *Singapore: The Pregnable Fortress*, Coronet Books, London, 1995, p. 479.

27   Ibid.

28   Ibid.

29   Edward Docker and Lynette Silver, *Fabulous Furphies: 10 Great Myths from Australia's Past*, 1997

Chapter 14: Inside Changi

1   Richardson, Bart, *The Army As I Saw It*, self-published, 2014.

2   Daldry, George, interview with author, Bondi, August 2006.

3   Kennedy, Arthur 'Bluey' George, *The Memoirs of Arthur George Kennedy*, unpublished, 1977.

4   Ibid.

5   Ibid.

6   Wall, Don, *Singapore and Beyond*, 2/20th Battalion Association, Cowra, NSW, 1985, p. 110.
7   Timbs, Kevin, interview with author, Dapto, May 2006.
8   Collins, Arthur 'Snowy', interview with author, June 2006.
9   Maynard, Roger, *Hell's Heroes*, HarperCollins, Sydney, 2009, p. 106.
10 Sweeting, A.J., *Prisoners of the Japanese*, p. 511, in Wigmore, Lionel, *The Japanese Thrust*, Australian War Memorial, Canberra, 1957.
11 Ibid.
12 Gaudry, Alan 'Butch', *What it was like to be a prisoner-of-war of the Japanese 1942–1945*: Memoirs of the POW experience, 22nd Brigade Headquarters Association, 15 June 1998, pp. 6, 7.
13 Boardman, Jack, unpublished memoir, p. 25.
14 Richardson, Bart, interview with author, 12 October 2016.
15 Harrison, Noel, interview with author, 27 September 2016.
16 Kennedy, Arthur 'Bluey' George, interview with author, 24 September 2016.

Chapter 15: All at Sea
1   Legg, Frank, *The Gordon Bennett Story*, Angus & Robertson, Sydney, 1965, p. 257.
2   Ibid.
3   Ibid.
4   Ibid.
5   Legg, Frank, *The Gordon Bennett Story*, Angus & Robertson, Sydney, 1965, p. 261.
6   Bennett, H. Gordon, *Why Singapore Fell*, Angus & Robertson, Sydney, 1944, p. 210.
7   Legg, Frank, *The Gordon Bennett Story*, Angus & Robertson, Sydney, 1965, p. 262.
8   Bennett, H. Gordon, *Why Singapore Fell*, Angus & Robertson, Sydney, 1944, p. 210.
9   Ibid., p. 212.
10 Sir John Dudley Lavarack, *Australian Dictionary of Biography*, http://adb.anu.edu.au/biography/lavarack-sir-john-dudley-10790
11 Legg, Frank, *The Gordon Bennett Story*, Angus & Robertson, Sydney, 1965, p. 263.

12 Sir John Dudley Lavarack, *Australian Dictionary of Biography*, http://adb.anu.edu.au/biography/lavarack-sir-john-dudley-10790

13 Legg, Frank, *The Gordon Bennett Story*, Angus & Robertson, Sydney, 1965, p. 263.

14 Bennett, H. Gordon, *Why Singapore Fell*, Angus & Robertson, Sydney, 1944, pp. 214–5.

15 Ibid., p. 215.

16 Ibid., p. 216.

17 Ibid.

18 Legg, Frank, *The Gordon Bennett Story*, Angus & Robertson, Sydney, 1965, p. 264.

Chapter 16: Bennett's Fall from Grace

1 Legg, Frank, *The Gordon Bennett Story*, Angus & Robertson, Sydney, 1965, p. 265.

2 Ibid., pp. 267–8.

3 Ibid.

4 Bennett papers, Mitchell Library, Sydney, MSS 773.

5 Clisby, Mark, *Guilty or Innocent? The Gordon Bennett Case*, Allen & Unwin, Sydney, 1992, p. 21.

6 Ibid.

7 Bennett papers, Mitchell Library, Sydney, MSS 773.

8 Ibid.

9 Ibid.

10 Blamey papers, 3DR6 643; Lodge, A.B., *The Fall of General Gordon Bennett*, Allen & Unwin, Sydney, 1986, p. 230; Clisby, Mark, *Guilty or Innocent? The Gordon Bennett Case*, Allen & Unwin, Sydney, 1992, pp. 21–22.

11 Lodge, A.B., *The Fall of General Gordon Bennett*, Allen & Unwin, Sydney, 1986, p. 230.

12 *The Examiner*, Launceston, 2 May 1944.

13 Clisby, Mark, *Guilty or Innocent? The Gordon Bennett Case*, Allen & Unwin, Sydney, 1992, p. 22; Australia Archives, Victoria: Department of Defence (III) – Army Headquarters, MP 7 2/1.

14 Letter from Blamey to Forde, 10 October 1945; MP 742, item B/3/2265; Lodge, A.B., *The Fall of General Gordon Bennett*, Allen & Unwin, Sydney, 1986, p. 250.

15 Clisby, Mark, *Guilty or Innocent? The Gordon Bennett Case*, Allen & Unwin, Sydney, 1992, p. 23.

16 Arneil, Stan, *Black Jack*, Macmillan, Melbourne and Sydney, 1983, p. 119.

17 Boardman, Jack, interview with author, August 2016.

18 Clisby, Mark, *Guilty or Innocent? The Gordon Bennett Case*, Allen & Unwin, Sydney, 1992, p. 72. Based on an interview between Moses and author Mark Clisby in May 1986.

19 Richardson, Bart, *The Army As I Saw It*, self-published, 2014, p. 81.

20 Lodge, A.B., *The Fall of General Gordon Bennett*, Allen & Unwin, Sydney, 1986, p. 245.

21 Mant, Gilbert, *Daily Telegraph*, 30 August 1945.

22 Ibid.

23 Lodge, A.B., *The Fall of General Gordon Bennett*, Allen & Unwin, Sydney, 1986, p. 246.

Chapter 17: Living Cadavers in Filthy Rags

1   Gaudry, Alan 'Butch', *What it was like to be a prisoner-of-war of the Japanese, 1942–1945*: Memoirs of the POW experience, 22nd Brigade Headquarters Association, 15 June 1998.

2   Ibid.

3   Ibid.

4   Ibid.

5   Ibid.

6   Ibid.

7   Sweeting, A.J., 'Prisoners of the Japanese', p. 523, in Wigmore, Lionel, *The Japanese Thrust*, Australian War Memorial, 1957.

8   Official 2/26 Battalion website: http://www.2-26bn.org/salarang.html

9   Sweeting, A.J, 'Prisoners of the Japanese', in Wigmore, Lionel, *The Japanese Thrust*, 1957, p. 523.

10 Ibid.

11 Kennedy, Arthur 'Bluey' George, *The Memoirs of Arthur George Kennedy*, unpublished, 1977.

12 Ibid.

13 Ibid.

14 Chippendale, John, unpublished memoir, December 1997, p. 8.

15 Ibid.

16 Ibid.

17 Arneil, Stan, *Black Jack*, Macmillan, Melbourne, 1983, p. 121.

18 Ibid.

19 Daldry, George, interview with author, Bondi, August 2006.

20 Byrne, Joe, interview with author, Ramsgate, June 2006.

21 Boughton diary extracts courtesy of David Boughton and members of the Boughton family.

22 Boughton, Dudley, unpublished memoir, courtesy David Boughton.

23 Timbs, Kevin, interview with author, Dapto, May 2006; Byrne Joe, interview with author, Ramsgate, June, 2006.

24 Cook, John, interview with author, Sydney, 2006.

25 Houston, Jimmy, unpublished diary, courtesy Pamela and Henning Nielsen.

26 Cook, John, interview with author, Sydney, April 2006.

27 Maynard, Roger, *Ambon*, Hachette Australia, Sydney, 2014.

28 Godfrey, Ralph interview with author, Melbourne, April 2013.

29 Swanton, Stuart, personal diary, AWM67 3/387/DPI300, courtesy Lloyd Swanton.

30 Smith, Windas, interview with Ralph Godfrey.

31 Maynard, Roger, *Ambon*, Hachette Australia, Sydney, 2014, p. 222.

32 Ibid.

33 Gilbert, Max 'Eddie', interview with author, Melbourne, 8 June 2012.

34 Gaudry, Alan 'Butch', *What it was like to be a prisoner-of-war of the Japanese 1942–1945: Memoirs of the POW experience,* 22nd Brigade Headquarters Association, 15 June 1998.

Chapter 18: Bennett Pleads His Case

1 Clisby, Mark, *Guilty or Innocent? The Gordon Bennett Case*, Allen & Unwin, Sydney, 1992, p. 23.

2 Legg, Frank, *The Gordon Bennett Story*, Angus & Robertson, Sydney, 1965, p. 280.

3 Military Court, sheet no. 17.

4 Legg, Frank, *The Gordon Bennett Story*, Angus & Robertson, Sydney, 1965, p. 281.

5   Ibid., p. 282.
6   Military Court, sheet no. 5.
7   Ibid.
8   Legg, Frank, *The Gordon Bennett Story*, Angus & Robertson, Sydney, 1965, p. 283.
9   Military Court, sheet no. 5.
10 Sydney *Sunday Telegraph*, 4 November 1945.
11 8th Division Association telegram to Prime Minister Ben Chifley on 5 November 1945, MP742/1, B/3/2265.
12 Lodge, A.B., *The Fall of General Gordon Bennett*, Allen & Unwin, Sydney, 1986, p. 262.
13 Bennett papers, Mitchell Library, Sydney, ML MSS 807/2.
14 *Commonwealth Gazette*, 17 November 1945, CRS A5954, item box 264.
15 *Manual of Military Law*, 1941 Australian edition, paragraph 30 http://trove.nla.gov.au/work/17732822?q&versionId=46287078 p. 407.
16 Fry, Thomas, 'Legal Aspects of the Departure of Major-General Gordon Bennett from Singapore', *University of Queensland Law Journal* 34, 1948, p. 44; http://www.austlii.edu.au/au/journals/UQLawJl/1948/9.html
17 *Japan Times and Advertiser*, 18 April 1942, p. 30.
18 Clisby, Mark, *Guilty or Innocent? The Gordon Bennett Case*, Allen & Unwin, Sydney, 1992, p. 35.
19 Ibid., p. 38.
20 Royal Commission transcript, Bennett Inquiry, transcript of evidence, CP 2910/19, item bundle 1, B/3/2265; AA. pp. 398–99.
21 Ibid., p. 399.
22 Ibid., pp. 363–66.
23 Royal Commission transcript quoted in Lodge, A. B., *The Fall of General Gordon Bennett*, p. 280.
24 Legg, Frank, *The Gordon Bennett Story*, Angus & Robertson, Sydney, 1965, p. 285.
25 Royal Commission transcript, p. 362.
26 Lodge, A.B., *The Fall of General Gordon Bennett*, Allen & Unwin, Sydney, 1986, p. 281.
27 Bennett, H. Gordon, *Why Singapore Fell*, Angus & Robertson, Sydney, 1944, p. 219.

28 Royal Commission transcript, pp 397–8.
29 Ibid.
30 Ibid., p. 550.
31 Ibid. pp. 574–75.
32 Ibid., p. 578.
33 Ibid. pp 8–11.
34 Ibid., pp. 11–13.
35 Ibid pp 19–21.
36 Melbourne *Age*, 7 January 1946.

Chapter 19: Rallying to Bennett's Defence

1   Melbourne *Sun*, 8 January 1946.
2   *The Argus*, Melbourne, 23 February 1952.
3   Galleghan, F., letter to Australian Staff College, Victoria, September 1969.
4   *The Age*, 20 April 1948.
5   Bennett papers, Mitchell Library, Sydney, 807/22.
6   Lodge, A.B., *The Fall of General Gordon Bennett*, Allen & Unwin, Sydney, 1986, p. 297.
7   Ibid.
8   Ibid., p. 305.
9   Fry, Thomas, 'Legal Aspects of the Departure of Major-General Gordon Bennett from Singapore', *University of Queensland Law Journal* 34, 1948, p. 35.
10 Ibid.
11 Ibid p. 34.
12 Ibid p. 56.
13 Ibid.
14 Ibid.
15 Ibid.
16 Ibid.
17 Ibid., p. 44.
18 Clisby, Mark, *Guilty or Innocent? The Gordon Bennett Case*, Allen & Unwin, Sydney, 1992, p. 114.
19 Percival, Arthur Ernest, *The War in Malaya*, Eyre & Spottiswoode, London, 1949.
20 Ibid.

21 Legg, Frank, *The Gordon Bennett Story*, Angus & Robertson, Sydney, 1965, p. 291.
22 *Sydney Morning Herald*, 4 August 1962.
23 Ibid.
24 Ibid.

Epilogue

1 Governor-General Sir Peter Cosgrove, Ballarat, 15 February 2017.
2 Email to author from Anthony Cassimatis, 26 February 2017.
3 Waddell, Jim, email to author, 28 February 2017.
4 Mead, L., email to author, 28 February 2017.
5 Email to author from Dianne Gallasch and Helen Macpherson, 15 February 2017.
6 Ibid.
7 Gaudry, Alan 'Butch', *What it was like to be a prisoner-of-war of the Japanese 1942–1945: Memoirs of the POW experience*, 22nd Brigade Headquarters Association, 15 June 1998.
8 Chippendale, John, unpublished memoir, 1997.
9 Boardman, Jack, interview with author, August 2016.
10 Harrison, Noel, interview with author, September 2016.
11 Kennedy, Arthur 'Bluey' George, interview with author, 24 September 2016.
12 Kennedy, Arthur 'Bluey' George, *The Memoirs of Arthur George Kennedy*, unpublished, 1977.
13 Richardson, Bart, *The Army As I Saw It*, self-published, 2014.

BIBLIOGRAPHY

Arneil, Stan, *Black Jack: The Life and Times of Brigadier Sir Frederick Galleghan*, Macmillan, Melbourne and Sydney, 1983.

Bean, C.E.W., *Official History of Australia in the War of 1914–1918, vol. I, The story of war to the end of the first phase of the Gallipoli Campaign*, 4 May 1915.

Bennett, H. Gordon, *Why Singapore Fell*, Angus & Robertson, Sydney, 1944.

Bose, Romen, *Secrets of the Battlebox*, Marshall Cavendish Editions, Singapore, 2005.

Churchill, Winston, *The Second World War*, vol. IV, *The Hinge of Fate*, Houghton Mifflin, London, 1950.

Clisby, Mark, *Guilty or Innocent? The Gordon Bennett Case*, Allen & Unwin, Sydney, 1992.

Corfield, Justin, & Corfield, Robin, *The Fall of Singapore*, Hardie Grant, Melbourne, 2012.

Elphick, Peter, *Singapore: The Pregnable Fortress*, Coronet Books, London, 1995.

Elphick, Peter, & Smith, Michael, *Odd Man Out: The Story of the Singapore Traitor*, Hodder & Stoughton, London, 1993.

Forbes, Cameron, *Hellfire*, Pan Macmillan, Sydney, 2005.

Ford, J. M., *Allies in a Bind: Australia and the Netherlands East Indies in the Second World War*, Australian Netherlands Ex-Servicemen and Women's Association, Loganholme, 1996.

Gilbert, Martin, *The Churchill Documents, Testing Times, 1942*, QLD College Press, Hillsdale, 2014

Hall, Timothy, *The Fall of Singapore*, Methuen Australia, 1983.

Horner, D.M., *Crisis of Command, Australian Generalship and the Japanese Threat 1941–1943*, Australian National University Press, Canberra, 1978.

Leasor, James, *Singapore: The Battle That Changed the World*, House of Stratus, Cornwall, 2nd edn, 2001.

Lee Kuan Yew, *The Singapore Story: Memoirs of Lee Kuan Yew*, Marshall Cavendish Editions, Singapore, 1998.

Legg, Frank, *The Gordon Bennett Story*, Angus & Robertson, Sydney, 1965.

Lodge, A.B., *The Fall of General Gordon Bennett*, Allen & Unwin, Sydney, 1986.

Manchester, William and Reid, Paul, *The Last Lion: William Spencer Churchill, Defender of the Realm, 1946–1965*, Pan Macmillan, London 2015.

Maynard, Roger, *Ambon: The Truth About One of the Most Brutal POW Camps in World War II and the Triumph of the Aussie Spirit*, Hachette Australia, Sydney, 2014.

Maynard, Roger, *Hell's Heroes: The Forgotten Story of the Worst POW Camp in Japan*, HarperCollins, Sydney, 2009.

Nelson, Hank, *Prisoners of War: Australians under Nippon*, ABC Enterprises, Sydney, 1985.

Newton, R.W., et al., *The Grim Glory: Official History of the 2/19th Battalion, Pt 1*, 2/19 Battalion AIF Association, 1st edn, 1975.

Oswald, Bruce & Waddell, Jim (eds), *Justice in Arms: Military Lawyers in the Australian Army's First Hundred Years*, Big Sky Publishing, Sydney, 2014.

Penfold, A.W., et al., *Galleghan's Greyhounds: The Story of the 2/30th Australian Infantry Battalion*, 2/30th Battalion AIF Association, Sydney, 1979.

Percival, Arthur Ernest, *The War in Malaya*, Eyre & Spottiswoode, London, 1949.

Smith, Colin, *Singapore Burning, Heroism and Surrender in World War II*, Penguin Books, Melbourne, 2005.

Thompson, Peter, *The Battle for Singapore*, Portrait, London, 2005.

Wall, Don, *Singapore and Beyond*, 2/20th Battalion Association, Cowra, NSW, 2000.

Wigmore, Lionel, *Official History of World War II, Part 2, South-East Asia Conquered, Vol. IV – The Japanese Thrust*, lst edn, Australian Memorial, Canberra, 1957.

INDEX